Trading **Democracy** for **Justice**

To Kristin,

Thank you for such a wonderful seminar and a visit! Good luck in your career ...I expect big things!

Traci

CHICAGO STUDIES IN AMERICAN POLITICS

A series edited by
*Benjamin I. Page, Susan Herbst,
Lawrence R. Jacobs, and
Adam Berinsky*

Also in the series:

Changing Minds or Changing
 Channels? Partisan News in
 an Age of Choice
 *by Kevin Arceneaux and
 Martin Johnson*
The Politics of Belonging:
 Race, Public Opinion, and
 Immigration
 *by Natalie Masuoka and
 Jane Junn*
Political Tone: How Leaders
 Talk and Why
 *by Roderick P. Hart, Jay P.
 Childers, and Colene J. Lind*
The Timeline of Presidential
 Elections: How Campaigns
 Do (and Do Not) Matter
 *by Robert S. Erikson and
 Christopher Wlezien*
Learning While Governing:
 Expertise and Accountability
 in the Executive Branch
 *by Sean Gailmard and
 John W. Patty*
Electing Judges: The Surprising
 Effects of Campaigning on
 Judicial Legitimacy
 by James L. Gibson

Follow the Leader? How
 Voters Respond to Politicians'
 Policies and Performance
 by Gabriel S. Lenz
The Social Citizen: Peer
 Networks and Political Behavior
 by Betsy Sinclair
The Submerged State:
 How Invisible Government
 Policies Undermine American
 Democracy
 by Suzanne Mettler
Disciplining the Poor:
 Neoliberal Paternalism and
 the Persistent Power of Race
 *by Joe Soss, Richard C. Fording,
 and Sanford F. Schram*
Why Parties? A Second Look
 by John H. Aldrich
News That Matters: Television
 and American Opinion,
 Updated Edition
 *by Shanto Iyengar and
 Donald R. Kinder*

*Additional series titles follow
 index*

Trading
Democracy
for
Justice

CRIMINAL

CONVICTIONS

AND THE

DECLINE OF

NEIGHBORHOOD

POLITICAL

PARTICIPATION

Traci Burch

THE

UNIVERSITY OF

CHICAGO PRESS

Chicago and

London

Traci Burch is assistant professor of political science at Northwestern University and research professor at the American Bar Foundation. She is a coauthor of *Creating a New Racial Order*.

The University of Chicago Press, Chicago 60637
The University of Chicago Press, Ltd., London
© 2013 by The University of Chicago
All rights reserved. Published 2013.
Printed in the United States of America

22 21 20 19 18 17 16 15 14 13   1 2 3 4 5

ISBN-13: 978-0-226-06476-5 (cloth)
ISBN-13: 978-0-226-06493-2 (paper)
ISBN-13: 978-0-226-06509-0 (e-book)

DOI: 10.7208/chicago/9780226065090.001.0001

Library of Congress Cataloging-in-Publication Data
Burch, Traci R., 1979–
   Trading democracy for justice : criminal
convictions and the decline of neighborhood
political participation / Traci Burch.
      pages. cm.—(Chicago studies in American
politics)
   ISBN 978-0-226-06476-5 (cloth : alk. paper)—ISBN
978-0-226-06493-2 (pbk. : alk. paper)—ISBN 978-0-226-
06509-0 (e-book) 1. Criminal justice, Administration
of—Social aspects—United States. 2. African
Americans—Suffrage. 3. Political participation—
United States. 4. Prisoners—Suffrage—United States.
5. Prisoners' families—Suffrage—United States. I. Title.
II. Series: Chicago studies in American politics.
HV9950.B867 2013
364.60973—dc23
                                    2013001977

Contents

Preface / VII

1 Introduction / 1

2 Theory / 15

3 A First Look:

Imprisonment and Community Supervision / 44

4 Neighborhood Criminal Justice Context and

Political Participation / 75

5 Exploring Mechanisms / 105

6 Can Mobilization Help? / 133

7 State Police Power and Citizen Political Power / 170

Appendix / 185

Notes / 205

References / 223

Index / 243

Preface

I grew up in a small city, Macon, Georgia, which is located in Bibb County. In my lifetime, Macon has declined significantly, like many cities. Its population is lower than it was in 2000. Most of the jobs and white people have left: Macon is 65 percent black, and the poverty rate is 31 percent. Things were so bad in Macon that this year, the city and county had to consolidate in order to keep basic services running.

My father works for one of the only booming businesses in town: the county jail. Over the last ten years the county jail has doubled in capacity, housing more than one thousand inmates. That's just big enough to hold about 1 percent of the adult population of the county at any given point. And it does seem like lots of people pass through the county jail at some point. It seems like my dad knows almost everyone in town, usually because of his work.

Obviously, my background contributes to my interest in criminal justice. Coming from a place like Macon, one cannot help but care about the young people who have no opportunities, no jobs, and no prospects other than death or prisons. And growing up with a father in law enforcement, one can't help but feel compassion for the thousands of guards, doctors, nurses, social workers, lawyers, and judges who work with inmates, probationers, and parolees each day. In a place like Macon, crime and punishment loom so large that almost everyone in town is involved: either as an offender, someone who knows an offender, or someone who works with offenders.

I wrote this book for the young people in Macon, people who are from the same place as me, and yet not. People who don't have fathers, husbands, children, or brothers in their lives because they are away in prison. Communities who are missing men, women, and children because of the violence and punishment that a lack of opportunity bring. Of course, one book can't tackle all the economic and social problems of Macon and places like it. But I hope I can help.

Several people have provided invaluable feedback on this manuscript as it grew into a book. Most important, my colleagues at Harvard, Jennifer Hochschild, Sidney Verba, and Gary King, provided significant guidance, advice, and encouragement in the production of this manuscript. In addition, I would like to thank Jamie Druckman, Vincent Hutchings, Michael Dawson, Dan Galvin, Kay Schlozman, Mark Peffley, and Taeku Lee for their comments, advice, and encouragement.

I am very blessed to have wonderful, encouraging, patient colleagues at both Northwestern University and the American Bar Foundation. I would like to especially thank Jamie Druckman for guiding me through this process. I would also like to thank Bonnie Honig, Dylan Penningroth, John Comaroff, and Susan Shapiro for their comments— and fieldwork training!

This book would not have been possible without the research assistance of several wonderful, hardworking graduate and undergraduate students from across the country. I would like to thank, in no particular order, Joshua Robison, Alan Ritchie, Mac LeBuhn, Dianna Coleman, Nathan Gannon, Adrienne DaGue, Chris Berk, Jeffrey Konowitch, Mneesha Gellman, Joseph L. Jones, Howard Polikoff, Damanvir Sidhu, Maavi Norman, Alanna Gunn, Fabiola Borel, James Miner, Jon Rogowski, Kevin Levay, and Gabriela Jara.

I presented various iterations and sections of this book in several places, including the University of Wisconsin, the University of Chicago, Northwestern University, the American Bar Foundation, the University of Pennsylvania, Yale University, Brown University, Marquette University, Loyola University at Chicago, the University of Illinois at Chicago, and the University of California at Berkeley.

Institutional support for this project was provided by Northwestern University and the American Bar Foundation.

The University of Chicago Press has done an outstanding job with this book. To that end, I would like to thank John Tryneski, Benjamin I. Page, Susan Herbst, Lawrence R. Jacobs, and James Druckman for their enthusiasm for this project. I would also like to thank the staff of the University of Chicago Press, particularly Rodney Powell and Erik Carlson, for working so hard to make this book come true.

I am especially grateful to the family and friends who put up with me during the six-year process of writing this book. I thank Marquis Parker, my new husband, for standing by me for the last part of this journey (and for postponing the honeymoon so that I could finish these revisions). I thank my parents, Freddie Burch and Alfred Burch, for their love and support. I also thank Jean Hodge, Susie Hodge, Ophelia Burch, Stephanie Bowman, Andrea Lewis, Russell Ellis, Garani Nadaraja, Ana

Aparicio, Nitasha Sharma, Todd Coleman, Melanie Penny, Francesca Soria Guerrero, Lauren Roberts, Antonia Henry, Richelle Williams, Bernadette Atuahene, Candace Jackson, Brigitte Anderson, Vicky DeFrancesco Soto, Leah Hobson, and LaShonda Hodge Johnson for their friendship and love.

1

Introduction

It was right there in prison that I made up my mind to devote the rest of my life to telling the white man about himself—or die.
— Malcolm X[1]

"Prior" incidents, which increased tensions and ultimately led to violence, were police actions in almost half the cases; police actions were "final" incidents before the outbreak of violence in 12 of the 24 surveyed disorders.
— Report of the National Commission on Civil Disorders, 1968

Imagine your hands callused, cramped, and swollen from writing each day for hours with the cartridge of a ballpoint pen—legal briefs, letters, essays, your master's thesis—and writing everything twice because the prison might "lose" the copies you send out.
— Noelle Hanrahan[2]

At first glance, these three quotations originate from disparate sources and describe markedly different phenomena. Yet each of these statements eloquently conveys the same sentiment: the criminal justice system has the power to mobilize, and demobilize, individual citizens and entire communities. The common sentiment expressed by these sources is that interactions with the criminal justice system shape the ability and desire of citizens to act in the political world. Political activism is intimately tied to state supervision and coercion: experiences with police, courts, judges, and state correctional bureaucracies can generate political activity by perpetuating the development of a revolutionary consciousness not only among convicts like Malcolm X, but also among other individuals who observe or experience varying degrees of contact with the criminal justice system, as the National Commission on Civil Disorders Report details. More commonly, however, the criminal justice system demobilizes citizens, taking away their ability and desire to participate in politics, as Hanrahan suggests. For the vast majority of citizens involved with the criminal justice system directly as suspects or convicts, or indirectly as the families, friends, and neighbors of suspects and convicts, interactions with the criminal justice system bring about their absence, rather than their presence, in mainstream political life.

At many points in the American past, various institutions of the criminal justice system—police, courts, jails, and prisons—have been used flagrantly to prevent political mobilization by certain groups or individuals. During the 1950s, for instance, suspected Communists were subjected to intense public harassment by Congress and even prosecutions under the Smith Act and other anti-Communist legislation.[3] The efforts made by the FBI and its COINTEL program to disrupt civil rights organizations provide another example of the use of law enforcement to demobilize citizens.[4] State-sanctioned vigilante violence also contributed to black disfranchisement in the South after Reconstruction.[5] South Carolina senator "Pitchfork" Ben Tillman, describing the effort to stop black voting after Reconstruction in his state, said, "We have done our level best. We have scratched our heads to find out how we could eliminate every last one of them. We stuffed ballot boxes. We shot them. We are not ashamed of it."[6]

The Civil Rights Act of 1964 and the Voting Rights Act of 1965, coupled with a constitutional ban on poll taxes, did much to eliminate the use of law enforcement for political subjugation. However, many people allege that the threat of state reprisal still restricts turnout among disadvantaged groups today, especially blacks and immigrants. A joint investigation by People for the American Way and the National Association for the Advancement of Colored People (NAACP) revealed reports of signs posted in black districts that attempted to mislead potential voters about elections using the threat of legal sanctions.[7] These signs, much like the historical one shown in figure 1.1, threatened potential voters with fines or imprisonment if they even attempted to vote.[8]

Despite such lingering examples of intimidation, the criminal justice system no longer plays such an obvious role in political repression. Government officials are not permitted to use legal institutions to punish their political enemies, and real protections for violations of civil rights have been instituted at the federal and state levels. For the most part, Americans are thought to experience state power through increasingly apolitical bureaucracies. At the same time, it is also true that governments in the United States supervise and imprison a higher proportion of their citizens than any other country in the world, including China and North Korea.[9] This high level of citizen criminal jus-

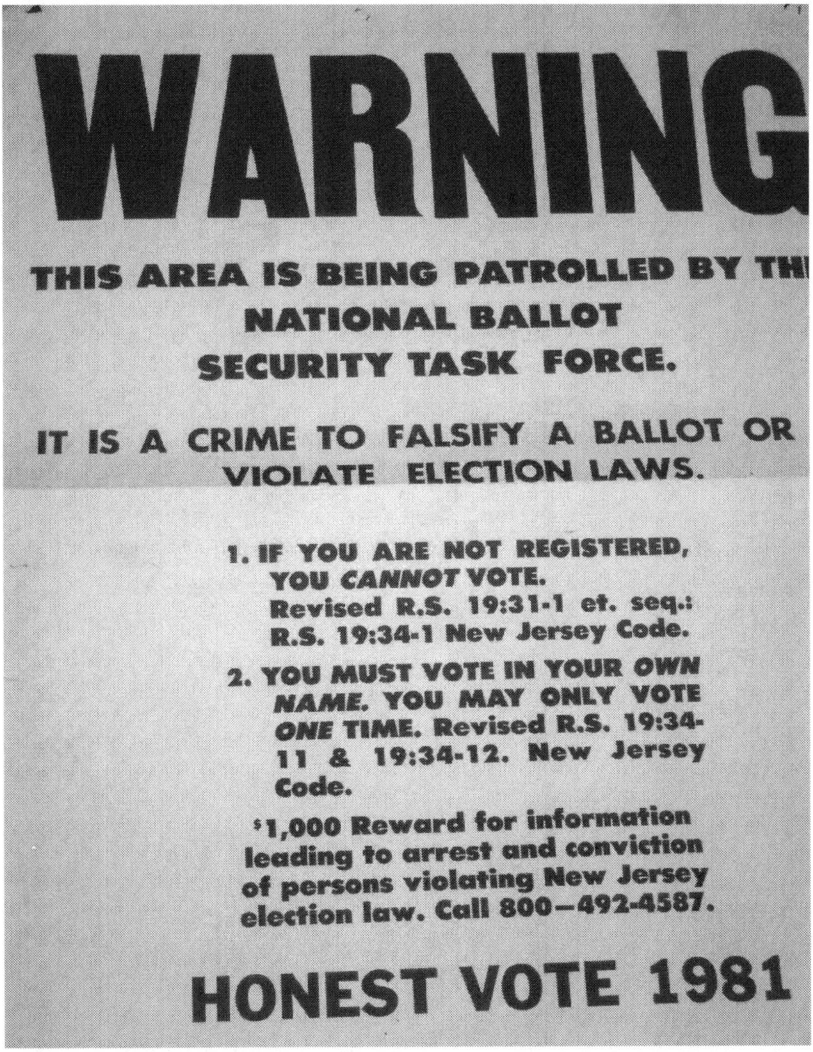

Figure 1.1: Poster found in a New Jersey district.

tice involvement may not have overt roots in the desire to subjugate political enemies; however, as this book will show, these punitive interactions between citizens and the criminal justice system still matter for politics.

This book explores the repercussions of the criminal justice system for American democracy. The central premise of the book is that the government, by punishing citizens, affects politics by defining who belongs to the political community, specifying how and when citizens can participate in politics, redistributing resources among individuals and social groups, and determining the balance of power and influence among citizens.[10] This effect on the political community occurs because criminal convictions destroy the social and human capital of individual offenders and, by extension, that of their families and neighbors. Regardless of one's normative position on crime and justice, it is difficult to deny that the experiences of individuals with the criminal justice system forever change their relationship with the state and with other citizens. When such experiences involve incarceration, probation, or disfranchisement, they obviously diminish the ability of offenders to participate in politics and to influence government, at least for the duration of their punishment. What will become apparent from this text, however, is that our treatment of offenders decreases the power and influence not only of those people who are convicted or disfranchised, but also of citizens who never face such punishment themselves.

Most political scientists would argue that a criminal justice system that supervises a little more than 3 percent of the adult population should not affect political outcomes in any real sense. However, such arguments ignore the fact that criminal justice interactions are demographically and geographically concentrated. What appears to be a small percentage of adults nationally represents a high percentage of residents in many neighborhoods; because of the concentration of criminal justice interactions within these geographically bounded spaces, as many as one-third of residents in disadvantaged communities can be under criminal justice supervision at any given time. This book focuses on concentration effects as the central mechanism through which individual experiences with criminal justice shape the political outcomes of entire communities. Previous research has found that in high-incarceration blocks in Brooklyn, "about one in every eight parenting-age males is sent to prison or jail each year."[11] Similarly, Western, Pattillo, and Weiman argue that incarceration is fast becoming "a pervasive event" in the life cycle of young black men; 32.4 percent of young black male high school dropouts of ages 22–30 are in prison or jail; for comparable whites, the figure is 6.7 percent.[12] Current estimates project that almost one-third of black males born in 2001 will be incarcerated in a state or federal prison in their lifetimes, compared with 6 percent of white males.[13] Thus, the concentration of criminal justice interactions means that such contacts with state power are increasingly common in the lives of disadvantaged people, particularly minorities. The criminal justice system, in some instances, may even rival public assistance bureaucracies as the most prominent state actor in many of the most distressed communities in the United States, thus serving a primary role in shaping the relationship between citizens and the state in those communities.

This work measures the prevalence of contacts with the criminal justice system across neighborhoods and relates the frequency of those contacts to political outcomes, focusing on neighborhoods in two states: Georgia and North Carolina.[14] Keys to the strength of this enterprise are neighborhood-level data on political participation, political attitudes, crime, imprisonment, probation, parole, and disfranchisement constructed on the basis of data from state boards of elections, departments of corrections, departments of public health, market research firms, and the Census Bureau. These uniquely detailed data, when combined with survey data, allow for precise analyses of politics at the neighborhood level. The analyses presented in this work employ advanced statistical techniques such as matching and regression analysis to avoid problems such as selection and omitted-variable bias that often plague neighborhood-level studies, making it possible to make strong causal inferences. Never before has such a comprehensive project been undertaken to determine the causal influence of incarceration on neighborhood participation.

The data indicate that, in disadvantaged neighborhoods across several cities, the spatial concentration of imprisonment, probation, and parole far exceeds the national average concentration of 0.43 prisoners and 1.42 probationers and parolees per square mile. Neighborhoods experience the burdens of prison and community supervision unequally. In the block groups in this study, imprisonment density ranges from no prisoners to 470 prisoners per square mile in Georgia and from no prisoners to 260 prisoners per square mile in North Carolina. The density of community supervision ranges from zero to 330 probationers or parolees per square mile (community supervision data are available only for North Carolina). These high spatial concentrations reflect that fact that residents of disadvantaged neighborhoods experience imprisonment at rates almost ten times the national average in North Carolina and fourteen times the national average in Georgia.[15] Probation and parole rates are similarly high in both states. Among young adults between the ages of 18 and 34, the situation is more dire: the average imprisonment rate for young adults in North Carolina is twice the national average for all adults; for Georgia, the young adult imprisonment rate is four times the national average for all adults.

The analysis further demonstrates that such intensive involvement with the criminal justice system has a politically demobilizing effect on low-income and minority neighborhoods. Moreover, imprisonment, rather than community supervision, seems to stand out as the form of punishment that most influences participation. Voter turnout in the 2008 general election was about 6 percentage points lower in North Carolina and 2 percentage points lower in Georgia neighborhoods with the highest concentration of imprisonment than that in neighborhoods with average spatial concentrations of imprisonment. Likewise, each new prison admission prior to the election lowers overall neighborhood voter turnout by about 1.4 percentage points. Estimates produced from individual-level data confirm that people living in the highest-imprisonment neighborhoods are 74 percent less likely to vote than individuals living in neighborhoods with no prisoners. The effects of imprisonment are not limited to voter turnout, however: people who live in high-imprisonment neighborhoods also are 43.4 percent less likely to undertake other civic and political activities such as signing petitions and protesting; are members of 33 percent fewer groups; and volunteer 78 percent fewer times a year.

Although it is likely that the criminal justice system influences political participation through several mechanisms, the evidence points to its effects on the social dynamics and economic resources of communities as the most likely explanatory factors. Anecdotal evidence of the economic strain of imprisonment on the families and friends of offenders abounds. However, this study adds evidence that residents of high-imprisonment neighborhoods also are less likely to be involved with formal social networks such as intact families, churches, and membership organizations and demonstrate fewer informal ties to their neighbors as well. It is well established that financial resources and social involvement contribute to political involvement;[16] this study demonstrates that living in a high-imprisonment neighborhood influences political behavior by decreasing the economic and social resources available to citizens.

These findings are presented in three chapters. Chapter 3 introduces the 2008 Neighborhood Criminal Justice Involvement Data and uses it to measure variation in the frequency and spatial concentration of imprisonment, probation, and parole for felony convictions across neighborhoods in Georgia and North Carolina. The purpose of this chapter is to provide readers with a sense of how prominently criminal justice interactions feature in the lives of poor minority neighborhood residents relative to people living in other communities. To that end, the chapter presents visual evidence of the correlation between imprisonment and community supervision and the black percentage of a neighborhood population, the Hispanic percentage, the poverty rate, and the homicide rate. Maps of neighborhood imprisonment and community supervision are presented for several cities in both Georgia and North Carolina in order to provide further evidence that this inequality is not an isolated phenomenon. Chapter 3 also presents evidence of the effects of imprisonment and community supervision on young adults in each state. As these data show, in many neighborhoods, the political socialization of youth is taking place in a context in which anywhere from one-tenth to one-third of young people are under criminal justice supervision for felonies. Consequently, in these neighborhoods, one-tenth to one-third of young people is barred from voting and other aspects of civic life.

Chapter 4 presents three different tests of the effects of neighborhood criminal justice context on voter turnout and other forms of political participation. The first analysis shows a statistically significant and strongly negative relationship between the spatial concentration of imprisonment and voter turnout in Georgia and a curvilinear relationship in North Carolina. As was just noted, the expected turnout in neighborhoods at the upper end of the prison density scale is about 6 percentage points lower than that in a neighborhood with no prisoners in North Carolina and 2 percentage points lower in Georgia, even after controlling for homicide rates, poverty, median income, racial composition, and other characteristics of the neighborhood. The second analysis shows that prison admissions also seem to diminish voting: in 2008, neighborhoods from which at least one person was sent to prison before the general election had lower voter turnout than those neighborhoods from which a person was sent to prison after the general election, again, these results hold despite controlling for a number of neighborhood-related factors. Based on simulations, imprisoning neighborhood residents in Georgia before the 2008 election decreased neighborhood voter turnout by 1.4 percentage points. The third test switches the level of analysis from the neighborhood to the individual, attaching a version of the Neighborhood Criminal Justice Dataset generated for the year 2000 to the Saguaro Seminar's 2000 Social Capital Benchmark Survey. Those findings provide further support for the overall conclusion that imprisonment diminishes political participation: residents of high-imprisonment neighborhoods were statistically significantly less likely to vote and undertake other political activities than people living in lower-imprisonment neighborhoods. At moderate levels of imprisonment concentrations, these effects were minor: people living in neighborhoods with average spatial concentrations of imprisonment were only about 2 percentage points less likely to vote than people living in neighborhoods with no prisoners. However, living in a neighborhood at the highest level of imprisonment decreased the likelihood of voting by 73.4 percent. These data also show that imprisonment diminishes participation in political and civic activities.

Chapter 5 turns to explaining these findings by focusing on the potential mechanisms by which imprisonment might produce political demobilization. Again using the Saguaro Seminar's Social Capital Benchmark Survey, this analysis examines the relationship between neighborhood criminal justice context and attitudes such as political trust, generalized trust, and political efficacy, as well as organizational membership. The findings show that people living in high-imprisonment neighborhoods demonstrate lower levels of interpersonal trust and trust in their neighbors than people living in lower-imprisonment neighborhoods; they are also less likely to participate in church and other groups and are more likely to be separated or divorced. Interestingly enough, however, people living in high-imprisonment neighborhoods are not significantly less likely to feel a sense of efficacy or to trust the police or the national or local governments. This particular pattern of findings—that neighborhood residents express norms and attitudes consistent with those held by the wider society outside the neighborhood, yet lack the formal and informal social networks to put those beliefs into practice—is consistent with previous findings that high-imprisonment neighborhoods suffer from a lack of formal and informal social ties.[17]

The evidence of political demobilization presented in these chapters paints a grim picture of the future of political representation in disadvantaged communities. Chapter 6 takes up the issue of voter mobilization, showing how it can be affected by imprisonment. More important, chapter 6 also explores the possibility for other neighborhood institutions to mitigate or exacerbate the impact of criminal justice involvement on neighborhoods by remobilizing disadvantaged citizens. This chapter is based on interviews and observation of campaigns, county parties, and community organizations conducting voter mobilization during the 2008 presidential election. The discussion focuses on how the standard outreach procedures of these organizations reach, or fail to reach, individuals in low-income, high-incarceration neighborhoods. Traditional methods of voter mobilization involving at-home contacts do not work well in low-income communities, particularly with offenders. Instead, organizations that want to reach offenders and their families must start at the registration stage, reaching out through service providers and community events to provide legal advice and help with the registration process.

First, however, chapter 2 traces the mechanisms by which criminal justice supervision vicariously affects the community at large. As noted above, the key concept in this theory is the spatial concentration of imprisonment, probation, and parole. The main argument is that concentrating a large number of convicts whose civic and political capacity has been devastated by criminal justice supervision in a neighborhood diminishes the ability and desire of all neighborhood residents to participate in politics. To make this claim, the argument focuses first on the effects of criminal convictions and supervision on individual offenders, highlighting the effects of arrest, conviction, and punishment (incarceration and probation) on their political behavior and attitudes. After this brief discussion, the next step is to develop a theory of how criminal justice interactions at the individual level can affect the political attitudes and behavior of others in a neighborhood indirectly. This part of the chapter relies heavily on the neighborhood effects literature in sociology, plus work by Huckfeldt and Sprague in political science, to describe four mechanisms by which one individual's circumstances in turn produces spillover effects that matter for everyone around him. First, the cultural deviance model argues that individuals within communities engage in undesirable activities because they learn them from their neighbors.[18] The social disorganization model, in contrast, posits that individuals within communities engage in undesirable activities because their neighbors have no power to stop them due to weakened social networks.[19] Third, the institutional deprivation explanation suggests that incarceration hurts neighborhood participation by decreasing the availability of institutions that support voting.[20] Finally, the demobilization explanation would argue that high rates of criminal justice interactions make it less likely that parties, campaigns, interest groups, and local organizations will contact potential voters from a neighborhood.[21]

Contributions to Previous Literature

This book makes important contributions to political science, sociology, legal studies, and public policy debates. Sociologists have studied the impact of incarceration on phenomena other than political behavior, such as families, social disorganization, and crime rates, for decades.[22] Perhaps the most important contribution of this project is to introduce criminal justice interactions as increasingly important aspects of neighborhoods that need to be studied by political scientists, particularly those of us who study race politics and urban politics. Since the 1980s, the United States has experienced growth in the size and scope of the criminal justice system at the federal, state, and local levels; as measured by employment, criminal justice bureaucracies have expanded dramatically, as shown in figure 1.2. Today, the United States' system of criminal justice ranks among the world's most punitive. Between 1992 and 2000, 850,000 to 1 million felony convictions were handed down each year in the United States.[23] At the end of 2010, more than 7 million people were being supervised in prison, in jail, on probation, or on parole at all levels of government as a result of felony and misdemeanor convictions.[24] Since 1980, the incarcerated population and the number of inmates on death row have grown exponentially, as figures 1.3 and 1.4 show. Currently, more than 2.3 million adults are incarcerated in the nation's prisons and jails.[25] The US adult incarceration rate for all levels of government, at 731 per 100,000 adults as of 2010, is the highest in the world, surpassing even that of Russia.[26] Serving time in federal and state prison is becoming more commonplace, such that by the end of 2001, an estimated 5.6 million adults had done so.[27]

Despite the obvious increase in the size and scope of the criminal justice system over the past thirty years, scholars of American politics have yet to make the criminal justice system a central focus of inquiry in mainstream political science. Thus far, the primary discussion of the ways in which state action influences the polity can be found in the literature on policy feedback effects.[28] The policy feedback literature provides a useful starting point for thinking about the ways in

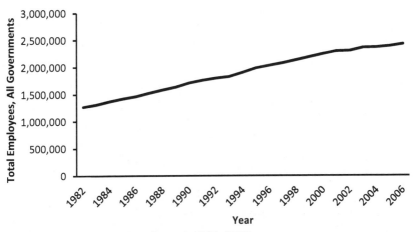

Figure 1.2: Criminal justice employment, 1982–2006.
Sourcebook of Criminal Justice Statistics Online 2009.

which state actions shape the relationships between citizens and the state, and among citizens themselves. However, the underlying theory of policy feedback has been developed and tested only with respect to policies concerned with redistributing material benefits across society. This book pushes the boundaries of this literature to question what happens when the government influences citizens not with monetary incentives, but with coercion.

Other scholars of American politics outside the policy feedback tradition gradually have begun studying some aspects of the criminal justice system. However, this work operates in a place outside mainstream discussions of the state and the citizen, which also tend to focus on the welfare state. Recent work highlights political explanations of criminal justice policy changes, measures the effects of public opinion on criminal justice severity, and explores variations in crime policies across states.[29] However, the criminal justice system has been not been studied in terms of its effects on the polity overall. Manza and Uggen's book *Locked Out* studies the impact of felon disfranchisement laws on ex-felon voting behavior.[30] However, Manza and Uggen's work is limited to the study of ex-felons, who tend to have low voter turnout regardless of their criminal convictions.[31] Moreover, disfranchisement laws represent only the tip of the iceberg with respect to how our policies toward offenders affect politics. Achieving a deeper understanding of how the criminal justice system affects citizen behavior and the

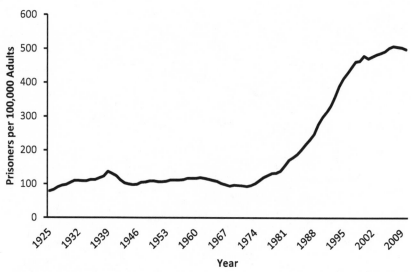

Figure 1.3: US incarceration rate, 1925–2009. Source: US Bureau of Justice Statistics.

broader polity requires neighborhood-level studies if we are to comprehend fully the significance of punitive justice policies.

For instance, most political science research on public opinion, trust in government, and other attitudes has been unable to account for the roles of either individual or neighborhood experiences with criminal justice in shaping those attitudes. American political scientists used to be quite interested in how interactions with the criminal justice system shaped political behavior and attitudes.[32] However, despite the fact that experiences with police and other officials have started riots and contributed to black mistrust of police and government,[33] few studies of public opinion and political behavior today directly examine personal or vicarious experiences of criminal justice supervision as an important predictor of outcomes.[34] Quite a few studies attempt to incorporate interactions with police into studies of public opinion on the criminal justice system.[35] However, most studies ignore just how prominently corrections (and most other aspects of the criminal justice system) feature in the everyday lives of disadvantaged citizens. This book demonstrates how vicarious neighborhood experiences with criminal justice supervision shapes participation in and perceptions of the polity, thus pointing out the importance of the experience of individuals and communities with criminal justice and convictions in research on political behavior.

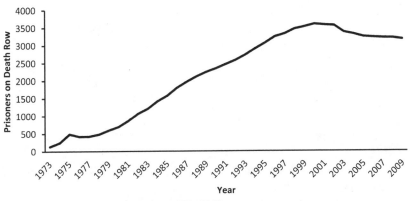

Figure 1.4: Prisoners on death row, 1973–2009.
Source: US Bureau of Justice Statistics.

The contribution of this book is to bring the state in its primary form, as the monopolizer of violence, back into discussions of American political behavior.[36] Political scientists cannot continue to focus on the role of the welfare state in shaping the polity while ignoring the role of the punitive state.[37] Redistribution and retribution cannot be treated separately, because our system of criminal retribution redistributes resources across individuals, families, and communities. Sociologists have shown that neighborhood interactions with the criminal justice system are related to individual and collective outcomes with respect to wealth, status, opportunity, and even health. This book adds politics to that list: the criminal justice system also redistributes political power within and across communities. This book is the first to look at the impact of modern correctional bureaucracies on neighborhood participation and attitudes. No other book offers such an extensive consideration of how criminal justice supervision shapes the political behavior of people who are not themselves under criminal justice supervision. By focusing on neighborhoods, it is easy to see how the criminal justice system contributes to structural political disadvantage.

It is important to note at the outset what this book does not do. This book does not argue for more lenient treatment of people who break the law. This book is not a manifesto for or against the prison boom, the war on drugs, or tough-on-crime policies. Individual offenders are discussed periodically throughout the manuscript; however, they are not the main focus of the book. Others have questioned the current justice system on any number of grounds, including racial bias,[38] fairness, and effectiveness in reducing crime.[39] Instead, the primary goal of this book is to help point out the negative externalities of mass supervision, the effects of which are felt by people who are not themselves convicted of crimes.

By focusing on the negative externalities of punishment, this book contributes to a growing literature that highlights the "collateral consequences" of the criminal justice system for communities and for society as a whole. This literature shows how the government, by punishing criminals, produces feedback effects that hurt not only individual convicts, but also the people who live around them. For example, many people have begun to suspect, and in some instances the evidence supports, that prisons are important to the transmission of infectious diseases among disadvantaged populations.[40] Incarceration also has been found to affect informal social control in neighborhoods, including the desire of neighbors to intervene when they see problems.[41] The evidence suggests that the criminal justice system destabilizes intimate partner relationships and promotes single parenthood as well.[42] Additional issues such as these make it important to consider more than just legal issues, potential victimizations, and notions of justice and desert when formulating crime and punishment policies. Rather, it is also important to weigh the negative consequences faced by the families and communities of the convicted, many of whom are innocent of wrongdoing.

Based on the discussion in the next chapter, it will become clear how the billions of dollars spent by federal, state, and local authorities on punishment could have an effect on the political participation of millions of men and women who live in disadvantaged communities. Because experiences with criminal justice supervision isolate, stigmatize, and exclude people categorized as offenders, it in turn decreases political participation within disadvantaged communities overall, thus keeping residents of those communities on the margins of the polity.

2

Theory

Yo I was born here, my momma was born here

Her momma was born here, my father was born here

And his father was born here, and we all here, livin' in fear

My peers are either dead or in prison for years

How many generations, get caught, in a perpetuation

Of poverty, robbery becomes a occupation

Look around, it's pure desolation

— Brand Nubian, "Still Livin' in the Ghetto"

The extent to which people feel acknowledged, respected, and included as equal members of the polity is a key measure by which to judge the health of a democratic society.[1] Political participation fosters this sense of belonging in citizens.[2] Laws, norms, and institutions encourage, and raise barriers to, voting and other forms of participation.[3] If such features of society privilege certain individuals and groups over others, they send different messages about the openness of the political system to citizen input to different groups.[4] They may also distribute participatory resources unequally across citizens.[5] Thus, it is important to study the different signals that key institutions in society send to citizens, because such signals can create disparities in political participation, and by extension, civic inequality.

Over time, scholars have identified many social, economic, and political institutions that encourage and discourage political participation by sending unequal messages and providing unequal resources to citizens. Almond and Verba identify schools as an important site of political learning to the extent that they encourage independent thought and self-determination among some young people and not others.[6] Employment that promotes subservience and dependence fosters a sense of political apathy among the lower classes.[7] Civic institutions such as churches, clubs, and membership organizations provide important resources such as leadership experience and social capital to those who have the money or free time to get involved.[8] Public bureaucracies often provide resources that can be used for political participation and that identify benefit recipients as deserving citizens who are entitled to make claims on the state.[9] Administrative and other restrictions on participation, such as time, place, and manner restrictions on assembly or poll taxes on voting often have been used to prevent political access for blacks and other groups.

In the same way, the criminal justice system also can create disparities in political behavior. As a result, it is important to view the criminal justice system as an institution, increasingly prominent in recent times, that has the potential to influence the sense that people are respected and included as citizens. Many scholars have made the point that the criminal justice system affects the quality of citizenship enjoyed by individual felons and ex-felons.[10] However, the criminal justice system plays a significant role in the political lives not only of disadvantaged citizens, but also of disadvantaged communities. The first chapter notes how experiences with law enforcement might trigger community protest or eliminate political mobilization. This chapter focuses on the final stage of the criminal justice process—punishment—as particularly important in shaping community political outcomes.

This chapter traces the mechanisms through which the punishment and supervision of individual neighborhood residents in prison, on probation, or on parole shapes political participation and thus political equality among neighborhoods. It will show how, for individuals living in disadvantaged communities, criminal justice supervision influences their experiences with the state and with fellow citizens, thus influencing the quality of democratic citizenship they enjoy. For convicts themselves, the mechanism through which this suppression occurs is obvious and will be outlined briefly in the following pages. However, for people without criminal backgrounds who merely share a common geographic or racial community with offenders, the role of punishment in influencing political participation and attitudes is less readily apparent. Thus, the bulk of this chapter is devoted to tracing the mechanisms by which individual convictions translate into community political disadvantage.

The main argument of this chapter is that neighborhood residents under criminal justice supervision are so disadvantaged and disaffected as a result of their punishment and its associated consequences that they cannot and, in many cases, do not want to contribute to the social, economic, and political life of the neighborhood. In many cases, these consequences include disfranchisement, labor market discrimination, social ostracism, and even expulsion from the neighborhood, as described below. These and other impediments placed by convictions in the way of individuals also matter for their families and neighborhoods as well, because the deteriorating circumstances of one neighborhood resident tend to affect the civic institutions and social life of the entire neighborhood. When only a few neighborhood residents bear the burdens of community supervision and incarceration, the community can overcome the inability of that small number of individuals to contribute. However, when larger numbers of residents face prison, probation, or parole, the impact of criminal convictions on community resources, attitudes, and mobilization is more widespread. This chapter presents four mechanisms through which high supervision rates might influence political behavior and attitudes: cultural deviance, social disorganization, resource deprivation, and demobilization.

However, before building the theoretical argument and outlining the four mechanisms, it is necessary to describe in detail the difficulties current and former offenders face as a result of conviction and punishment. The next section provides this important background information.

The Effects of Punishment on Individual Offenders

As Mayer and Jencks so succinctly stated, "Disadvantaged neighbors are a disadvantage."[11] It is difficult to find neighbors more politically, socially, and economically disadvantaged than those who are current and former offenders. For instance, it is no secret that people with convictions tend to have access to fewer resources than the rest of the population even prior to their convictions. For instance, in a national sample of state prisoners, about 70 percent of state inmates and 40 percent of state probationers did *not* have a high school diploma—in comparison, only 18 percent of the general population lacked high school diplomas.[12] Only 55 percent of state prisoners were employed full time at the time of their arrest, and only 15 percent reported earning more than $25,000 before their arrest.[13] In addition to resource disparities, prisoners tend to come from disadvantaged groups. The Bureau of Justice Statistics estimates that almost 60 percent of US inmates are under age 35.[14] Blacks and Hispanics each make up about

13 percent of the US population but are 37 percent and 22 percent of the nation's prisoners, respectively.[15]

Apart from the disadvantages that accrue disproportionately to the young, black, and poor, people convicted of crimes also face other problems that would affect their economic and social well-being. Because of their lower socioeconomic status and higher disease incidence, it could be that mortality rates are higher among offenders as well.[16] Psychological and emotional disturbances are more common among offenders.[17] Sexual abuse is high among these populations: 16 percent of male and 57 percent of female prisoners report having been victimized sexually prior to their entry into prison.[18] Drug and alcohol dependence is high among people who are convicted of crimes: one-third of federal and more than half of state prisoners reported committing their crimes while under the influence of alcohol or drugs.[19] Twenty-one percent of state and 16 percent of federal prisoners showed signs of past alcohol abuse, while 57 percent of state and 40 percent of federal inmates had used drugs in the month prior to committing their offense.[20] These types of physical and mental health concerns often render political, economic, and social life difficult, even impossible.

To be sure, people who have been convicted of crimes often face many disadvantages that would lower their turnout relative to the rest of the population. However, as a result of their involvement with the criminal justice system, convicted offenders also face a unique set of constraints that dramatically affects their propensity to participate in politics even long after their sentences are complete. Being convicted of a crime exacerbates the problems of poverty and isolation that have already dampened the civic capacity of these individuals prior to their conviction in several ways, as described below.

CIVIL, ECONOMIC, AND SOCIAL EXCLUSION

Once an individual becomes a criminal, often he or she becomes identified as an enemy of the state, a traitor unfit for and incapable of living up to the demands of citizenship. As a result, public policies are designed to exclude offenders from membership in the political community. Such policies are deemed just because the enemy of the state voluntarily forfeits his or her citizenship and thus no longer deserves to be treated the same as a member of the political community.[21] Rousseau argues that when a person chooses to violate society's laws, "he ceases to be a member; he even wages war with it."[22] Exclusion from the political community serves as a "quarantine" designed to protect virtuous citizens from dangerous criminals and to prevent their disorder from spreading. As noted above, this exclusion may involve the actual removal of individual bodies through exile, deportation, confinement, or, ultimately, execution. Conversely, political membership may be rescinded symbolically through the denial of political, economic, and social rights.

While people convicted of crimes can be physically removed from membership in the polity for a time, more often they are excluded symbolically from the polity in the sense that they are stripped of many of the basic rights and privileges afforded to other citizens in society. Aside from the loss of liberty, many of those who are convicted of crimes are denied the right to vote, run for office, receive social welfare benefits, participate in the labor market, and serve on juries. Regardless of whether they are physically present in the polity, the deprivation of civil, political, and social rights sends important messages about the exclusion of people convicted of crimes from the polity.[23]

The deprivation of the basic rights of citizenship, such as voting, jury service, and officeholding is the primary mechanism by which people convicted of crimes are excluded from civic membership. Apart from the direct effect of defining how and under what circumstances people convicted of crimes can participate in influencing their government, the loss of civic privileges associated with criminal convictions also conveys important symbolic meanings:

> It was the denial of the suffrage to large groups of Americans that made the right to vote such a mark of social standing. To be refused the right was to be almost a slave, but once one possessed the right, it conferred no other personal advantages. Not the exercise, only the right, signified deeply. Without the right, one was less than a citizen. Once the right was achieved, it had fulfilled its function in distancing the citizen from his inferiors, especially slaves and women.[24]

Similarly, the ability to serve on juries distinguishes the citizen from the powerless. Tocqueville argues that "the man who judges the criminal is really the master of society" and that "the institution of the jury, therefore, really puts the direction of society into the hands of the people."[25] Thus, the deprivation of civil rights implies that the primary mechanisms of influencing government—voting, holding office, and serving on juries—are closed to people convicted of crimes. Justice Thurgood

Marshall writes in his dissent in *Richardson v. Ramirez*, "There is certainly no basis for asserting that ex-felons have any less interest in the democratic process than any other citizen. Like everyone else, their daily lives are deeply affected and changed by the decisions of government."[26] However, depriving offenders of their civil rights renders them powerless to influence the trajectories of their own lives. The denial of civil rights deprives a person "of his civic personality and social dignity" and demonstrates society's "indifference to his interests."[27] Moreover, depriving people of their civil rights denies them the benefits that accrue from the act of participating, such as personal efficacy and a belief in the legitimacy of the political system.[28] The denial of civil rights also decreases respect for the rights of others. Tocqueville writes, "In America, the man of the people has conceived a lofty idea of political rights because he has political rights; so that his own are not violated, he does not attack those of others."[29]

Often, social membership is rescinded after a person is convicted of a crime. A person attains social membership in the polity to the extent that society cares about that person's interests and well-being.[30] Social membership is closely tied to the idea of social rights—that is, "rights to a minimum standard of welfare and income."[31] Access to jobs, education, and the social safety net are the quintessential expression of social membership. Mettler argues that such access includes people in the polity, writing that "the extension of social provision may not only ensure them some modicum of well-being but also convey to them a sense of dignity and value as citizens."[32]

The treatment of people convicted of crimes demonstrates their exclusion from social membership and society's indifference to their interests and well-being. Current public policies sharply delineate the subordinate, almost alien status of people with convictions in the United States. For instance, Wacquant, writing of the criminal conviction as the equivalent of civic death, points out that felons can be denied access to public funding for higher education, welfare payments, disability support, veterans' benefits, and food stamps as well.[33] People convicted of crimes also are discriminated against in the labor market.[34] Exclusionary policies such as these reflect society's view that people who have been convicted of crimes are thus "irredeemably different and dangerous" in a way that releases society from its obligations to them.[35] Such marginalization may hinder the ability of an offender to reenter society; the symbolic expulsion from the polity renders offenders less than human in the eyes of people who have not been convicted of crimes.

Of course, some may argue that people convicted of crimes do not deserve to have their needs taken into account, especially when those needs are perceived to conflict with those of people who have not violated the social contract. In this way, policies that exclude criminals from the polity are seen not only as punishments but also as "safeguards . . . interposed to prevent the lowest class of our people from exercising the highest and most important duty and privilege of a citizen."[36] A more recent opponent of the enfranchisement of offenders writes,

> [Advocates of voting rights for felons] maintain that felons who have rejected the rule of law for themselves should, by retaining the vote in prison, continue to take part in making laws for others to obey. The folly of this notion is self-evident to the citizens of all but three states. In most of the country, the exercise of the vote is understood not merely as conferring the right to govern oneself, but a right to share in the governing of others. When felons demand the right to vote, they demand the right to govern others while rejecting the right of others to govern them. In this they exhibit patent hypocrisy. When we deny felons the vote, we merely hold them to the logic of their own position on the law and maintain a minimum respect for the process by which laws are made.[37]

Ignoring the interests and well-being of people convicted of crimes keeps them from having status and priority equal to that of law-abiding citizens. Under this view, the unfair position is to allow a "good citizen of the State, who is interested in the common welfare" to "have his vote and power as a citizen neutralized by a convict, who is one of the vilest of the vile."[38]

DECREASING POLITICAL PARTICIPATION

By denigrating and rejecting people classified as criminals, American criminal justice policies should decrease the political participation of these individuals. In order to understand why these policies might affect participation, it first is necessary to explore the factors affecting an individual's decision to participate in politics. Explaining political participation is an inexact science, and even the most elegant theoretical models have difficulty predicting individual political involvement in practice. Still, these theories should prove helpful for understanding the decisions of people with convictions to participate in politics.

Rational choice models provide one way of thinking about the decision to engage in political activity. Simply put, rational choice theory posits that individuals choose to participate in or abstain from politics based on whether or not they believe the benefits they receive from participation will outweigh the associated costs of activity.[39] Most acts of participation are costly in that the tasks of acquiring political information, attending meetings, registering, or donating to campaigns require time and money.[40] Because the likelihood that one individual will make a difference is small, calculations based solely on this expected benefit mean that no one would ever participate.[41] However, social, economic, emotional, and other institutional factors also can enter the calculus and make the decision to participate more or less rational for a given individual. Such factors tend to have the effect of increasing or decreasing the benefits and costs of political activity.[42]

Being convicted and punished decreases the political participation of offenders because such an event dramatically affects the calculus of political participation. For these negatively constructed outsiders, participation in politics becomes an extremely costly act that confers few benefits. On the one hand, because of symbolic exclusion, people with criminal records are prevented from receiving many of the benefits of social and political membership that motivate participation. Moreover, their negative association and perceived powerlessness leads them to believe that their likelihood of success is small. On the other hand, the stigma and exclusion associated with convictions make the cost of participating high by erecting barriers to participation and then removing access to the resources to overcome those barriers. The costs of participating for these individuals are staggering.

Institutional factors limit political participation by making it even more costly in time, effort, and resources.[43] As described previously, people convicted of crimes lose the right to participate in elections; perhaps the most obvious barrier to the political participation of current and former offenders is legal disfranchisement.[44] The practice of legal disfranchisement dates back to antiquity.[45] In the United States, states first adopted disfranchisement statutes after the Revolutionary War; these statutes were extended after Reconstruction to deny the right to vote for convictions for minor offenses.[46] Over time, disfranchisement statutes became more restrictive even as the right to vote was extended to new segments of the population.[47] Currently, forty-eight states retain some restriction on the voting rights of felons and/or misdemeanants while they are serving their sentences; twelve states bar some or all ex-offenders from the ballot box, at times for life.[48]

Once the period of disfranchisement ends, institutional barriers still make electoral participation costly. Reregistration requirements may discourage participation for ex-offenders. The amount of time a person is required to register before an election may discourage turnout, as can the amount of bureaucratic hassle involved with registering.[49] Residency requirements for registration matter as well; criminal offenders tend to be less residentially stable and thus may not be allowed to register because of recent moves.[50] Poll locations and opening hours may not be convenient for people unable to afford childcare, time off from work, or decent transportation.[51]

Aside from institutional factors, according to Verba, Schlozman, and Brady, one of the primary factors affecting political participation is access to resources; people undertake political activities because they have resources such as time, money, education, and civic skills.[52] Because they decrease the costs of participating, such resources make political activity more likely. For instance, wealthy people have more disposable income to contribute to causes that concern them; they do not feel the burdens of campaign contributions as glaringly as do the poor.[53] People with higher levels of education know more about politics and find it easier to acquire new political information.[54] Likewise, individuals with high civic skills might find it easier to navigate the bureaucratic barriers associated with voting and other forms of participation.[55]

The social and economic exclusion associated with criminal convictions severely restricts the ability of offenders to gather resources that could be used for political participation after they have served their sentences. This statement is particularly true for offenders who face economic penalties as a result of their convictions. The unemployment rate among ex-offenders is much higher than that of the general population, implying that members of this group have less access to financial resources than their counterparts in the general population.[56] This high unemployment rate is partly due to discrimination in the private sector: employers use criminal background in making hiring decisions and many refuse to hire people with criminal records.[57]

Moreover, a criminal record tends to hurt black applicants more than whites, as employers are more likely to hire white ex-offenders than even blacks without any criminal history.[58] Such findings reflect the fact that stereotypes and convictions interact to influence the assignment of criminal labels and the imposition of the associated penalties. Often, because of social exclusion, ex-offenders have no recourse to other sources of income, especially if they have been convicted of drug offenses. All federal programs such as Temporary Assistance for Needy Families (TANF) and Supplemental Security Income (SSI) deny benefits to people convicted of drug crimes, sometimes permanently.[59] Drug offenders especially are limited in their ability to acquire civic skills, as they also are denied access to government grants for higher education. People with criminal convictions also are barred from federal public housing.[60] Some states deny public assistance for other types of offenses as well.

In addition to institutional barriers and resources, communities and social networks affect political participation. Processes of exclusion and stigmatization decrease the ability of offenders to form and maintain the networks that encourage political participation. This phenomenon especially affects offenders who experience periods of physical exclusion from their communities. Already-fragile social networks "are made tenuous by the distance between home and prison."[61] If they are released, inmates tend to return to the low-income, minority communities from which they came, which further depresses their individual civic capacities.[62] It is likely that the problems that ex-offenders face in reintegrating into their communities results in a lack of connection to the peer networks that reinforce the norm of political participation.[63] Although many nonpartisan groups, such as the NAACP and the American Civil Liberties Union (ACLU), attempt to register and mobilize ex-offenders, particularly those who have been legally disfranchised, most politicians and other groups ignore ex-offenders, often out of concern that associating with them would be portrayed as soft on crime. Because they are not as connected to peer networks or political parties, ex-offenders are less likely to be mobilized and therefore less likely to vote.

SHAPING INDIVIDUAL POLITICAL ATTITUDES

The experience of punishment also affects the relationship between citizens and government because punishments that involve supervision, unlike fines or corporal punishment, require repeated interactions with criminal justice bureaucracies. These experiences with punishment teach important lessons about how the government relates to citizens. As Soss writes, people tend to extrapolate their experiences with one aspect of the government to the entire government, and these experiences then "become the basis for broader orientations toward government and political action."[64] Experiences with government through public policies influence people's perceptions of the "general responsiveness of government to people like them."[65] For instance, Soss noted that clients of Aid to Families with Dependent Children (AFDC) viewed the agency "as a pervasive threat in their life, as a potent force whose limits were unclear," and as "an autonomous power over them."[66] Moreover, they saw their interactions with the agency "as one-way transactions in which the agency had the authority to issue directives."[67] As a result, AFDC clients believed "that speaking out is both ineffective and risky" and that they do not have the ability to influence government.[68]

Insofar as AFDC and criminal justice authorities both supervise and control underclass populations, one should expect people who experience criminal justice supervision to exhibit beliefs similar to those of welfare recipients regarding their relationship to government and personal efficacy.[69] When people experience policies "as fair and efficient, managed through procedures that made them feel treated as respected citizens," they view the government more positively.[70] Conversely, when policies assign burdens to people arbitrarily or according to a rule they do not accept, they foster the idea that the government does not care about people like them. As Abu-Jamal writes, "For those people, almost a million at last count, who wear the label 'prisoner' around their necks, there is no law, there is no justice, there are no rights."[71] Manza and Uggen find that such beliefs are common among offenders, who are more likely to agree with statements like "people like me have no say" and that they would "get nowhere talking to public officials."[72]

Studies of legal consciousness also find that people who have been involved with the criminal justice system have much lower levels of trust in government and politicians than those who have not had such experiences.[73] Perhaps this is because they perceive the government as arbitrary or unfair. The perceived fairness or injustice associated with a policy provides important information to citizens about the workings of government.[74] Thus, the appearance of differential treatment based on race, class, or gender by criminal justice policies has important implications for the political engagement of individual offenders. Many offenders are aware of the disparities in criminal justice, according to Davis: "Prisoners—especially blacks, Chicanos and Puerto Ricans—are increasingly advancing the proposition that they are *political* prisoners. They contend that they are political prisoners in the sense that they are largely the victims of an oppressive politico-economic order, swiftly becoming conscious of the causes underlying their victimization."[75] Perceived injustices in criminal justice policies also send messages to the broader society about the quality of the social and civil rights enjoyed by targeted groups such as minorities and the poor.

Racial disparities in criminal justice are especially problematic to the extent that they send the message that racial minorities are targeted by the state. The growth in criminal sanctions discussed in the previous chapter has a racially disparate impact. Blacks are 13 percent of the US population but are overrepresented among those who are arrested for crimes.[76] Blacks continue to be incarcerated at rates much higher than whites and Hispanics and make up a disproportionate share of federal and state prisoners, as noted above. Seventeen percent of black and 8 percent of Hispanic men have served time in federal or state prison in their lifetimes, compared with 2.6 percent of white men.[77] More than half the inmates legally executed since the 1930s have been black.[78] Current estimates project that almost one-third of black males born in 2001 will be incarcerated in a state or federal prison in their lifetimes, compared with 6 percent of white males.[79] Although involvement with the criminal justice system remains mostly a male phenomenon, racial disparities also exist among women. Black women are incarcerated at a rate more than twice that of Hispanics and five times that of whites.[80]

Disproportionate involvement in crime partially may explain the racial disparities in criminal justice involvement, but discrimination by law enforcement and courts may also contribute to this disparity. By many accounts, racial profiling by law enforcement is a persistent problem in many communities; blacks are often stopped and searched for traffic and other offenses at higher rates than whites.[81] These assumptions about individual behavior based on race may occur at the organizational level, or at the level of individual officers or agents. For instance, at the individual level, when confronted with targets of different races, both police officers and community members shoot faster when confronted with a black suspect than a white one, at times with tragic circumstances.[82] No one can forget the shocking killing of Amadou Diallo, an unarmed, 23-year-old African immigrant, by New York City police officers who reportedly assumed that Diallo was reaching for a gun. At the organizational level, legally, race can be used in an investigation when an agency has reliable information about the race of a perpetrator or suspect—that is, when a victim identifies a perpetrator as a member of a particular race.[83] More young black men report having been stopped by police than their white counterparts, often for no reason or for a reason perceived to be illegitimate.[84] As one college student reports, "They'll pull me aside sometimes because they say I fit the description. Yeah. Young black male. I always 'fit the description.'"[85]

The state also defines and discriminates against particular racial groups through another practice: selective enforcement. Although such practices are associated with Jim Crow–era racial discrimination, the rise of aggressive policing, border controls, and counterterrorism activities have led to disparities in arrests, prosecution, and convictions for crimes. The most widely acknowledged disparity is in the penalties for and enforcement of crack and powder cocaine violations at the federal level. The federal mandatory minimum for crack cocaine trafficking is ten years in prison, or twenty years if someone you sold to died, while possession of crack cocaine until recently incurred a five-year sentence.[86] In contrast, one had to possess 500 grams of cocaine powder to trigger the five-year mandatory minimum. The crack cocaine laws were thought to disproportionately target minorities.[87]

Since 1970, arrests for drug trafficking and possession have risen exponentially, so that now almost 2 million drug arrests take place each year. Almost all of the recent spike in convictions in federal court is for these new drug violations. In federal court, where penalties are most severe, people convicted of drug and weapons offenses are disproportionately minority—black and Hispanic. Among all prisoners, black and Hispanic prisoners are more likely to be in prison for drug crimes than property crimes; the opposite is true for whites. However, there are no statistically significant differences between reported drug use among blacks, whites, and Hispanics in the wider population; moreover, whites are more likely to report trying cocaine and other drugs than other groups. The disconnect between punishment rates and crime rates might be due to disparities in stops and arrests. Bob Herbert reports that 84 percent of the 450,000 people stopped by the

New York Police Department last year were black or Hispanic. Of those stopped, only 1.5 percent of blacks and 1.6 percent of Hispanics carried contraband, compared with 2.2 percent of whites. Nearly 60 percent of blacks and Hispanics who were stopped were also frisked, compared with only 46 percent of whites.[88]

Pretextual stops are becoming another source of selective enforcement in many cities.[89] In 1996, the Immigration and Nationality Act was amended to allow local law enforcement to be trained in immigration control.[90] Since then, local agencies have taken on a more active role in detaining illegal immigrants. Many of these detentions result from pretextual stops. In Maricopa County, Arizona, Sheriff Joe Arpaio uses traffic stops to arrest and detain immigrants.[91] To date, Arpaio has taken responsibility for 31,868 suspected illegal immigrants being held and questioned by Immigration and Customs Endorcement.[92] In Escondido, California, police use road blocks to check for drivers' licenses.[93]

Like "driving while Mexican," "driving while black" remains a widespread a problem. Studies by John Lamberth of New Jersey, Maryland, and other states plainly show that black drivers are stopped more often than whites, even though drivers in the two groups violate traffic laws at roughly the same rates.[94] In 2003, Maryland settled a lawsuit filed by the NAACP alleging racial profiling in traffic stops. As a final example, "flying while Arab" is yet another form of the race-based pretextual stop. Federal guidelines permit Transportation Security Administration and other law enforcement officers to subject members of certain ethnic groups to heightened scrutiny at airports. This policy has led to many humiliating and intrusive searches of Muslims and Arabs based on their appearance, religion, and ethnic origin.

Finally, racial disparities in sentencing also persist. Numerous studies have chronicled the racial gap in sentencing at both the federal and state levels; oftentimes, race has a persistent, direct effect on sentencing even when taking legally relevant characteristics such as the defendant's prior record and offense severity into account.[95] For instance, at the federal level, black drug offenders received harsher punishments than similarly situated whites, even while taking socioeconomic status, offense severity, criminal history, plea agreements, and sentencing departures into account.[96] This finding holds across all types of federal offenses, with blacks convicted of nondrug offenses receiving sentences that are five months longer, on average, than whites in comparable

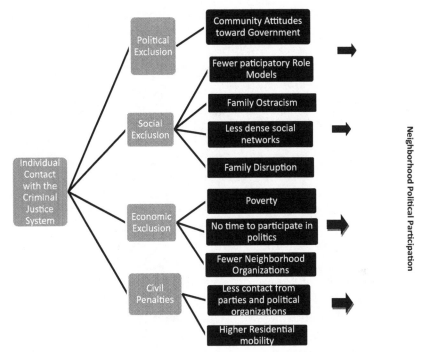

Figure 2.1: Path diagram of relationship between individual convictions and neighborhood political participation.

situations.[97] Similar evidence of the direct effects of race on sentencing can be shown at the state level, as well.[98]

The preceding discussion shows how personal characteristics, legal impediments, civil exclusion, mistreatment, and discrimination combine to establish current and former offenders as a group that is particularly prone to disadvantage. First, processes of stigmatization and exclusion delegitimize the standing of offenders to make demands of their fellow citizens and the government and sharply proscribe the mechanisms by which they may contribute to their neighborhoods. Second, the experience and appearance of injustice or unfairness in the routine interactions of individual convicts with the state further alienate offenders and diminish their belief in their capacity to influence government. Figure 2.1 summarizes the discussion. As a result of convictions, individual offenders face a number of consequences, labeled "political exclusion," "social exclusion," "economic exclusion," and "civil penalties," that can affect their social, economic, and political well being. The next section describes how this effect on offenders can translate into neighborhood effects through the processes in the third section of the diagram, which describes effects on communities.

The Neighborhood Effects of Supervision, Voting, and Prior Research

A variety of factors influence citizen participation in politics. As Verba and Nie argue, citizen participation is a function of individual social circumstances (such as age and race), attitudes (such as efficacy and group consciousness), and mobilization by voluntary associations or political parties.[99] However, political scientists have always recognized that "external social factors," or context, matter for political behavior.[100] A citizen's participation is a function of "the nature of the polity within which he lives."[101] While Verba and Nie primarily test whether the size of the polity itself decreases participation, other factors such as voting registration rules and other institutional barriers vary across localities and may also affect participation rates.[102]

Where a person lives affects political behavior not just through institutions, but also through social interactions. For some citizens, living in an area in which their views are in the minority, or having friends with different viewpoints, may discourage participation.[103] Citizen inactivity may result from living around others who "under-value participation."[104] Huckfeldt argues that being around others who participate may "encourage participation through the informal trans-mission of group based norms which turn participation into a social obligation."[105]

This theory adds the geographic concentration of imprisonment to the list of ways in which where a person lives might affect his or her political participation. There is evidence that imprisonment is con-centrated not only among certain social groups, but also in particular communities. For instance, incarceration rates vary across neighbor-hoods throughout New York City.[106] In Brooklyn, "eleven percent of the block groups in that borough . . . account for 20 percent of the popu-lation, yet they are home to 50 percent of the parolees."[107] Individuals within these communities tend to cycle in and out of justice supervi-sion; in the blocks mentioned in Brooklyn, "about one in every eight parenting-age males is sent to prison or jail each year."[108] In Cuyahoga County, Ohio, less than 1 percent of the county's block groups account for 20 percent of the county's prisoners.[109] Also at the local level, Lynch et al. find evidence of clustering of incarceration in Baltimore.[110]

In thinking about the ways in which such high concentrations of imprisonment might affect individual outcomes, it may be useful to "distinguish the effects of neighborhoods from the effects of neighbors."[111] That is, one should differentiate between contextual effects, which are based on the characteristics of an area's structural or institutional environment, and concentration effects, which result from having a large number people with similar personal characteristics in a single area or demographic group.[112] The presumption of concentration effects implies a "difference in behavior between a person who is alone in being exposed to certain macrostructural constraints, on the one hand, and a person, on the other hand, who is influenced both by these constraints and by the behavior of others who are also affected by them."[113] For instance, all other factors being equal, people who are poor are likely to adopt different behaviors if they live around affluent people than if they lived around other poor people.

The concentration and contextual effects associated with mass imprisonment are many and varied. First, with respect to concentration effects, recall the pithy point that "disadvantaged neighbors are a disadvantage."[114] As noted above, it is difficult to find neighbors more disadvantaged than those who are current and former offenders. To be sure, prisoners tend to have access to fewer resources than the rest of the population even prior to being convicted of crimes. However, as the previous discussion shows, prisoners are physically and psychically excluded from social, economic, and political life through the actions of the state.[115] Having a high concentration of convicted offenders in a neighborhood means having a large number of individuals who share a problematic relationship with the state in one space. As noted above, such concentration effects may alter the behavior and attitudes of other neighborhood residents. For instance, neighborhoods that have fewer voters as role models may fail to transmit norms of participation effectively even to enfranchised residents and future voters because people tend to "learn the community's participatory values as they observe ample instances of engagement among their family members and peers."[116] Spouses of convicted offenders also miss out on the participatory effects of having a partner that votes.[117] These effects might be further exacerbated by the experience and appearance of injustice or unfairness in the criminal justice system.[118]

These concentration effects, in turn, reinforce aspects of the neighborhood structural and institutional context that might further decrease voting. Communities pay an economic and social price for having a large proportion of their members, particularly parenting-age males, convicted of felonies each year. The impact of convictions on communities is separate from that of crime and is well documented. Although it seems counterintuitive to suggest that it is "bad for neighborhood life to remove people who are committing crimes," it may not be the case that arresting, convicting, and punishing offenders will increase safety by incapacitating criminals.[119] First, it often is the case that people who commit crimes "contribute both positively and negatively toward family and neighborhood life."[120] Convicting these individuals or removing them from the community may help eliminate the scourge of crime at the cost of breaking up families.[121] Often, people convicted of crimes have both legitimate and illegitimate sources of income that they use to support their families.[122] Imprisoning people prevents them from contributing to family and community upkeep altogether during the course of their sentences, thus increasing neighborhood and family poverty.[123] Convictions may affect voter mobilization; parties, interest groups, and campaigns are more likely to reach out to registered voters and are less likely to contact households where voters have been removed from the registration rolls because of felony convictions.[124] Finally, convictions have important effects on neighborhood social life. Imprisonment has been shown to increase neighborhood social disorganization; disorganized communities cannot exert informal controls over their members, because they lack informal ties such as friendships and formal social ties such as stable families that help socialize people into desirable behavior.[125]

These concentration and contextual effects occur through four mechanisms: cultural deviance, social disorganization, resource deprivation, and political demobilization. Each mechanism is discussed in more detail below.

CULTURAL DEVIANCE

One definition of culture is "modes of behavior learned within the community."[126] The adoption of deviant behaviors (such as crime or nonvoting) may thus be explained as a process of "socialization to subcultural values condoning as right conduct" what the dominant culture thinks of as deviance.[127] Culture-of-poverty theorists first developed this notion to explain why social problems affected residents of the ghetto at high rates. As an example, Lewis writes, "By the time slum children are age six or seven, they have usually absorbed the basic values and attitudes of their subculture and are not psychologically geared to take full advantage of changing conditions or increased opportunities which may occur in their lifetime."[128] Massey and Denton also argue that segregation "concentrates male joblessness, teenage motherhood, single parenthood, alcoholism, and drug abuse, thus creating an entirely black social world in which these oppositional states are normative."[129] As an example from politics, Verba and Nie argue that a person who lives around others who do not participate "would violate the norms of those around him if he tried to participate."[130]

In this context, however, cultural deviance provides a mechanism by which the experiences with and attitudes toward government of individual offenders can vicariously affect the people around them. The term "cultural deviance" refers to shared attitudes in a subculture or subpopulation that differ from those held by the wider, mainstream society.[131] These "deviant" attitudes might arise not in a vacuum but rather in response to the common experiences of policy targets with government bureaucracies. In this way, the arguments presented here dovetail with those of the policy feedback literature presented earlier. However, the original theoretical contribution of this section is the *extension* of the policy effects on individual targets to the entire community. Unlike the policy feedback literature, the focus here is not on the effects of policies on individual targets (in this case, offenders who directly encounter the criminal justice system) but rather on people who are not policy targets themselves.

The cultural deviance argument relies on a mechanism of cultural transmission—the adoption of norms and beliefs based on contact with others who hold and communicate those beliefs. People tend to adopt the culture of their communities either through explicit transmission and teaching or passively through the presence of role models; the transmission of cultures should be "efficient when a mode of behavior is encountered frequently and in many different persons.[132] Wilson agrees that "a person's patterns and norms of behavior tend to be shaped by those with which he or she has had the most frequent or sustained contact and interaction."[133] Cultural transmission is not always a function of geography; it may also occur via contact among members of different racial and ethnic groups who share the same "counterpublic spaces" even if they do not share geographic spaces.[134]

As noted in the previous section, direct experiences with the criminal justice system impart lessons to individuals about their relationship with the government. People who have been convicted, based on their negative experience with law enforcement and other agencies, most likely do not believe that they have the ability to influence government actions. They are also likely to be alienated from the government altogether or reluctant to provide information or make contact with government officials voluntarily. "Because the larger society has clearly rejected him," a convicted individual may in turn reject "the values, the aspirations, and the techniques of that society."[135] Citizens who have negative experiences with the criminal justice system, "scornful of what they consider the hypocrisy and the dishonesty of the larger society," may develop and transmit oppositional cultures that devalue participation in mainstream politics to other community residents.[136] In this way, increasingly negative interactions with state authorities that are focused on a particular area may cause many residents in a community to develop negative orientations toward government.[137] Such negative views of the government have been shown to decrease voting.[138] Other work shows how direct experiences with other bureaucracies including police,[139] courts,[140] corrections,[141] the Veterans Administration,[142] and the Social Security Administration[143] influence political attitudes such as perceptions of legitimacy, efficacy, and trust in government.

To the extent that convicts come from a spatially concentrated area, these attitudes are more likely to be shared with and by other family and community members through the process of accidental or nonconscious cultural transmission.[144] These antigovernment attitudes spread throughout communities more quickly as more convictions take place. Children are especially vulnerable to this process and "are disadvantaged because the social interaction among neighbors tends to be confined to those whose skills, styles, orientations, and habits are not as conducive to promoting positive social outcomes" or positive relationships with government.[145] Because "children and newcomers learn the community's participatory values as they observe ample instances of engagement among their family members and peers," neighborhoods that have fewer voters as role models may fail to transmit norms of participation effectively even to enfranchised residents and future voters.[146] Spouses of convicted offenders also miss out on the participatory effects of having a partner that votes.[147]

However, it is also important to note that cultural transmission is not the only factor shaping attitudes toward the government and other formal political institutions. Previous research shows that other factors such as fear of crime,[148] positive personal experiences with police and courts,[149] or unfair treatment by police[150] also have strong effects on attitudes toward the openness of government among people who live in high-crime and high-conviction neighborhoods.

SOCIAL DISORGANIZATION

In contrast to cultural deviance theories, social disorganization models do not presume that people adopt the norms of deviant subcultures. Instead, most people accept the values of the wider society but fail to live up to those standards of behavior because deviations from norms are not costly.[151] Disorganized communities cannot exert informal controls over their members because they lack informal ties such as friendships and formal social ties such as stable families and membership organizations that help socialize people into desirable behavior.[152] In contrast to disorganized neighborhoods, Wilson argues, "Neighborhoods that feature higher levels of social organization—that is, neighborhoods that integrate the adults by means of an extensive set of obligations, expectations, and social networks—are in a better position to control and supervise the activities and behavior of children. Youngsters know they will be held accountable for their individual and group action; at the same time, they know they can rely on neighborhood adults for support and guidance."[153] Social disorganization theories recognize that individual behaviors are shaped by those around them not only through the transmission of cultural ideals but also through their enforcement.

A growing incidence of convictions may increase social disorganization or the ability to enforce community norms by disrupting social networks. Residential instability in a community often leads to social disorganization.[154] Drug convictions in particular increase residential mobility for families because people with drug convictions are not allowed to live in public housing.[155] Moreover, exits and entries to communities because of imprisonment also disrupt family and friendship networks.[156]

A second factor in the breakdown of social networks is stigma.[157] Families with convicted members often avoid contacts with friends and family. As one woman whose husband was incarcerated says, "You isolate yourself because, you know, even though the other person don't know what you going through, you really don't want to open up and talk to them about it. You don't want them knowing your business. Or it's a certain amount of respect you want them to have. I just don't like the idea of people knowing that he's incarcerated. . . . You know. So I live a lie."[158] Convictions may be less stigmatizing as more and more community members experience them, at least within the community.[159] However, contacts with higher-status outsiders may still provoke encounters that prove awkward and demoralizing for offenders and their families.

Finally, to the extent that an increase in convictions implies an increase in the number of unemployed and unstable residents, people may choose to isolate themselves from their less desirable neighbors. As Wilson writes, residents of a public housing project in Denver "resisted casual contact with their neighbors, established few friendships, and did not get involved with neighborhood problems," because they were concerned about safety and suspicious of their neighbors.[160] Victims of crime demonstrate lower levels of social trust; likewise, community residents who experience harassment also may withdraw from public spaces.[161] As one woman interviewed in Chicago explains, "Sometimes I walk out of my house and start to try to walk down the street, and a gang will cross the street and try to scare me and my mother. . . . Actually, we're afraid to walk around in the neighborhood after it gets dark. I stay right in front of the house where my parents can see me."[162] In many instances, deteriorating neighborhood conditions and fear of crime can push community members to move away entirely, spurring a process of depopulation.[163]

Social organization is particularly important in disadvantaged neighborhoods. Although many of the networks in disadvantaged communities lack social capital,[164] they still can provide important resources to neighborhood residents. Women in particular often rely on social networks to help with caring for children and fulfilling other family responsibilities.[165]

RESOURCE DEPRIVATION

Living near people with the same characteristics also affects the institutional context of behavior. Wilson stresses that the "constraints and opportunities associated with living in a neighborhood in which the population is overwhelmingly socially disadvantaged" are primarily institutional in nature.[166] The concentration of joblessness, for instance, means that a community lacks the economic resources to sustain "basic institutions" like "churches, stores, schools, recreational facilities" and voluntary associations.[167] These basic institutions facilitate individual and collective life, enabling people to build social networks, transmit community norms, educate children, and access the labor market.[168] Thus, concentration effects may create contextual effects; neighborhoods with a large number of disadvantaged residents produce an environment adverse to individual development, not because of peer pressure or interpersonal interactions, but because such neighborhoods are devoid of the resources that promote success.

A community pays not only a social price, but also an economic price for having a large proportion of its members convicted each year. The impact of convictions on communities is separate from that of crime and is well documented. As noted above, people who commit crimes "contribute both positively and negatively toward family and neighborhood life," and a criminal conviction might harm the ability of offenders to continue to support their families and neighborhoods.[169] Second, people who are convicted and incarcerated usually come back to the community worse off than when they left, unable to find employment and "socialized into prison subcultures."[170] As Travis notes, "The significant increases in arrests, removals, imprisonment, and return of large numbers of individuals, mostly males, have placed severe additional burdens on the capacity of those communities to do what communities should do—namely, exist as places where individuals, families, and civic institutions can thrive."[171] Each of these factors contributes to the decline in the norms, institutions, and social controls that facilitate participation.

The economic resources of a community are affected by its members' experiences with criminal justice supervision. As was just noted, people convicted of crimes have both legitimate and illegitimate sources of income that they use to support their families.[172] Incarcerating people prevents them from contributing to family and community upkeep altogether during the course of their sentences. Likewise, once people are convicted of crimes, it is much more difficult for them to find and keep legitimate employment after their sentences due to the reluctance of employers to hire them, even if they are not sent to prison.[173] Moreover, employers may be less inclined to hire *any* individuals from particular communities based on the reputation of their neighborhood. According to Wilson, many employers "express concerns about [inner city poor blacks'] honesty, cultural attitudes, and dependability—traits that are frequently associated with the neighborhoods in which they live."[174] Several employers in Wilson's study associated people with such crimes as stealing, dishonesty, robbery, and drug abuse just by virtue of the neighborhoods in which they lived.[175] Thus, communities that have had large numbers of people convicted of crimes may experience high rates of joblessness. Joblessness, in turn, increases the isolation of community members.[176] Because of this increased isolation, the unemployed not only miss out on many opportunities to find work, but also miss out on the political discussions and mobilization that take place through work.[177]

Imprisonment especially contributes to family poverty both by removing income and by breaking up families. Convictions are costly, especially when then involve incarceration. Simply communicating with an incarcerated family member over the phone can be expensive—visits even more so if the family member is imprisoned far away from home.[178] Strong evidence suggests that, because of this disruption of family ties, increases in incarceration rates depress marriage and increase rates of single parenthood.[179] Incarceration also tends to diminish ties between parents and their children.[180] Living with a convicted offender makes life difficult:

> The already overburdened role of caretaker in low-income families is further complicated by the constant threat women face of possible arrest and detention of a family member, chaotic trials, long prison sentences, expensive visits and phone calls from correctional facilities, confusing parole hearings, probation requirements that may involve making a change in household arrangements if more than one family member has a felony conviction, and the ever present risk of rearrest.[181]

Families in public housing are especially vulnerable, because in many cases, family members with convictions are barred from these facilities.[182]

This increase in joblessness and family poverty leads to an increase in neighborhood poverty. At the same time, out-migration of stable residents due to the increase in convictions further diminishes the resources available to sustain communities. "Economically stable and secure families" provide financial support to voluntary associations, schools, and other institutions that facilitate individual and collective political activities.[183] Neighborhood poverty has important implications for community institutions and thus participation. In neighborhoods where many of the members are poor and unemployed, the resources to support social and financial institutions are unstable. The lack of resources available to support community institutions especially hurts churches, which are particularly important in mobilizing African Americans.[184] Cohen and Dawson find that living in an impoverished neighborhood decreases the probability that a person will belong to a church or other voluntary organization.[185] Residence in a high-poverty neighborhood (where more than 20 percent of residents live below the poverty line) decreases the likelihood that an individual will talk about politics, attend public meetings, or give money to candidates.[186]

DEMOBILIZATION

The demobilization explanation would argue that punishing residents hurts a neighborhood to the extent that such negative interactions with the government make it less likely that parties, campaigns, interest groups, and local organizations will contact potential voters from that neighborhood. Mobilization—activities designed to get people to register, vote or otherwise participate in politics—is undertaken most visibly by campaigns, parties, interest groups, and nonpartisan organizations, but it also occurs through person-to-person contacts. Large-scale mobilization efforts are costly, and organizations employ time and resources strategically in order to reach those voters most likely to participate (and participate on behalf of the right side).

Punishment damages both the partisan and the interpersonal mechanisms of mobilization. Political parties, campaigns, and interest groups tend to concentrate their efforts in places where mobilization is more effective. For instance, parties often fail to mobilize communities with members of low socioeconomic status.[187] They tend to contact people who have voted before, especially those who have voted in primaries.[188] Using voter registration lists to mobilize citizens makes it unlikely that people who have never voted will be contacted or mobilized. Although this technique is most effective for mobilization, going door-to-door may yield fewer voters in high-conviction neighborhoods if residents are afraid to open their doors to strangers.[189] Interpersonal networks of mobilization may also falter in communities where many citizens have been sent to jail or prison

Theory 39

or been disfranchised. There are fewer voters available to serve as discussion partners in high-conviction neighborhoods.[190] Potential voters that live in these communities may be less exposed to placards, yard signs, and bumper stickers, all of which communicate important political information.[191] The disruption of social networks that occurs because of imprisonment or social ostracism may also impede the dissemination of political information.[192]

Aside from these more practical aspects of mobilization, it is also important to recognize such outreach as a way for political parties and other elites to invite citizens to participate in politics. However, because their primary interest is in reelection, parties and politicians have no incentive to encourage the participation of individuals who cannot help and may even hurt them in this goal.[193] Politicians often find it politically advantageous to adopt "tough on crime" positions.[194] When a large percentage of community residents is perceived as criminals, politicians not only lack any incentive to pursue policies in the interests of the neighborhood, they also have clear incentives to punish the neighborhood by imposing burdensome policies.[195] The experience of the Massachusetts Prison Association illustrates the difficulty of mobilizing offenders and the people closely associated with them.[196] When these inmates attempted to register their political action committee with the State Office of Campaign and Political Finance, Acting Governor Paul Cellucci denounced the group, issued an executive order barring prisoners from forming PACs, and filed a constitutional amendment designed to strip inmates of their right to vote.[197] Other officials refused to accept campaign donations from the group. In this prominent instance, politicians ignored the needs of inmates and their families and friends, thus denying political access to the convicted offenders and demobilizing innocent bystanders.

Alternative Hypotheses

Although it seems obvious that the growing incidence of criminal justice supervision among neighborhood residents would decrease political participation and affect citizen attitudes, it is entirely plausible that the number of people from the community who are being punished for felonies would have no effect or even the opposite effect in the aggregate once intervening factors are taken into account. The apparent relationship between punishment and participation could be spurious. Several factors could account for both community supervision rates and political outcomes, including racial composition, poverty, and crime rates. Once these factors are taken into account, voting may be unrelated to convictions. Alternatively, the conviction of neighborhood residents may *increase* voter participation by making neighborhoods safer and by restoring social trust among law-abiding community members.[198]

Similarly, social capital theorists rely on social disorganization models to link crime rates with the level of civic engagement in a community. However, in these arguments, the causal direction is *reversed*: civic engagement, often measured as an index of voting and other political activities, decreases the crime rate and, by extension, the supervision rate.[199] Rising crime, in turn, further decreases civic engagement in communities. Thus, social capital researchers also find a negative correlation between crime and voting and other forms of civic engagement. However, the suppression operates solely through the inability of low-engagement communities to enforce social norms or due to the breakdown of social networks. Such analyses fail to take supervision into account and ignore the ways in which frequent negative interactions with state authorities as a result of crime suppress civic engagement.[200]

Finally, communities with many convicted members may in fact participate less or have negative political attitudes even after accounting for poverty and other factors. However, this finding may be explained by a sorting effect. Perhaps there is some underlying quality of people such that those who commit crimes also do not want to participate in politics. If people who tend to commit crimes tend to live together in the same neighborhoods and sort themselves accordingly, then the neighborhood itself does not change individual behavior; rather, the concentration of certain behaviors in the neighborhood is the result of sorting.[201]

Conclusion

The consensus among anthropologists and sociologists is that the concentration of social ills matters for communities. As Massey and Denton argue with respect to neighborhoods, "Identical individuals with similar family backgrounds and personal characteristics will lead very different lives and achieve different rates of socioeconomic success depending on where they reside."[202] While the evidence suggests that this finding is true for crime, poverty, teenage motherhood, and contagious diseases, the *political* effects of living in a neighborhood where many people have been convicted of crimes has been little studied, despite the fact that criminal convictions have grown over the past three decades.[203] The impact of convictions on neighborhood politics, then, deserves further attention.

This chapter presents a theory of why criminal convictions matter for local politics. At the national and state levels, the number of individuals that experience convictions may be too small to matter for electoral outcomes. However, because of the concentration of criminal justice supervision, supervision rates in particular local areas may be high enough to produce political effects by producing important spillover effects that marginalize the people in the neighborhood who are not under criminal justice supervision. The individual consequences of criminal justice involvement might spread by several possible mechanisms.

First, cultural deviance theories suggest that convicted individuals, because they tend not to vote, influence the voting patterns of those around them by providing examples of nonvoting to their partners, children, and friends. Experiences with criminal justice also promote negative attitudes toward government and a belief that participation is futile among convicted individuals; offenders may communicate these attitudes to other neighbors and friends, thus influencing their levels of trust in government and efficacy as well.

Second, the conviction of neighborhood residents also may destroy a community's ability to enforce norms of voting and political participation. Incarceration is perhaps the best example of how the conviction of individual offenders can affect the social organization of entire neighborhoods. Incarcerated people are removed from their families and friendship networks, thereby destroying links among neighborhood residents through which social and civic norms are enforced. Convictions also impose stigmas on offenders and their families; the shame of convictions might lead families to withdraw from community life and positive influences.[204] Convicted individuals and their families may be ostracized involuntarily by other neighborhood residents, removing them from the formal and informal networks that provide political information and encourage voting.

Third, when residents of a neighborhood are excluded from the labor market and denied access to public assistance because of criminal convictions, the neighborhood as a whole suffers because those offenders cannot support themselves or their families. The economic strain on the families of offenders means that they cannot contribute their fair share of financial resources to neighborhood institutions. As a result, churches, neighborhood associations, and schools are deprived of the resources they need to adequately serve the needs of community members. Because they are important loci of mobilization efforts, depriving neighborhoods of these important resources diminishes the voter participation of all residents, including those who have not experienced criminal convictions.

Finally, political elites—parties and individual politicians—tend not to reach out to residents of high-supervision neighborhoods. This political exclusion can occur incidentally through the standard operating procedures of mobilization that these organizations undertake. Political exclusion might also take place intentionally because political elites have an incentive to ignore residents of high-supervision neighborhoods. Interpersonal mobilization may take place less often in high-supervision neighborhoods as well.

Testing the claim that high supervision rates suppress political participation and affect the relationship between citizens and the state will be the subject of the next three chapters. Chapter 3 presents a new collection of imprisonment and community supervision data for neighborhoods in two states: Georgia and North Carolina. The highlight of this chapter will be the presentation of maps and tables that illustrate the variation in the extent to which neighborhood residents experience prison, probation, and parole either themselves or vicariously. These maps and tables show the geographic concentration of both community supervision and imprisonment. These measures of neighborhood community supervision and imprisonment, coupled with other block group-level measures such as crime, poverty, and median income, will be used to predict neighborhood political behavior in chapter 4 and to test possible mechanisms in chapter 5. Finally, chapter 6 focuses on mobilization as a way to counter the effects of the criminal justice system on political participation.

3

A First Look
Imprisonment and Community Supervision

I see a lot of people there from my old neighborhood.
— Tangenea Miller, Houston Corrections Officer[1]

In 2006, only 5 percent of respondents to the General Social Survey reported that they knew someone from their neighborhood who was currently in state or federal prison.[2] Only 19 percent of respondents reported that they knew anyone in prison at all.[3] Most Americans, then, rarely experience imprisonment either themselves or vicariously through their friends or neighbors. However, when these same questions are asked among people living in poor and minority communities, people report that many members of their families and communities are locked up. For instance, 37 percent of respondents to the African American Men Survey (also conducted in 2006) reported that they had had a close friend or family member in prison.[4] Anecdotal evidence also suggests that prison and community supervision are common occurrences in poor and minority neighborhoods. Kenneth Barber, a native of the Frenchtown community in Tallahassee, Florida, was quoted in *Newsweek* as saying "I don't think you're going to find anybody in the neighborhood who doesn't have a relative who's in prison or been in prison."[5] Toylean Johnson, quoted in the same article, reports, "I personally know of at least 40 or 50 kids . . . who are either locked up, who've been in prison and are back on the street or on paper."[6] In such communities, "prison time can seem as inevitable as the rain."[7]

These claims are no exaggeration, as this chapter will show. It begins the work of matching the theoretical concerns about differences in the quality of citizenship enjoyed by different segments of the polity presented in chapter 2 to empirical investigation of the presence of such inequality. It presents an original and extensive collection of data on the imprisonment and community supervision rates of neighborhoods, or block groups, in two states: Georgia and North Carolina. These data were assembled from records of departments of corrections, public health data, and proprietary estimates of 2008 population and other block group characteristics from Scan/US and Geolytics. In later chapters, these data will be used to explore the relationship between neighborhood criminal justice characteristics and political participation and attitudes. However, the goal of this chapter is to introduce the data, discuss its assembly, and use it to produce a snapshot of criminal justice supervision at the neighborhood level.

These data richly describe the context of criminal justice supervision for nearly ten thousand neighborhoods across these two states. The chapter presents the variation in the extent to which adult and young adult residents of different neighborhoods experience prison, probation, and parole visually in maps of four major cities in each state, plus a table of descriptive statistics. To explain this variation, scatterplots and correlations between community supervision and imprisonment rates and poverty, homicide rates, black percentage of the population, and Hispanic or Latino percentage are introduced. Block groups with high community supervision and imprisonment rates are presented and discussed in detail as well, with an eye toward explaining these more extreme outliers.

To preview the key findings, imprisonment and community supervision are distributed unevenly across neighborhoods. Most block groups in this study have above-average concentrations of prisoners (measured as imprisoned residents per square mile). Moreover, as we might expect from previous research, there are many outlier block groups with extremely high concentrations of prisoners. For example, 6,681 of the 9,486 block groups in the final sample have prisoner densities higher than the national average of 0.43 prisoners per square mile. There are also many neighborhoods, 3,508, that have prisoner densities that are ten times the national average. Five hundred forty block groups have no residents in prison. Black neighborhoods experience much higher concentrations of prisoners. For the 25 percent of neighborhoods in which blacks represent less than 7.5 percent of the population, the average prisoner density is about 1.81 prisoners per square mile. However, in the 25 percent of neighborhoods in which blacks represent more than 42 percent of the population, the average prisoner density is 41.66 prisoners per square mile.

Community supervision density (measured as the number of people on probation or parole per square mile) is also concentrated, as data from the 4,948 North Carolina block groups show. Three quarters, or 3,741, block groups in North Carolina have community supervision densities greater than 1 probationer or parolee per square mile, while 1,518 have densities greater than 10 probationers or parolees per square mile. Only 10 of the 4,948 block groups have no one under community supervision.

Though these figures seem astonishingly high, the analysis reveals that the circumstances of young adults of ages 18–34 are much more dire in many neighborhoods. Ninety-six block groups across Georgia and North Carolina had young adult imprisonment rates higher than 10 percent, while 86 block groups (North Carolina only) have young adult community supervision rates higher than 10 percent. Only 1,296 block groups had no young adults in prison, and only 117 block groups had no young adults on probation or parole.

As might be expected, this pattern of imprisonment and community supervision is related to race, crime, and poverty. The percentage of neighborhood residents who are black is highly and positively correlated with imprisonment and moderately positively correlated with community supervision rates. Likewise, poverty and homicide rates are positively correlated with both imprisonment and supervision rates. Interestingly enough, the relationship between imprisonment and community supervision rates and Latino ethnicity is mixed.

These and other findings are discussed more fully in the remainder of this chapter. First, however, the data are described in more detail in the next section.

The Data

One of the most exciting facets of this study is that it explores neighborhood politics and criminal justice involvement using administrative data on actual offenders, voters, and crimes maintained by various state agencies. The data for this study took several years to construct and were obtained by combining updated demographic estimates for block groups with data on prison inmates, probationers, parolees, voters, and, where available, crimes. The result of this massive effort is the combining of voter registration and history records, criminal records, and geographic data into a dataset on which spatial analyses can be performed.

DEMOGRAPHIC DATA

As a reminder, block groups constitute neighborhoods throughout this book. In this chapter, block groups are the units of analysis.[8] Estimates for the 2008 demographic characteristics of block groups were obtained from Scan/US and Geolytics.[9] Because of population changes since the decennial census, population data at the block group level from the 2000 census may be inaccurate.[10] Scan/US produces updated estimates of block group populations each year using US Postal Service delivery statistics, direct marketing databases, credit bureau reporting agencies, and other data sources.[11] Geolytics produces profiles of the relative economic characteristics of block groups using similar methods.[12]

For each block group, the proportion of vacant housing units, the female-to-male ratio, the black proportion of the population, the Hispanic or Latino proportion, the other minority proportion, the percentage of households with incomes under $10,000, the proportion of adults under age 25, the proportion in group quarters, the total population, the adult population, and the population density were obtained using the data from Scan/US. The proportions of noncitizens and unemployed residents and the female high school completion rates for each block group were provided by Geolytics. Two hundred seventy-five block groups were excluded from the data because they contained large numbers of ineligible adults, based on the group quarters and citizenship measures. An additional 181 block groups were excluded from the data because the number of voters exceeded the estimated adult population size due to errors in the population estimates. Finally, 109 block groups were excluded because they contained no household population (either no people or all members in group quarters).

DEPARTMENT OF CORRECTIONS DATA

In each state, the department of corrections maintains highly detailed data on all offenders convicted of felonies who are sentenced to state supervision in prison or in the community through probation or parole. People convicted of felonies in federal court who served sentences under federal authorities and people convicted of misdemeanors or infractions in municipal court who served time in the county jail are not included in the analysis.[13] In all states in this analysis, all offenders accused of state felonies are tried, convicted, and punished by state authorities, such that the files represent a complete list of people who have or are being supervised for felony convictions by that state. People with misdemeanor convictions who were supervised by local authorities are absent from the data, as are people convicted under Federal law.

The North Carolina Department of Correction provided deindividuated data on the race, gender, offense, age, sentence length, punishment type, and address for all individuals under state supervision for felonies as of October 8, 2008 (that state's voter registration closing date that year), as well as a separate file of individuals who were admitted to state prison, probation, or parole between August 1, 2008, and February 4, 2009. The Georgia Department of Corrections provided demographic, crime, and criminal history information on all offenders ever supervised by the Georgia Department of Corrections up to September 2009, making it possible to select a range of dates for the offender population. However, last-known-address data are available only for prisoners.

As described here, address data for prisoners, probationers, and parolees were provided unevenly across states. As a result, complete information on both imprisonment and community supervision rates is available only for North Carolina block groups. For Georgia block groups, only the imprisonment rate can be calculated. Thus, throughout this chapter, unless otherwise noted, data on current imprisonment rates include block groups from North Carolina and Georgia, while data on community supervision rates include block groups from North Carolina only.

CRIMINAL JUSTICE CONTEXT VARIABLES

These data from the departments of corrections, along with supplementary information from other agencies, were used to construct several measures of criminal justice context at the neighborhood level. The most important variables, *prisoner density* and *community supervision density*, measure the spatial concentration of people serving time in prison from the neighborhood and people serving probation and parole sentences in the neighborhood at the close of voter registration, respectively. These variables are constructed as the number of prisoners per square mile or the number of probationers and parolees per square mile. The demographic concentration of imprisonment and community supervision are also presented as the percentage of the population in prison or under community supervision. These percentages are calculated for all adults as well as for young adults between the ages of 18 and 35.

Uniform data on violent crimes are not available at the block group level. Instead, data on 2008 homicides were obtained from the Georgia and North Carolina Departments of Public Health.[14] The *homicide rate* for each block group is then defined as the number of fatal intentional injuries sustained among residents living in the block group, divided by the block group adult population. The count of fatal intentional injuries excludes self- and state-inflicted injuries (such as suicides, executions, and police shootings). One might think of the homicide rate as a purer measure of violent crime, as homicides are not usually subject to reporting or other biases.[15]

Ex-felons deserve special discussion, because the number of ex-felons in a community should also matter for political outcomes for several reasons. First, in Georgia and North Carolina, ex-offenders regain their voting rights once they fulfill all the terms of their punishments. Second, labor market discrimination and other disadvantages continue after the official punishment ends, such that many ex-felons remain unable to contribute financially to their families and neighborhoods and may even turn or return to crime.[16] Third, ex-offenders may continue to share their negative experiences and beliefs about government with those around them—in particular, returning prisoners have even more opportunity than current prisoners to share their now-past experiences and attitudes with their neighbors.

All of these factors make the presence of ex-felons within a community an additional contextual variable that is worth studying. Failing to control for the presence of ex-felons in a community might confound the results, but administrative data on former offenders are difficult to obtain. With the exception of sex offenders, departments of corrections rarely keep track of offenders after their sentences end and usually do not release what little data they do have. Released prisoners who do not serve their complete sentences remain under supervision as parolees for a time; these offenders are available in community supervision data for North Carolina. Nevertheless, once all time is served, finding information about the residence and movement of ex-felons is nearly impossible. Because of these difficulties, rather than attempting to estimate the number of ex-felons living in a neighborhood, instead the dataset includes a measure of institutions that are likely to attract released prisoners and other ex-felons. This measure of *ex-felon-serving institutions* is a dummy variable that indicates whether the block group is located within half a mile of a halfway house, residential reentry center, transitional facility, or other nonprofit group whose primary mission is to provide housing, training, or services to ex-felons. This indicator was constructed using the Federal Bureau of Prisons list of residential reentry centers, departments of corrections lists of transitional centers, and the IRS Master List of Exempt Organizations.

GEOCODING

Addresses for prisoners, probationers, parolees, ex-felon-serving institutions, and, later, voters were converted to points with latitudes and longitudes and then to census blocks by geocoding with ArcGIS. Ninety-seven percent of Georgia and North Carolina voters with valid addresses were successfully geocoded. Matching prisoners and probationers to valid addresses was more difficult. In each state, about 10 percent of offenders indicated temporary housing (such as hotels, motels, or shelters), correctional facilities, or the streets as their last known address. Of the remaining prisoners, probationers, and parolees, about 90 percent with valid in-state addresses were geocoded successfully. The remainder includes offenders matched to out-of-state addresses, including foreign countries, and offenders who provided incomplete information or post office boxes.

Descriptive Findings

ALL ADULTS

The descriptive statistics for each criminal justice supervision measure, by state, can be found in table 3.1. This table paints the same overall picture of inequality as that presented in the introduction to this chapter. The median neighborhood prisoner density for both Georgia and North Carolina block groups is well above the national average of 0.43 prisoners per square mile, with a maximum prisoner density of 470 prisoners per square mile in Georgia and 260 prisoners per square mile in North Carolina.[17] Likewise, the community supervision density in North Carolina block groups is above the national average of 1.42 probationers and parolees per square mile, reaching a maximum of 330 probationers and parolees per square mile.

These high spatial concentrations of prisoner and community supervision reflect high concentrations of prisoners, probationers, and parolees demographically. Georgia's average imprisonment rate for all adults is more than double the national imprisonment rate of 506 per 100,000 adults, reaching a maximum of 14.3 percent of neighborhood

Table 3.1: Descriptive statistics of block group neighborhood criminal justice context, by state

Supervision Measure	Minimum	1st Quartile	Median	Mean	3rd Quartile	Standard Deviation	Maximum	N
Georgia:								
Prisoner density (all adults)	0.000	0.588	3.647	21.130	20.000	44.820	470	4,536
Imprisonment rate (all adults)	0.000	0.004	0.008	0.013	0.016	0.015	0.143	4,536
Imprisonment rate (adults ages 18–34)	0.000	0.005	0.012	0.020	0.025	0.025	0.389	4,536
North Carolina:								
Prisoner density (all adults)	0.000	0.217	0.924	7.344	5.304	18.670	260	4,948
Imprisonment rate (all adults)	0.000	0.002	0.004	0.006	0.007	0.007	0.057	4,948
Imprisonment rate (adults ages 18–34)	0.000	0.003	0.007	0.011	0.014	0.014	0.168	4,948
Community supervision density (all adults)	0.000	1.031	3.479	15.240	15.710	29.245	330	4,948
Community supervision rate (all adults)	0.000	0.007	0.012	0.014	0.018	0.011	0.081	4,948
Community supervision rate (adults ages 18–34)	0.000	0.015	0.025	0.030	0.039	0.023	0.203	4,948

Source: Results from the 2008 Neighborhood Criminal Justice Involvement Data.

residents in one block group.[18] North Carolina's imprisonment rate is only slightly above the national imprisonment rate; however, in one block group, the imprisonment rate reaches nearly 6 percent. The community supervision rate in North Carolina is lower than the national average of 2.15 percent.[19] However, in one North Carolina block group, more than 8 percent of adults are on probation or parole, nearly four times the national average.

Figures 3.1–3.3 present maps of supervision density and imprisonment density for selected local areas in within each state. These maps show great variation in both imprisonment and community supervision in several cities in North Carolina and Georgia. In figures 3.1 and 3.2, block groups from four cities in North Carolina and Georgia, respectively, are shaded based on prisoners per square mile, with darker shading representing higher imprisonment densities. Both the descriptive statistics table and figure 3.1 show that the prisoner densities in North Carolina block groups range from 0 to 260 prisoners per square mile, while both table 3.1 and figure 3.2 show that prisoner densities in Georgia block groups range from 0 to about 470 prisoners per square mile. Imprisonment is highly concentrated within certain areas of each city. Neighborhoods with high prisoner densities are concentrated north of the city center in Charlotte, North Carolina, and far south and southwest of the city centers in Greensboro and Raleigh, North Carolina. High-imprisonment neighborhoods are more dispersed throughout Durham, North Carolina. Similarly, high-imprisonment neighborhoods are concentrated in the southern half of the Atlanta metropolitan area in Georgia, the north and west parts of Savannah, and northeastern Augusta. In Macon, the few low-imprisonment areas are located north of the city center.

Community supervision density varies more than imprisonment density. Figure 3.3 again depicts block groups in four cities, this time shaded by community supervision density in North Carolina, the only state for which these data are complete. As shown in table 3.1 and reflected in figure 3.3, statewide community supervision density in North Carolina ranges from 0 to 330 prisoners per square mile. Figure 3.3 also shows a pattern of concentrated community supervision. Southern Charlotte has the lowest community supervision rates in that city; all high probation and parole areas in Greensboro and Raleigh are in the southern and eastern parts of these cities. In Durham, some areas west of the city have below-average levels of community supervision, but

Charlotte

Raleigh

Durham

Greensboro

Legend
0.000000 - 13.157895
13.157896 - 47.500000
47.500001 - 115.000000
115.000001 - 260.000000

Figure 3.1: Imprisonment density in selected North Carolina metro areas, 2008. Block groups shown in white were excluded from the data due to a lack of eligible voters or adult population in households. Source: Neighborhood Criminal Justice Involvement Data.

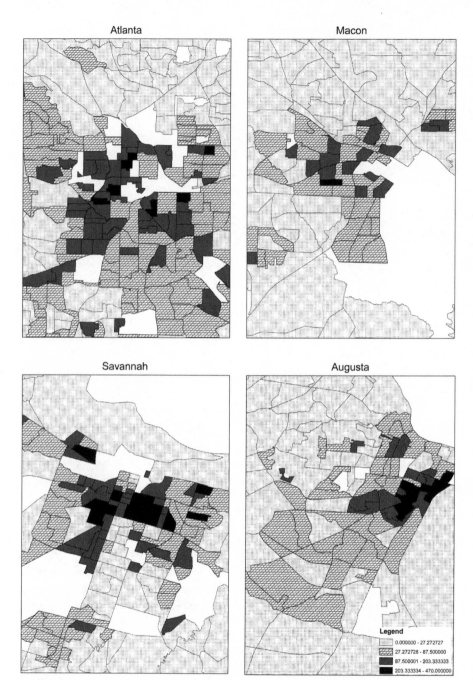

Figure 3.2: Imprisonment density in selected Georgia metro areas, 2008. Block groups shown in white were excluded from the data due to a lack of eligible voters or adult population in households. Source: Neighborhood Criminal Justice Involvement Data.

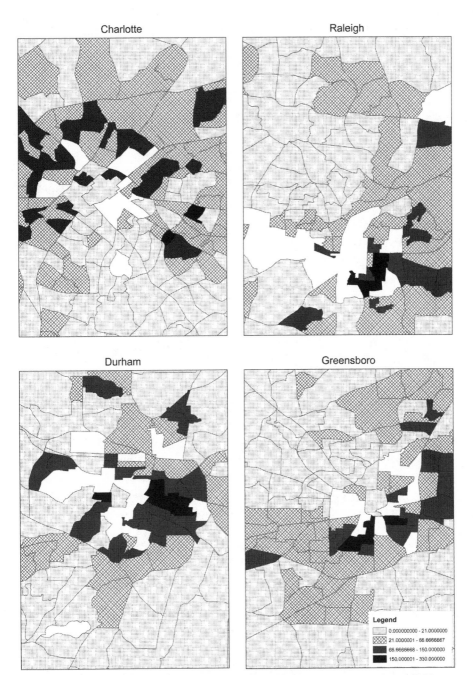

Figure 3.3: Community supervision density in selected North Carolina metro areas, 2008. Block groups shown in white were excluded from the data due to a lack of eligible voters or adult population in households. Source: Neighborhood Criminal Justice Involvement Data.

the northern, eastern, and southern quadrants of the city have higher levels of community supervision.

These particular patterns of criminal justice involvement across cities mirror inequalities in the wider society and within the criminal justice system. To state the claim bluntly, criminal justice involvement is concentrated in neighborhoods where black people and poor people live. A number of factors may account for this reality, as discussed in chapter 2. These communities may be policed more aggressively.[20] Residents of these communities may commit more crimes.[21] Blacks and the poor may face discrimination in charging, conviction, and sentencing outcomes.[22] Imprisonment is particularly concentrated in black communities, perhaps reflective of crime patterns, but also of the fact that blacks more often get prison sentences than whites and other groups for similar crimes.[23] The relationship between race and imprisonment is readily apparent in the maps of Charlotte (fig. 3.4) and Atlanta (fig. 3.5), which depict imprisonment incidents over a six-month period superimposed over block groups that have been shaded by the percentage of black residents.

More general evidence makes it clear that predominantly black neighborhoods, high crime neighborhoods, and high-poverty neighborhoods tend to have higher spatial concentrations of imprisonment and community supervision than other neighborhoods. As shown in the scatterplot of the black percentage of the neighborhood versus the neighborhood's prisonerdensity for North Carolina and Georgia block groups in figure 3.6, there are many majority-black neighborhoods with low concentrations of imprisonment, just as there are some majority-nonblack neighborhoods with high imprisonment. However, the general pattern emerges that black neighborhoods experience high concentrations of imprisonment more often than neighborhoods in which other racial groups are the majority. The black percentage of the population is highly correlated with prisoner density in both states; Pearson's R = 0.566 in Georgia and 0.510 in North Carolina. Interestingly, as figure 3.7 shows, the Hispanic or Latino percentage of the neighborhood population is less strongly correlated with prisoner density, at least in Georgia and North Carolina (Pearson's R = 0.191 in North Carolina and –0.027 in Georgia).[24]

Similarly, the percentage of households with incomes under $10,000 is also positively correlated with imprisonment, though not as strongly

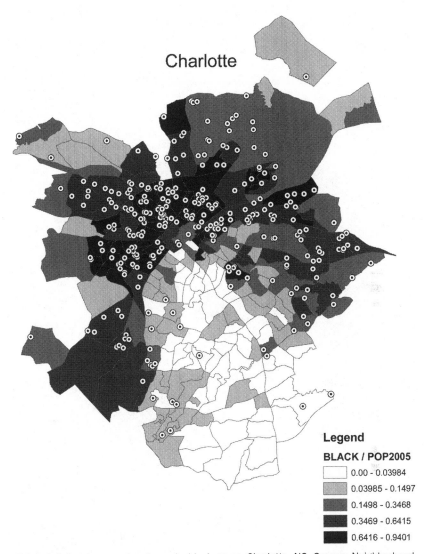

Charlotte

Legend

BLACK / POP2005

☐	0.00 - 0.03984
▨	0.03985 - 0.1497
▨	0.1498 - 0.3468
▨	0.3469 - 0.6415
■	0.6416 - 0.9401

Figure 3.4: Imprisonment and race by block group, Charlotte, NC. Source: Neighborhood Criminal Justice Involvement Data.

as race (Pearson's R = 0.436 in Georgia and 0.384 in North Carolina). Figure 3.8 depicts the scatterplot of neighborhood poverty versus prisoner density. Although most neighborhoods have fewer than 40 percent of households with incomes under $10,000, it is clear that prisoner density tends to increase as neighborhood poverty rates approach that threshold. As with race, there are neighborhoods with high poverty and

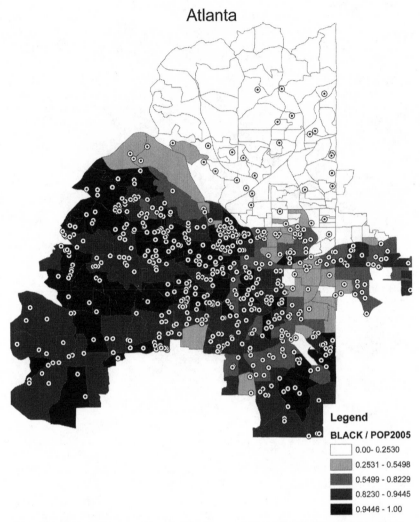

Figure 3.5: Imprisonment and race by block group, Atlanta, GA. Source: Neighborhood Criminal Justice Involvement Data.

low imprisonment, and neighborhoods with low poverty and high imprisonment. However, relatively poor neighborhoods tend to experience higher imprisonment.

Homicide rates, as expected, are also positively correlated with prisoner density (Pearson's R = 0.177 in Georgia and 0.187 in North Carolina). As figure 3.9 shows, most neighborhoods did not experience the murder of any residents during 2008. However, for those few

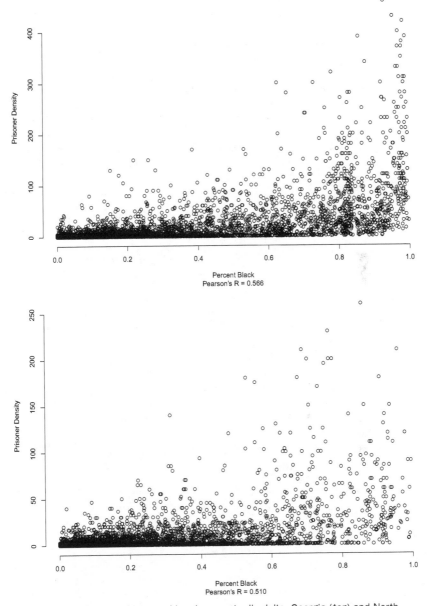

Figure 3.6: Scatterplot of race and imprisonment, all adults, Georgia (*top*) and North Carolina (*bottom*). Source: Neighborhood Criminal Justice Involvement Data.

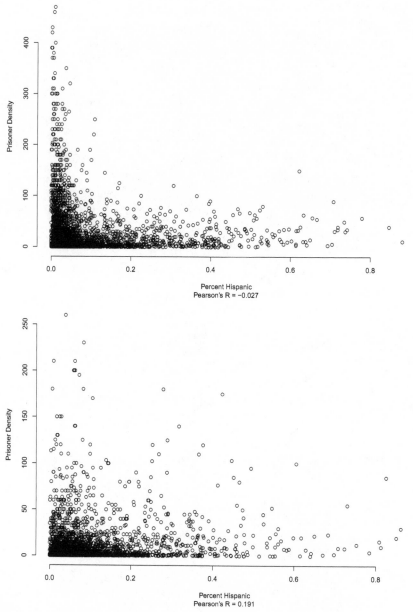

Figure 3.7: Scatterplot of ethnicity and imprisonment density, all adults, Georgia (*top*) and North Carolina (*bottom*). Source: Neighborhood Criminal Justice Involvement Data.

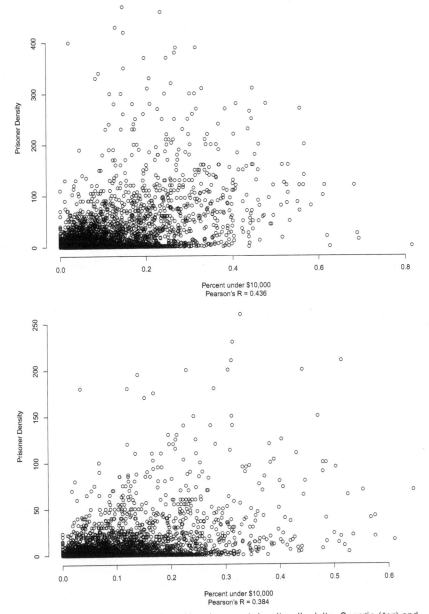

Figure 3.8: Scatterplot of poverty and imprisonment density, all adults, Georgia (*top*) and North Carolina (*bottom*). Source: Neighborhood Criminal Justice Involvement Data.

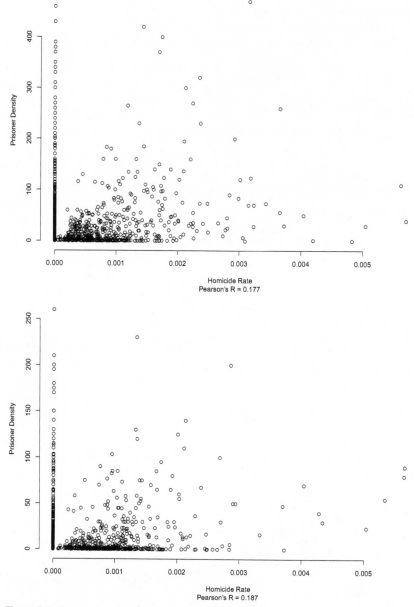

Figure 3.9: Scatterplot of homicide and imprisonment density, all adults, Georgia (*top*) and North Carolina (*bottom*). Source: Neighborhood Criminal Justice Involvement Data.

neighborhoods that did experience homicides, prisoner density tends to be higher than in those neighborhoods that did not.

The relationships among race, poverty, homicide, and community supervision density (data available only for North Carolina) are similar to those found for incarceration, perhaps because community supervision and imprisonment are so highly correlated with each other. Again, this pattern mostly reflects differences in the type and frequency of crimes committed by residents of different communities, but also certainly is related to the racial and ethnic discrimination in prison and probation sentences noted above. The black percentage of the block group population is positively correlated with community supervision density, as shown in figure 3.10 (Pearson's R = 0.506). Figure 3.11 shows that the Hispanic percentage of the block group population is much more correlated with community supervision density than with prisoner density (Pearson's R = 0.234). Community poverty is positively correlated with community supervision density, as shown in figure 3.12 (Pearson's R = 0.372). Finally, figure 3.13 shows that homicide rates are also positively associated with community supervision density (Pearson's R = 0.194).

It is also useful to pay attention to those block groups with especially high imprisonment and community supervision levels. Tables 3.2 and 3.3 list the ten block groups with the highest imprisonment densities in Georgia and North Carolina. These block groups have imprisonment densities ranging from 370 to 470 prisoners per square mile in Georgia and from 200 to 260 prisoners per square mile in North Carolina. All of these block groups are majority African American; the average for the Georgia block groups is about 95.5 percent black and .004 percent Hispanic, while the average among the North Carolina block groups is 78.5 percent black and 5.3 percent Hispanic. These block groups are low income, with an average 19.1 percent of households in the Georgia block groups and 35.0 percent of households in the North Carolina block groups making less than $10,000. Homicides occurred in four of the Georgia block groups and two of the North Carolina block groups.

The North Carolina block groups with the worst community supervision densities are shown in table 3.4. The lowest of these block groups has a community supervision density of 260 probationers or parolees per square mile; the highest community supervision density is 330 probationers or parolees per square mile. The average black composition

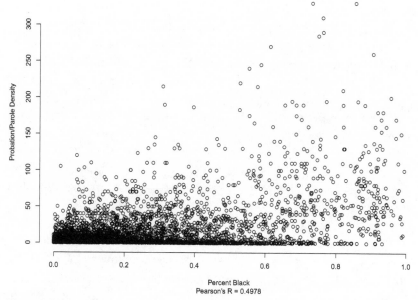

Figure 3.10: Scatterplot of race and community supervision density, all adults, North Carolina. Source: Neighborhood Criminal Justice Involvement Data.

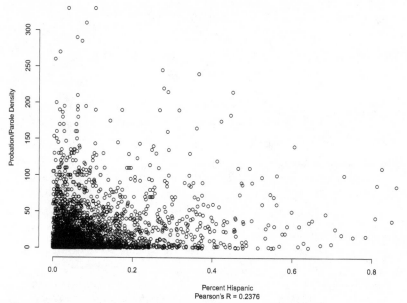

Figure 3.11: Scatterplot of ethnicity and community supervision density, all adults, North Carolina. Source: Neighborhood Criminal Justice Involvement Data.

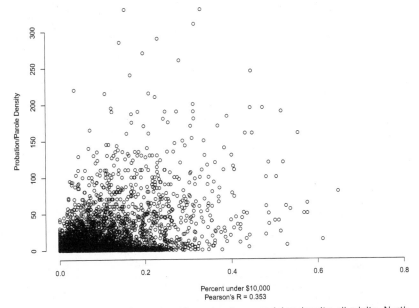

Figure 3.12: Scatterplot of poverty and community supervision density, all adults, North Carolina. Source: Neighborhood Criminal Justice Involvement Data.

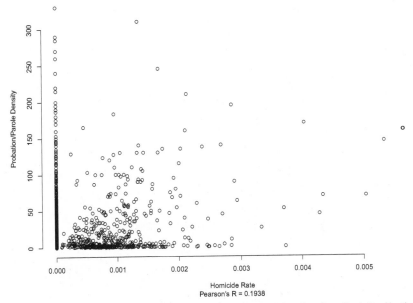

Figure 3.13 Scatterplot of homicide and community supervision density, all adults, North Carolina. Source: Neighborhood Criminal Justice Involvement Data.

Table 3.2. Georgia block groups with the highest prisoner densities, all adults

Rank	County	Tract	Block Group	Prisoners per Square Mile
1	Chatham	002300	3	470
2	Chatham	002400	2	460
3	Chatham	002600	1	430
4	Chatham	002800	1	420
5	Chatham	002700	4	400
6	Chatham	001800	2	390
7	Chatham	002000	1	390

Source: Results from the 2008 Neighborhood Criminal Justice Involvement Data.

Table 3.3: North Carolina block groups with the highest prisoner densities, all adults

Rank	County	Tract	Block Group	Prisoners per Suare Mile
1	Guilford	011400	6	260
2	Wake	050800	3	230
3	Forsyth	000500	2	210
4	Guilford	011400	4	210
5	Forsyth	000301	1	200
6	Wake	050700	4	200
7	Wake	050900	3	200

Source: Results from the 2008 Neighborhood Criminal Justice Involvement Data.

of the population in these ten block groups 76.8 percent. The average Hispanic composition of these block groups is 5.4 percent. The average poverty rate, at 23.4 percent, is lower than that found among the North Carolina block groups with the highest imprisonment density, as is the average homicide rate. In fact, only one block group on this list had any homicides at all.

YOUNG ADULTS

Many of the adults under correctional supervision in the United States are young adults, under the age of 35. About half of state prisoners are between the ages of 18 and 35, and imprisonment rates among people in these age groups are much higher than those among older adults.[25]

Table 3.4: North Carolina block groups with the highest community supervision densities, all adults

Rank	County	Tract	Block Group	Community Supervision per Square Mile
1	Guilford	011400	6	330
2	Wake	050700	3	330
3	Wake	050800	3	310
4	Wake	050700	4	290
5	New Hanover	011100	3	285
6	New Hanover	010200	5	270
7	New Hanover	011100	2	260

Source: Results from the 2008 Neighborhood Criminal Justice Involvement Data.

Thus, it makes sense to examine imprisonment and community supervision in this subgroup more closely.

Returning to the descriptive statistics in table 3.1, it is clear that the discussion of neighborhood criminal justice interactions so far, though thorough, does not tell the full story. Examining the community supervision and imprisonment rates by state for 18–34-year-olds reveals high imprisonment and community supervision rates at the block group level among young adults. The median community supervision rate for North Carolina's young adults is 2.49 percent, meaning that more than half of North Carolina's block groups have young adult community supervision rates above the national average for all adults of 2.41 percent. In one block group, the youth community supervision rate exceeds 20 percent. Even worse, imprisonment rates at the block group level also are high among young adults in North Carolina: the average block group imprisonment rate for young adults is almost three times as high as the average for all adults in that state. Likewise, young adult imprisonment rates are high in Georgia: the median young adult imprisonment rate in Georgia's block groups is 1.2 percent, meaning that half of Georgia's block groups have young adult imprisonment rates that are twice the national average imprisonment rate for all adults of 0.5 percent.

Despite the more extreme extent of supervision among young adults in both states, the distribution of imprisonment and community supervision across block groups by geography, race, ethnicity, and socioeconomic status is similar to that for all adults. Across cities, the areas of high young adult imprisonment and community supervision match the areas of high imprisonment and community supervision for all adults (figs. 3.14–3.16). The black percentage of the block group is positively correlated with young adult imprisonment in Georgia and North Carolina (Pearson's R = 0.588 and 0.575, respectively) and with young adult community supervision (Pearson's R = 0.19) in North Carolina (scatterplots not shown). The Hispanic percentage of the block group is slightly correlated with young adult imprisonment (Pearson's R = –0.116 in Georgia and 0.058 in North Carolina) and is uncorrelated with young adult community supervision (Pearson's R = 0.003; scatterplots not shown). Finally, poverty is positively associated with young adult imprisonment rates in Georgia and North Carolina (Pearson's R = 0.492 in Georgia and 0.437 in North Carolina) and with young adult community supervision rates in North Carolina (Pearson's R = 0.451; again, scatterplots not shown).

Turning to the worst block groups for young adult imprisonment listed in tables 3.5 and 3.6, it is clear that young adults in Georgia, particularly in Richmond County, face extremely high imprisonment rates in certain block groups. In the Georgia block groups in table 3.5, the young adult imprisonment rates range from a low of 20 percent to a high of 39 percent. The situation in North Carolina is less severe for young adults, but still troubling: young adult imprisonment rates in these block groups range from a low of 11.43 percent to a high of nearly 17 percent. Within the top five North Carolina block groups for young adult community supervision (table 3.6), community supervision rates range from 18 to 20 percent.

Implications

The maps, scatterplots, and tables presented here all provide strong evidence for the claims made at the beginning of this chapter: in some neighborhoods, prison, probation, and parole are commonplace. As these data show, neighborhood experiences with criminal justice interactions vary widely. Some neighborhoods have no individuals in prison, on probation, or parole, while in others the spatial concentration of imprisonment and community supervision is astonishingly high: 273 block groups in Georgia and North Carolina have prisoner densities higher than 100 prisoners per square mile, while 121 block groups in North Carolina have community supervision densities higher

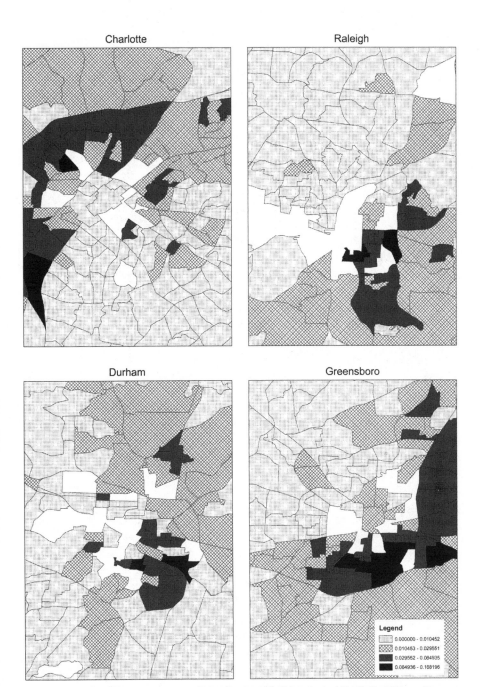

Figure 3.14: Imprisonment rates of people ages 18–34, selected North Carolina metro areas, 2008. Block groups shown in white were excluded from the data due to a lack of eligible voters or adult population in households. Source: Neighborhood Criminal Justice Involvement Data.

Figure 3.15: Imprisonment rates of people ages 18–34, selected Georgia metro areas, 2008. Block groups shown in white were excluded from the data due to a lack of eligible voters or adult population in households. Source: Neighborhood Criminal Justice Involvement Data.

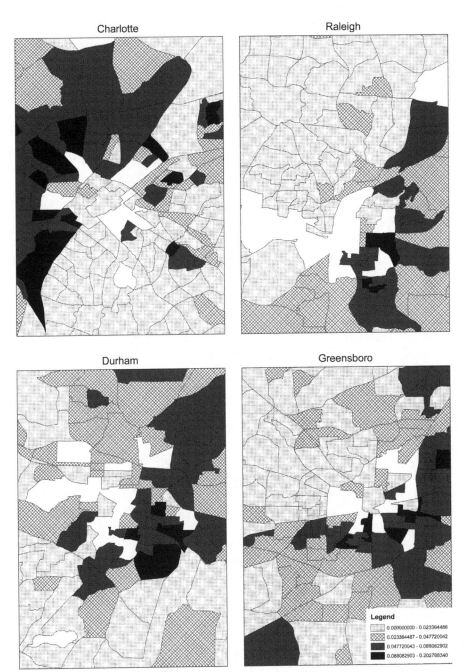

Figure 3.16: Community supervision rate in selected North Carolina metro areas, 2008. Block groups shown in white were excluded from the data due to a lack of eligible voters or adult population in households. Source: Neighborhood Criminal Justice Involvement Data.

Table 3.5: Georgia block groups with the highest imprisonment rates, young adults

Rank	County	Tract	Block Group	Percentage in Prison
1	Richmond	000700	1	38.86
2	Richmond	001500	2	22.25
3	Troupe	960600	4	21.65
4	Muskogee	003000	3	19.90
5	Richmond	010300	1	19.87

Source: Results from the 2008 Neighborhood Criminal Justice Involvement Data.

Table 3.6: North Carolina block groups with the highest imprisonment rates, young adults

Rank	County	Tract	Block Group	Percentage in Prison
1	Lenoir	010200	3	16.82
2	Lenoir	010300	4	16.77
3	Wake	052805	2	16.13
4	New Hanover	011100	1	12.39
5	Pitt	000702	1	11.43

Source: Results from the 2008 Neighborhood Criminal Justice Involvement Data.

Table 3.7: North Carolina block groups with the highest community supervision rates, young adults

Rank	County	Tract	Block Group	Percentage under Community Supervision
1	New Hanover	011200	2	20.28
2	Pitt	010300	4	19.82
3	New Hanover	011100	1	19.68
4	Craven	960800	6	18.60
5	Craven	960800	3	18.06

Source: Results from the 2008 Neighborhood Criminal Justice Involvement Data.

than 100 probationers or parolees per square mile. Overall, 46 percent of North Carolina block groups have community supervision rates at least three times as high as the national average, while 54.9 percent of block groups in Georgia and North Carolina have prisoner densities at least three times the national average. These findings echo those reported previously in other studies.[26]

The central claim of this book is that life in high-imprisonment and high-community-supervision block groups differs from that in low-imprisonment and low-supervision block groups in ways that matter for politics. As discussed in chapter 2, previous research argues that neighborhoods in which a large number of residents are serving time in prison, on probation, or on parole are poorer because fewer individuals are available to contribute to family incomes and community upkeep. Higher imprisonment and community supervision also lead to more political disfranchisement: more people are absent from the neighborhood voter rolls due to disfranchisement, and more people are absent from official statistics due to imprisonment. Even social interactions are different because of high community supervision and imprisonment: the likelihood of having met someone who is now in prison, on probation, or on parole is much higher in these neighborhoods. Measuring neighborhood heterogeneity as the likelihood that of two randomly drawn individuals from a neighborhood, one will be a convicted offender reveals that people living in high community supervision and imprisonment neighborhoods are much more likely to have encountered offenders.[27] For those neighborhoods at the very top of the scale, with imprisonment rates greater than 10 percent, the likelihood of having encountered someone who is now a prisoner is 20 percent or higher. Similarly, for those North Carolina neighborhoods at the top of the community supervision scale, the likelihood of having encountered someone who is on probation or parole exceeds 14 percent.

The results provide a sense of how prominently criminal justice interactions feature in the lives of people who live in black and poor neighborhoods relative to people living in other communities. Thus, the problems associated with community supervision and imprisonment—social disorganization, cultural deviance, and the like—should be felt more acutely in these neighborhoods. In particular, with respect to imprisonment, residents of black neighborhoods see a degree of punitive interactions with the state that residents of other neighborhoods do not. For instance, among the neighborhoods in this study where fewer than 7.9 percent of residents are black, the median likelihood of having encountered someone who is now in prison is only 0.7 percent. However, in the quarter of neighborhoods in which more than 42 percent of the residents are black, the likelihood of having encountered someone who is now in prison is about 5 percent. It is also important to remember that all of the high-imprisonment neighborhoods in North Carolina and Georgia are majority black.

It is also important to note that imprisonment and community supervision rates for young adults are both more varied and more severe than those just noted for the general adult population. Within the cohort of young adults, the median likelihood of having met a neighbor within the same age group who has been sent to prison is about 1.5 percent. The situation is especially dire for young adults living in black neighborhoods, whose median likelihood of having met neighboring peers who have been sent to prison is 7 percent. In the neighborhoods where blacks make up three quarters of the population, the likelihood that young blacks will know someone in prison is higher than 11 percent, and in one case, nearly 55 percent.

Conclusion

The purpose of this chapter was to develop and describe the key causal independent variables that will be used throughout the remainder of this book: neighborhood prisoner and community supervision density. The data show the spatial concentration of these two phenomena differs across neighborhoods. In many instances, neighborhood residents, particularly residents of black and poor neighborhoods, vicariously experience imprisonment and community supervision at alarming rates. Young adults are also especially likely to encounter examples of imprisonment and community supervision among their peers in the neighborhood.

It is troubling to think about how these differential experiences with government supervision across neighborhoods might shape political advantages and disadvantages across cities and states, yet these effects are the subject of the remainder of the book. Chapter 4 begins the work of estimating the effects of neighborhood criminal justice involvement on political participation.

4

Neighborhood Criminal Justice Context and Political Participation

I'm a Muslim, and I don't vote. We don't support a system that is
oppressive. They're spending millions for prisons while putting nothing
to rehabilitate people who come out.
— Mark St. John, New York City Resident.[1]

To many readers, the views of Mr. St. John might seem militant
or extreme. However, the sentiments expressed by him may be all too
common among residents in low-income communities. As noted in
chapter 2, the problems and stresses that come from living in a high-
supervision community might lead people to drop out of politics for
any number of reasons. Some may be protesting perceived unfairness,
like Mr. St. John. Others may be too busy or too poor to devote the time,
money, and other resources to political participation. Still others may
be ignored by campaigns afraid to mobilize voters in "neighborhoods
where even police fear to go."[2]

Chapter 5 will return to these questions in greater detail. For now,
it is important to note that whatever the reason, the main conclusion
of this chapter is inescapable: living in a high-imprisonment neighborhood demobilizes citizens. People who live in high-imprisonment
neighborhoods vote less than people who live in neighborhoods with
fewer prisoners. This statement is true even when other individual-
and neighborhood-level phenomena such as race, poverty, ethnicity, and citizenship that might have explained this result have been
accounted for. What's more, individuals living in neighborhoods
with a high spatial concentration of prisoners are less active in politics and in their communities in other ways, too. People in high-
imprisonment neighborhoods participate in fewer political activities
such as marching or signing petitions and volunteer less frequently
than do their counterparts in neighborhoods with lower imprisonment levels. There is also evidence that they join fewer groups.
There is, however, little evidence that a neighborhood's experience

with community supervision (probation and parole) affects political participation.

The effects of living in a high-imprisonment neighborhood are both statistically and substantively significant. The results of three different tests strongly support the conclusion that imprisonment reduces voter turnout. Beta regression models of block group prisoner density (measured as prisoners per square mile) on block group voter turnout in the 2008 general election reveals a complex relationship between imprisonment and voter turnout.[3] It is clear that at high concentrations, imprisonment has an unequivocally demobilizing effect on neighborhoods. In North Carolina, block groups with a prisoner density of 250 prisoners per square mile are expected to vote at a rate of 57.0 percent, a rate that is 6.1 percentage points lower than that of block groups without any prisoners even after holding constant factors including race, residential mobility, poverty, crime, county, and citizenship. Similarly, in Georgia, block groups at 250 prisoners per square mile are expected to turn out at 44.5 percent, a figure that is 2.1 percentage points lower than that expected in block groups with no prisoners.[4]

However, at lower concentrations of imprisonment, the relationship between imprisonment and voter turnout varies by state. In North Carolina, imprisonment seems to have a curvilinear relationship with turnout, such that at low levels of prisoner density, imprisonment seems to help turnout, increasing it by up to 8 percentage points before it begins to have a detrimental effect. In Georgia, a curvilinear relationship is not statistically significant, and increasing imprisonment seems to hurt voter turnout at all levels, even in neighborhoods with a relatively low concentration of prisoners.

Based on these outcomes, the results of the second test are not surprising. In Georgia, the consistently negative relationship between neighborhood imprisonment and neighborhood voter turnout holds for new instances of imprisonment. The evidence suggests that imprisoning new inmates in Georgia up to three months prior to the 2008 election decreases voter turnout by 1.4 percentage points from what it would have been had those inmates been sent to prison after the election. In North Carolina, as might be expected, there is no apparent relationship between new imprisonments and voter turnout.

The third test reveals that individual-level effects match up with the aggregate-level effects found in the first two tests. Individuals living in high-imprisonment neighborhoods are less likely to vote, undertake other political activities, volunteer, or join groups than people living in low-imprisonment neighborhoods. With respect to voting, the results support the aggregate-level tests: people who live in neighborhoods with a prisoner density of 110 prisoners per square mile (the highest in the Charlotte sample for which these data were available) are 73.8 percent less likely to vote than people who live in neighborhoods without any prisoners, even after controlling for individual-level and neighborhood-level factors that might confound the analysis.

The individual-level data reveal that imprisonment shapes other forms of participation as well. Individuals in the neighborhoods with the highest concentrations of prisoners participate in 43.4 percent fewer political activities than people who live in neighborhoods with no prisoners. Likewise, people who live in neighborhoods with a prisoner density of 110 prisoners per square mile are members of only two-thirds as many groups and volunteer 78 percent less than people who live in neighborhoods with no prisoners. However, the results of the group membership analysis are significant only at the traditional $p > 0.10$ level, but not at the traditional $p > 0.05$ level.

The argument employed in this chapter uses multiple data sources and multiple methods, each of which points to the same conclusion. These results were produced using the 2008 demographic data on block groups introduced in chapter 3, along with individual survey data from the 2000 Social Capital Benchmark Survey. The neighborhood prisoner density, neighborhood prison admissions, and individual-level analyses are discussed separately in three separate sections in the remainder of this chapter. Each section will briefly describe the research methods, data, and results, in some cases referring readers to separate papers or the appendix for more detailed information.

The First Test: Voter Turnout and Neighborhood Prisoner Density

The first analysis of the effects of neighborhood criminal justice context on political participation uses the dataset on block group demographics first introduced in chapter 3. As a reminder, this dataset combines information on the prison, probation, and parole population during the 2008 general election from the Georgia and North Carolina Departments of Corrections, information on block group homicide rates from the Georgia and North Carolina Departments of Public Health, and updated estimates of block group demographic characteristics from Scan/US and Geolytics. Voter turnout in the 2008 general election for each block group was produced by geocoding with ArcGIS the street addresses of registered voters provided by the Georgia secretary of state and the North Carolina State Board of Elections. Just over 97 percent of voter addresses were successfully geocoded to block groups within each state.[5] The final data contain 9,484 block groups: 4,948 from North Carolina and 4,536 from Georgia. See appendix table A.1 for the descriptive statistics of the block groups in this sample.

These data provide evidence that the hypothesized effects of neighborhood criminal justice context do operate in the real world, at least with respect to imprisonment. As the scatterplots of neighborhood prisoner density vs. neighborhood voter turnout for each state in figure 4.1 show, the relationship between neighborhood imprisonment and voter turnout is clear in the raw data for Georgia; voter turnout is negatively correlated with prisoner density (Pearson's R = −0.1). In North Carolina, the relationship is very weak, but positive (Pearson's R = 0.026). Figure 4.2 shows that in North Carolina, the only state for which these data are available, the number of probationers and parolees per square mile is also only weakly related to voter turnout (Pearson's R = 0.026).

Simply identifying the aggregate relationship between prisoner density and voter turnout does not provide sufficient evidence that prisoner density matters for turnout, because these simple bivariate correlations might be masking other, more complex phenomena. There may be other factors that are related to both prisoner density and voter turnout that might be driving this apparent relationship. These factors must be taken into account in a multivariate model of these effects. Poverty, violent crime, the presence of young residents, and racial and ethnic diversity have been shown to influence neighborhood outcomes including voter turnout; thus, they are included in this analysis as the poverty rate,[6] homicide rate, proportion of adults under age 25, black percentage of the population, Hispanic percentage, and other minority percentage.[7] To control for the influence of ex-offenders on turnout, the model identifies block groups with inmate-serving organizations such as halfway houses, residential reentry centers, transitional centers, and other facilities that provide housing, jobs, and other assistance to ex-offenders. Education affects voter turnout at the individual level; it stands to reason that block groups with more educated individuals would be more likely to vote, so Geolytics' measure of the

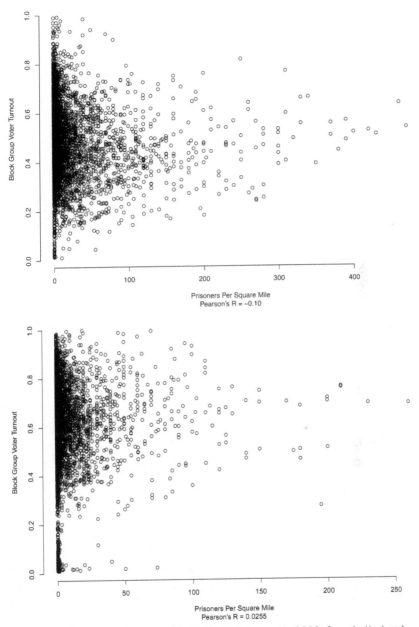

Figure 4.1: Scatterplot of prisoner density vs. voter turnout in 2008, Georgia (*top*) and North Carolina (*bottom*). Source: Neighborhood Criminal Justice Involvement Data.

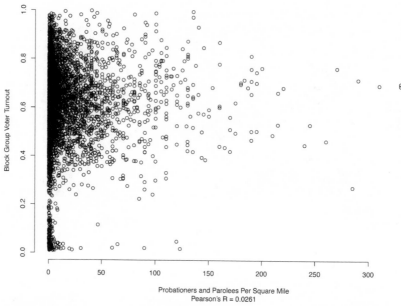

Figure 4.2: Scatterplot of community supervision density vs. voter turnout in 2008, North Carolina. Source: Neighborhood Criminal Justice Involvement Data.

female high school graduation rate is included in the models.[8] Residential mobility also reduces voter turnout, so the models include the percentage of vacant housing units as a proxy for residential mobility. Only citizens are allowed to vote; for this reason, the relative proportions of US-born and naturalized citizens and noncitizens are included in the regressions as well.[9] Further, the presence of college students, nursing home residents, or others in group quarters might affect voter turnout, so the percentage of the population in group quarters is included in the models. Finally, the male-to-female ratio and the relative proportion of residents who are unemployed are included in the models.[10]

Throughout this chapter, the prisoner density variable is a measure of the number of adult residents of the block group who were in state prison during the 2008 general election, divided by the area of the block group in square miles. The dependent variable, voter turnout, was obtained by geocoding the addresses of voters obtained from the North Carolina and Georgia State Boards of Elections and represents the number of people from the block group who voted in the November general election divided by the 2008 adult population of the block group. Because the dependent variable is continuous but bounded between 0 and 1, beta regression is used to estimate the effects of prison density.[11] Block groups from both states are modeled separately, and the models control for county fixed effects. For both states, a linear model and a curvilinear model (that includes the variable prisoner density squared) are presented.

RESULTS

At first glance, the results of the beta regression models shown in table 4.1 seem to point in different directions. In the linear models, the relationship between voter turnout and prisoner density is *positive* and statistically significant in North Carolina, while the relationship is *negative* but not statistically significant in Georgia.[12] In the curvilinear models, the coefficients of both prisoner density and the squared prisoner density are statistically significant in North Carolina, meaning that increasing the concentration of prisoners increases voter turnout at low levels of prisoner density but begins to decrease voter turnout at higher levels.[13] However, only the prisoner density is statistically significant in Georgia, indicating that the effect of prisoner density is negative at all levels of prisoner density. Further testing reveals that the curvilinear models fit the data better than the simple linear models.[14]

Regression coefficients are not easily interpreted, so it is easier to discuss the predicted block group voter turnout using simulations for the curvilinear models.[15] As shown in figure 4.3, which presents the estimated range of block group voter turnout for each level of prisoner density in the data separately for each state, prison density had a negative, statistically significant effect on neighborhood voter turnout in Georgia in the 2008 general election. Voter turnout in a block group with no prisoners was expected to be 4.56 percent higher than voter turnout in a neighborhood with 250 prisoners per square mile.[16] This effect persists even after controlling for the potentially confounding factors listed above. The predicted turnout reflects the fact that the curvilinear relationship is statistically insignificant; the results show that it is likely that as prisoner density increases, its effects on turnout level off or continue to decrease but at a slower rate. For North Carolina, the curvilinear relationship shown in figure 4.3 shows that at low levels of prisoner density, increasing the concentration of prisoners actually appears to *help* voter turnout. This phenomenon is consistent with the alternative hypothesis presented in chapter 2. However, the

Table 4.1: Effects of imprisonment on voter turnout

	Georgia Linear Model	North Carolina Linear Model	Georgia Curvilinear Model	North Carolina Curvilinear Model
Prisoner density squared			2.414×10^{-06}	-3.27×10^{-05}***
			(0.0000)	(0.000)
Prisoner density	-2.715×10^{-04}	2.29×10^{-03}***	-9.576×10^{-04}**	7.00×10^{-03}***
	(0.0002)	(0.001)	(0.0005)	(0.001)
Vacancy rate	-0.641***	-0.129	-0.647***	-0.138
	(0.1361)	(0.092)	(0.1369)	(0.092)
Relative proportion noncitizen	-0.088***	-0.012	-0.088***	-0.016
	(0.0140)	(0.016)	(0.0140)	(0.016)
Relative proportion unemployed	-0.036***	-0.029*	-0.035***	-0.033**
	(0.0105)	(0.011)	(0.0105)	(0.011)
Median income (in 1,000s)	0.007***	0.004***	0.007***	0.004***
	(0.0004)	(0.001)	(0.0004)	(0.001)
Ratio of women to men	0.529.	0.732*	0.528.	0.707*
	(0.2850)	(0.320)	(0.2849)	(0.319)
High school completion rate (female)	1.046***	0.888***	1.047***	0.883***
	(0.0816)	(0.089)	(0.0815)	(0.089)
Proportion of adults under 25	-3.099***	-1.584***	-3.088***	-1.581***
	(0.1922)	(0.187)	(0.1916)	(0.187)
Homicide rate	55.170***	6.710	55.400***	2.958
	(15.9500)	(17.640)	(15.9100)	(17.620)
Proportion other minority	-110.000	-18.380	-101.600	-87.580
	(103.8000)	(121.300)	(103.4000)	(121.600)

Proportion black	0.420***	0.302***	0.436***	0.229***
	(0.0433)	(0.056)	(0.0442)	(0.057)
Presence of ex-felon-serving Institutions	0.009	0.072*	0.009	0.062*
	(0.0254)	(0.028)	(0.0254)	(0.028)
Proportion Hispanic	-0.816***	-1.494***	-0.811***	-1.517***
	(0.1493)	(0.151)	(0.1490)	(0.151)
Proportion in group quarters	-1.441***	-1.418***	-1.451***	-1.442***
	(0.2234)	(0.219)	(0.2229)	(0.219)
Poverty rate	0.340**	0.310*	0.360**	0.305*
	(0.1155)	(0.136)	(0.1159)	(0.135)
Intercept	-2.206***	-5.70×10^{-01}**	-1.969***	-5.69×10^{-01}**
	(0.1803)	(0.188)	(0.1931)	(0.188)
phi	20.670***	19.080	20.802***	19.205
	(0.425)	(0.376)	(0.427)	(0.378)
N	4,536	4,948	4,536	4,948
Pseudo-R^2	0.535	0.648	0.539	0.649

Note: The first and third columns present estimates by state from unmatched beta regressions on a linear model for all block groups, with prisoner density as the key causal variable of interest. The second and fourth columns present estimates by state from unmatched beta regressions on a curvilinear model for all block groups, with prisoner density as the key causal variable of interest. Standard errors are in parentheses. County fixed effects were included in the models but are not shown here.

. $P < .10$

* $P < .05$

** $P < .01$

*** $P < .001$

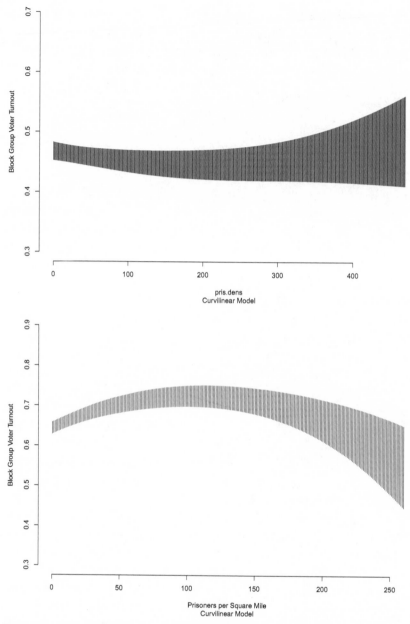

Figure 4.3: Expected voter turnout by block group prisoner density in 2008, Georgia (*top*) and North Carolina (*bottom*). Source: Neighborhood Criminal Justice Involvement Data.

North Carolina data also show that at higher concentrations of imprisonment, imprisonment suppresses voter turnout. In North Carolina, voter turnout in a block group with no prisoners is expected to be about 14 percent higher than that in a block group with 250 prisoners per square mile. Thus, the findings are clear with respect to high levels of imprisonment: they suppress voter turnout.[17]

DISCUSSION

The results of this first study confirm that, on average, the imprisonment of neighborhood residents by criminal justice authorities suppresses voter turnout among those they leave behind. In Georgia and North Carolina neighborhoods with the highest imprisonment rates, voter turnout was lower on average than that in neighborhoods with low imprisonment rates even after controlling for potentially confounding factors. While this analysis cannot shed much light on the particular mechanisms by which this suppression occurs, by controlling many of the neighborhood characteristics that would confound the analysis, the results at least provide compelling evidence that *something* is happening at the neighborhood level because of the criminal justice system.

Some might argue that the findings presented here are the result of bias. With respect to geographic data, it may be the case that the clustering of high-imprisonment neighborhoods in space might bias the results. However, tests for spatial autocorrelation reveals that the results are not caused by this phenomenon.[18] Outliers, or extreme values that can skew results, are also a common concern when working with criminal justice data, since neighborhoods that have high concentrations of prisoners are thought to be qualitatively different from low-imprisonment neighborhoods in many ways. One way to evaluate extreme values is to calculate Cook's d, which is a measure of how influential each observation is on the estimates. Evaluating each observation for which Cook's d is greater than 0.005 reveals that these most influential observations are all for neighborhoods with low imprisonment levels and low voter turnout, suggesting that if any outliers are present, the bias causes this analysis to underestimate the effects of prisoner density.[19] Omitted variables could present a final source of bias. However, Ramsey's RESET test for functional form reveals that the neither the North Carolina nor the Georgia models demonstrate omitted-variable bias.[20]

The Second Test: Voter Turnout and New Prison Admissions

Another way of studying the relationship between imprisonment and political participation tests the effect of new prison admissions on voter turnout. The ideal test of this relationship would randomly assign neighborhoods to experience the imprisonment of residents independently of poverty rates, racial heterogeneity, and other potentially confounding factors. Of course, such an experiment is impossible in the real world, but this research approximates such random variation by taking advantage of variation in the timing of criminal sentences.[21]

This analysis uses the timing of prison admissions to set up a natural experiment in which turnout rates of voters in neighborhoods that experience imprisonment prior to the 2008 general election are compared with those in control neighborhoods matched in terms of homicide rates, poverty rates, racial composition, education, and the other potentially confounding factors that were discussed in the previous section. The control neighborhoods also have residents sent to prison, but only after the election is over. For North Carolina and Georgia, the analysis compares neighborhoods from which prisoners were incarcerated within ninety days of election day with neighborhoods from which prisoners were incarcerated up to ninety days after the election.

The key innovation of this research design involves the analysis of a reduced sample of neighborhoods in which the comparison group, like the treatment group, includes only neighborhoods that have residents sent to prison. Neighborhoods that do not have residents imprisoned during the six-month time period are excluded. Comparing neighborhoods that experience imprisonment within this narrow window around the election further lessens the impact of unmeasured differences across neighborhoods that help determine which neighborhoods experience imprisonment and which do not. Arguably, within a small time frame, the date on which a community member actually is sentenced is random, dependent on factors such as individual officers' schedules, the date the offender committed the crime, the court docket, the length of the trial, and the like. Within the set of communities that experience imprisonment around election day, one could compare communities that receive the treatment before the election with those that receive the treatment afterward as a way of testing the effects of incarceration on turnout. The random assignment of the neighborhoods to the treatment and control conditions (residents sentenced to prison before or after election day, respectively) along with controlling for potentially confounding factors in a regression model should produce unbiased estimates of the effects of sending people to prison on neighborhood voter turnout.[22]

Limiting the treatment and control groups in this analysis to include only neighborhoods that experience imprisonment makes it more likely that the treatment and control communities have the same underlying distribution of factors that lead to the conviction and sentencing of their members; the actual timing of the treatment within the small window around the election is random and thus independent of those confounding factors. As a result, unless there is some systematic process that determines both the particular week or month that an individual from a given neighborhood is incarcerated *and* that neighborhood's voter turnout rate, any differences in the dependent variables across the treated and control groups should be due to imprisonment. To reiterate, within the reduced sample, any differences across neighborhoods would have to be correlated with *both* the timing of the sentence and voter turnout in order to bias the results.[23]

With respect to mechanisms, the reason that imprisonment might affect voter turnout even in this short time period are similar to those described in chapter 2. To summarize the extant literature, incarceration is so disruptive to communities that its effects could influence turnout even in the span of a few months. This explanation fits well with the Civic Voluntarism Model outlined by Verba, Schlozman, and Brady, which argues that people fail to participate in politics because they cannot, were not asked, or do not want to.[24] Much of the impact of sending people to prison stems from the fact that incarceration leaves the families and friends of inmates in emotional and financial chaos and thus unable to participate. For instance, a woman may not have time to vote because she is working more hours to make up for the lost income of her convicted spouse.[25] Foster parents struggling to care for a convicted mother's children might be too overwhelmed with their new responsibilities to make it out to the polls. In general, the spouses and families of individuals who are convicted of crimes often are disconnected from the typical avenues of political mobilization because they move often or are ostracized from their communities.[26] Similarly, households may be less likely to be contacted by parties and interest groups if their incarcerated members are removed from the voter rolls, a phenomenon that is discussed more fully in chapter 6. Finally, imprisonment may decrease the desire to vote within the neighborhood. The accomplices of an inmate might be reluctant to contact any public officials, including the board of elections. Even among neighbors without an explicit connection to an offender, a highly publicized, contentious, or controversial imprisonment might decrease efficacy or trust in government.[27] In these ways, imprisoning individuals may lead to measurable differences in turnout even in the short term.

METHODS

In order to make the treated block groups as similar to the control groups as possible, the data are preprocessed using MatchIt.[28] The nearest-neighbor method without replacement is used, which matches each treated neighborhood with the comparison unit with the closest propensity scores.[29] Matching makes it possible to compare similarly situated neighborhoods to each other—apples to apples. The process discards incomparable data points that may bias the results. For instance, neighborhoods full of millionaires may be different from more heterogeneous communities; if there were no corresponding high-income neighborhoods in the treatment group, this outlier neighborhood might be discarded. More formally, this process discards neighborhoods outside the range of common support, because including these neighborhoods in the analysis could bias the results.[30] The neighborhoods were matched on several control variables for which the treated and control groups differed significantly, including the number of inmates sent to prison during the study period, black percentage of the neighborhood population, existing level of incarceration, homicide rate, median income, and proportion of adult residents under age 25. The descriptive statistics for the full and matched samples are provided in appendix table A.2.

As in the multivariate analysis of the effect of incarceration on turnout in the previous section, the data were analyzed at the block group level. Many of the same control variables used in the previous analysis are included in the models presented in this analysis: the poverty rate, homicide rate, presence of ex-inmate-serving organizations, housing unit vacancy rate, proportion of adult residents under age 25, relative proportion of noncitizens, male-to-female ratio, relative proportion unemployed, female high school completion rate, percentage in group quarters, black percentage of the population, Hispanic percentage, and other minority percentage. The states are analyzed separately. However, the key causal independent variable differs in an important way. The *inmates* variable is a measure of the number of people imprisoned from each block group between August 4, 2008, and February 4, 2009. The treatment variable, *convicted before election*, is an indicator of whether a neighborhood had inmates sent to prison in the ninety days prior to the election. As with the previous analysis, the dependent variable, *voter turnout*, is the number of people from the block group who voted in the November general election divided by the 2008 adult population of the block group. As a robustness check, the analysis also includes the same models estimated for a sixty-day window around the election. The relationship between voter turnout and incarceration at the neighborhood level was tested using ordinary-least-squares regression on the matched data.

RESULTS

The findings presented in the first and second columns of table 4.2 indicate that sending individuals to prison decreases neighborhood voter turnout, at least in Georgia. Georgia neighborhoods that experienced the imprisonment of residents ninety days before the November general election voted at lower rates than those neighborhoods that had not had residents imprisoned before the election, even after controlling for racial composition, poverty rates, median age, the percentage of people living in group quarters, home vacancy rates, homicide rates, citizenship, and educational attainment in the neighborhood. Based on simulations, imprisoning neighborhood residents in Georgia decreased turnout about 1.4 percentage points on average when all other variables were held constant at their means. About 47.1 percent of adults voted in the 2008 general election in the typical Georgia block group that experienced the imprisonment of a resident in the three months prior to the election. In contrast, the analysis suggests that turnout in that block group would have been 48.5 percent had that resident been sent to prison after the election. The findings do not hold for the sixty-day window, perhaps because the number of neighborhoods that experience imprisonment before or after the election is smaller in this shorter time span.

In North Carolina, turnout in neighborhoods that experienced imprisonment was no different from turnout in those neighborhoods that did not. However, this finding is not surprising, given that the effects of imprisonment in North Carolina seem to be mixed, as shown in the previous section.

Table 4.2: Estimated effect of incarceration on neighborhood voter turnout

	Georgia Whole Sample, 90 Days	Georgia Reduced Sample, 90 Days	Georgia Whole Sample, 60 Days	North Carolina Whole Sample, 90 Days	North Carolina Reduced Sample, 90 Days	North Carolina Whole Sample, 60 Days
Intercept	0.192**	0.195**	0.177***	0.062	0.011	0.027
	(0.060)	(0.060)	(0.048)	(0.092)	(0.098)	(0.073)
Convicted before election	-0.014*	-0.014.	0.000	-0.007	-0.005	-0.002
	(0.007)	(0.007)	(0.005)	(0.012)	(0.012)	(0.007)
Number of Inmates convicted	-0.002	-0.002	-0.005***	-0.001	-0.001	-0.001
	(0.002)	(0.002)	(0.001)	(0.002)	(0.002)	(0.002)
Relative proportion unemployed	-0.011**	-0.011**	-0.007*	-0.010.	-0.010.	-0.008.
	(0.004)	(0.004)	(0.003)	(0.005)	(0.006)	(0.005)
Homicide rate	10.200.	10.060.	11.650*	1.272	2.760	0.810
	(5.348)	(5.341)	(4.567)	(7.918)	(8.434)	(6.722)
High school completion rate (female)	0.268***	0.267***	0.229***	0.249***	0.254***	0.285***
	(0.031)	(0.032)	(0.024)	(0.043)	(0.045)	(0.035)
Imprisonment rate	0.569*	0.566*	0.414*	3.591***	3.712***	3.362***
	(0.221)	(0.222)	(0.185)	(0.630)	(0.665)	(0.555)
Ratio of women to men	0.160	0.155	0.253**	0.496**	0.583***	0.549***
	(0.108)	(0.109)	(0.085)	(0.162)	(0.172)	(0.129)
Median Income (in 1,000s)	0.002***	0.002***	0.002***	0.002***	0.002***	0.002***
	(0.000)	(0.000)	(0.000)	(0.000)	(0.000)	(0.000)
Poverty rate	0.115**	0.120**	0.047	0.045	0.069	-0.020
	(0.043)	(0.043)	(0.035)	(0.067)	(0.070)	(0.054)

Proportion of adults under 25	-0.735***	-0.738***	-0.677***	-0.066	-0.098	-0.095
	(0.080)	(0.080)	(0.065)	(0.111)	(0.116)	(0.083)
Proportion black	0.113***	0.114***	0.107***	0.100***	0.087***	0.111***
	(0.013)	(0.013)	(0.010)	(0.021)	(0.022)	(0.017)
Proportion Hispanic	-0.152**	-0.155**	-0.221***	-0.516***	-0.475***	-0.462***
	(0.052)	(0.052)	(0.041)	(0.076)	(0.079)	(0.057)
Proportion other minority	-94.290	-94.600	-97.160*	108.300.	104.000.	112.100*
	(64.010)	(63.970)	(49.500)	(60.120)	(62.240)	(47.550)
Vacancy rate	-0.108*	-0.108*	-0.058	-0.046	-0.054	-0.034
	(0.043)	(0.043)	(0.035)	(0.054)	(0.055)	(0.041)
Proportion in group quarters	-0.275**	-0.270**	-0.333***	-0.170	-0.195	-0.203*
	(0.090)	(0.090)	(0.070)	(0.118)	(0.122)	(0.093)
Presence of ex-felon-serving institutions	0.003	0.002	-0.007	0.013	0.014	0.033**
	(0.009)	(0.009)	(0.007)	(0.013)	(0.014)	(0.011)
Relative proportion noncitizen	-0.021***	-0.021***	-0.016***	0.016*	0.014.	0.007
	(0.006)	(0.006)	(0.004)	(0.008)	(0.008)	(0.006)
N	1,591	1,591	2,481	1,529	1,455	2,581
Adjusted R^2	0.484	0.484	0.469	0.224	0.220	0.224

Note: Figures are results of OLS regression on matched data. Standard errors are in parentheses.

. $P < .10$

* $P < .05$

** $P < .01$

*** $P < .001$

DISCUSSION

The analysis presented in this section adds to the mounting evidence that high imprisonment decreases voter turnout, not just for prisoners themselves, but also for the families, friends, and neighbors they leave behind. This analysis takes a different approach from the previous one, however, by attempting to estimate only the marginal effect of new incarcerations that take place right before the election. In setting up the research in this way, the intervention is to measure the average effect of imprisoning additional people in the short term rather than the effects of a longer history of imprisonment, which is better captured by the analysis from the previous section. The design is based on the assumption that this effect occurs within a short time frame: if this theory is correct, sending another person to prison, no matter how many people were imprisoned previously, on average will result in a measurable decrease in voter turnout within three months of sentencing. It is plausible that some people who might have voted do not because someone in their neighborhood or household is sent to prison. Do these short-term suppressions of political activity add up to a permanent decrease in voter turnout in subsequent elections? Perhaps, but it is likely that the hypothetical individuals described in the previous section would eventually vote in the future. Longer-term effects, should they exist, might be driven by different processes.

The Third Test: Individual-Level Analyses

It stands to reason that the result described in the previous two sections—that neighborhood imprisonment decreases neighborhood voter turnout—reflects the influence of the neighborhood criminal justice context on the behavior of all individual neighborhood residents. Therefore, it seems sensible to expect that at an individual level, a person who lives in a neighborhood with a higher spatial concentration of prisoners would be less likely to vote, and maybe even to participate in other forms of political and community activities, than a person who lives in a neighborhood with fewer prisoners. This final section undertakes this analysis, translating the turnout patterns observed at the broader block group level into individual political behavior. As noted in the introduction to this chapter, this final piece of the puzzle fits well with the phenomenon observed in the aggregate: living in a high-imprisonment neighborhood stifles political participation.

This research makes use of the restricted Social Capital Community

Benchmark Survey conducted by the Saguaro Seminar at the John F. Kennedy School of Government at Harvard University.[31] Unlike most public opinion data, this survey comprises both a national sample of some 3,000 respondents and representative samples of 26,700 respondents in forty-two communities nationwide, making it ideal for neighborhood-level analyses. This analysis uses the Charlotte-Mecklenburg area sample, which has a sample size of 1,266. However, due to missing data, the final sample size can be as low as 1,037.

For each Charlotte-Mecklenburg respondent, block group characteristics similar to those used in the preceding block-group-level analyses were added to the data. However, because the respondents were surveyed in 2000, census counts, rather than proprietary estimates, were used to provide data on vacant housing units, the black percentage of the population, the Hispanic percentage, the median age, the percentage in group quarters, the adult population, the block group high school completion rate, and citizenship. Using census data also allowed for the inclusion of variables, such as the block group unemployment rate, median income, and percentage receiving public assistance. The block group 2000 homicide rate and information about ex-inmate-serving institutions in 2000 were obtained from the departments of public health in each state and from departments of corrections and the IRS Master List of Exempt Organizations, as described for all other analyses.

The key causal variable, prisoner density, was calculated from North Carolina department of corrections data based on the prison population as of November 2000 in that state. This analysis tests the effects of neighborhood prisoner density on four measures of individual participation: voter registration and turnout, political activities, volunteering, and group membership. The voter registration question asks each respondent whether he or she was registered to vote at the time of the survey. The voter turnout question asks each eligible respondent whether he or she voted in the 1996 presidential election. The political activities scale counts responses on several questions with yes or no answers: whether the respondent voted in the last election, whether the respondent participated in a march in the past twelve months, whether the respondent signed a petition in the past twelve months, whether the respondent participated in a community project in the past twelve months, whether the respondent attended a rally in the past twelve months, whether the respondent is a member of a political group, and whether the respondent is a member of any group that took local action for reform. This variable falls along a 0–7 scale, with 0 representing participation in no activities and 7 representing participation in all activities. The group membership index was constructed by the survey's principal investigators based on membership in nineteen different types of groups, including churches, youth groups, and professional organizations. This variable ranges from 0, or no group memberships, to a high of 19, or membership in all nineteen organizations. The last dependent variable is a count of the number of times the respondent reports volunteering in the past twelve months. The responses range from 0, or no volunteering, to 60, or volunteered sixty times in the past twelve months. Descriptive statistics for the individuals and neighborhoods included in the analysis can be found in appendix table A.3.

METHODS

Because the voter registration and turnout dependent variables each take on only two values, these relationships are best estimated with logit models. Likewise, the political activities, volunteering, and group membership scales are counts and are best estimated using a negative binomial model. Often, researchers would use hierarchical models to analyze nested causal structures such as individuals situated in neighborhoods. However, in this case, the geographic units share too few individuals to estimate the fixed effects of different block groups using hierarchical models. Instead, the characteristics of the block groups are included in the models as separate variables.

The model accounts for both individual-level[32] and neighborhood-level influences on these activities. At the individual level, age, race, gender, ideology, educational attainment, political knowledge, political interest, and income all have been shown to influence individual political activity.[33] Consequently, age is included in the model as a continuous variable. Total household income is included as a categorical variable with the highest category being "$100,000 or more." Education is a seven-part variable, where 1 = "high school or less" and 7 = "graduate or professional training." Gender and race are included as dummy variables for female, black, and Hispanic, respectively. Ideology is a five-category variable with responses ranging from 1, "very liberal," to 5, "very conservative." The political knowledge scale is based on responses to questions about the elected officials in the respondents' states; respondents receive a 1 if they were unable to name either of their US senators and a 5 if they were able to name both correctly. The political interest scale is a four-point scale ranging from 1, "not at all interested," to 4, "very interested" in politics and national affairs. Newspaper reading is measured as a simple count of the number of days in the past week the respondent reports having read a newspaper.

At the neighborhood level, many neighborhood characteristics might influence individual behavior while being correlated with neighborhood incarceration rates; these factors must be taken into account in any model of these effects. Thus, like the previous models, these models also control for the median income, percentage receiving public assistance, poverty rate, unemployment rate, percentage of housing units that are vacant, presence of ex-inmate-serving institutions, homicide rate, median age, citizenship rate, black percentage of the population, Hispanic percentage, and percentage of the population in group quarters.

RESULTS

The results of the individual-level analyses confirm the block group analyses. Individuals are much less likely to participate in politics when they live in high-imprisonment neighborhoods. Table 4.3 presents the results of the models of voter registration, voter turnout, political activities, volunteering, and group involvement.

With respect to voting, the data in table 4.3 clearly show the effects of neighborhood criminal justice context on both registration and turnout. The evidence supports the claim that people who live in a high-imprisonment neighborhood are less likely to be registered voters than those who live in lower-imprisonment neighborhoods; however, this result is significant only at the $p = 0.079$ level and does not reach traditional levels of statistical significance. The estimate of the effect of prisoner density on voter turnout is negative and statistically significant ($p = 0.004$). This estimated difference is also substantively meaningful, as shown in figure 4.4, which plots the probability of having voted in 1996 for blacks and whites at different levels of neighborhood prisoner density, holding all other individual and neighborhood-level characteristics at their means. As shown in the figure, the difference in the probability of voting among people living in a community with the average prisoner density and people living in a community with no prisoners is small, only about 1 percentage point. However, for people

Table 4.3: Effects of imprisonment on turnout and political activity in Charlotte

	Number of Activities (Negative Binomial)	Voter Turnout (Logit)t	Voter Registration (Logit)	Number of Times Volunteered (Negative Binomial)	Number of Groups (Negative Binomial)
Block group variables:					
Prisoners per square mile	-0.006*	-0.031**	-0.022.	-0.016*	-0.004.
	(0.003)	(0.011)	(0.013)	(0.007)	(0.002)
Proportion noncitizen	1.601	-2.123	-2.235	1.618	0.580
	(1.587)	(6.378)	(7.495)	(3.999)	(1.425)
Percentage foreign born	-1.027	-0.256	-1.781	1.417	-0.650
	(1.358)	(5.293)	(6.349)	(3.352)	(1.208)
Homicide rate	59.169	433.900	642.988.	199.800	78.315**
	(70.344)	(281.600)	(367.312)	(181.400)	(63.968)
Proportion receiving public assistance	0.418	0.147	1.506	8.340**	2.878
	(1.310)	(4.349)	(5.129)	(3.013)	(1.109)
Poverty rate	-0.152	1.848	0.984	-0.952	0.084
	(0.525)	(1.811)	(2.171)	(1.206)	(0.447)
Median income (in 1,000s)	-0.001	-0.010*	-0.011*	-0.001	0.001
	(0.001)	(0.005)	(0.005)	(0.003)	(0.001)
Median age	-0.005	0.017	0.003	0.018	0.001
	(0.006)	(0.021)	(0.026)	(0.014)	(0.005)
High school completion rate	0.066	-0.133	-0.122	-1.089	0.194
	(0.310)	(1.073)	(1.281)	(0.729)	(0.271)
Proportion black	0.225	1.034	0.753	-0.380	-0.027
	(0.200)	(0.753)	(0.918)	(0.479)	(0.175)

	(1)	(2)	(3)	(4)	(5)
Proportion Hispanic	0.265	1.324	0.218	-3.059	1.133.
	(0.770)	(2.887)	(3.393)	(1.927)	(0.685)
Presence of ex-felon-serving institutions	0.097	0.142	-0.259	0.525	0.277*
	(0.151)	(0.541)	(0.605)	(0.365)	(0.126)
Proportion in group quarters	0.196	0.582	0.596	0.660	-0.608
	(0.563)	(2.228)	(2.658)	(1.432)	(0.531)
Vacancy rate	-0.235	-3.502	-3.661	-1.666	0.331
	(0.609)	(2.146)	(2.511)	(1.446)	(0.524)
Unemployment rate	-0.220	1.679	0.459	0.001	0.200
	(0.899)	(3.540)	(4.481)	(2.190)	(0.804)
Individual-level variables:					
Economic satisfaction	0.020	0.246.	0.284.	-0.029	0.175***
	(0.039)	(0.140)	(0.165)	(0.093)	(0.047)
Home Internet access	0.114*	0.000	-0.148	0.425***	0.047
	(0.054)	(0.188)	(0.229)	(0.126)	(0.034)
Income	0.062***	0.145**	0.211**	0.050	0.040**
	(0.016)	(0.056)	(0.066)	(0.038)	(0.014)
Political interest	0.266***	0.537***	0.647***	0.122.	0.202***
	(0.030)	(0.095)	(0.114)	(0.065)	(0.025)
Political knowledge	0.035*	0.346***	0.384***	0.003	-0.012
	(0.016)	(0.074)	(0.109)	(0.043)	(0.015)
Reads paper	0.009	0.051.	0.023	0.054**	0.022**
	(0.009)	(0.031)	(0.038)	(0.021)	(0.008)
Gender	0.090.	0.168	0.300	0.386***	0.108**
	(0.047)	(0.171)	(0.202)	(0.113)	(0.041)
Ideology	0.006	-0.036	-0.007	-0.080	-0.010

(continued)

Table 4.3: *continued*

	Number of Activities (Negative Binomial)	Voter Turnout (Logit)	Voter Registration (Logit)	Number of Times Volunteered (Negative Binomial)	Number of Groups (Negative Binomial)
Educational attainment	0.102*** (0.020)	0.345*** (0.076)	0.331*** (0.089)	0.139*** (0.049)	0.091*** (0.018)
	(0.015)	(0.065)	(0.086)	(0.039)	(0.014)
Age	0.003.	0.049***	0.033***	-0.003	0.005**
	(0.002)	(0.007)	(0.008)	(0.004)	(0.002)
Hispanic	-0.016	0.080	0.355	-0.497	-0.032
	(0.197)	(0.557)	(0.521)	(0.349)	(0.143)
Black	0.154*	0.768**	0.471	0.102	0.283***
	(0.071)	(0.255)	(0.301)	(0.171)	(0.061)
Citizenship	0.838***	3.930***	3.982***	0.382	0.434**
	(0.238)	(1.080)	(0.720)	(0.366)	(0.153)
Intercept	-1.940***	-9.572***	-7.574***	0.423	-1.096**
	(0.436)	(1.754)	(1.769)	(0.932)	(0.352)
N	1,037	1,058	1,079	1,087	1,088

Source: These data rely on the Charlotte sample of the 2000 Social Capital Benchmark Survey.

Note: Standard errors are in parentheses.

. P < .10

* P < .05

** P < .01

*** P < .001

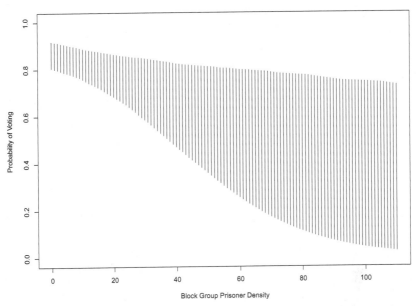

Figure 4.4: Effects of block group prisoner density on the individual probability of voting. Data from the Charlotte sample of the Social Capital Benchmark Survey.

living in neighborhoods with more extreme spatial concentrations of prisoners (the maximum in this sample is 110 prisoners per square mile), the effects on turnout are much more dramatic: the probability of voting among people living in block groups with the maximum prisoner density declines by two-thirds from the probability of voting among people who live in block groups with no prisoners.

Also from table 4.3, the relationship between the spatial concentration of prisoners and the general political activity scale is negative and statistically significant ($p = 0.042$). Figure 4.5 plots the expected range of political activity for individuals based on the prisoner densities of the block groups in which they live. As with the previous figures, these predictions were made holding all other individual- and neighborhood-level characteristics at their means. The graph shows the clear negative effect of prisoner density on the number of political activities undertaken by individuals: people are much less likely to engage in multiple forms of participation in high-imprisonment neighborhoods. An average person living in a block group with no prisoners is expected to undertake about two of the seven political activities in the index, while a person living in a neighborhood with the maximum

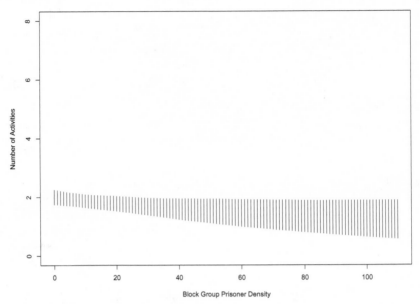

Figure 4.5: Effects of block group prisoner density on individual political activities. Data from the Charlotte sample of the Social Capital Benchmark Survey.

prisoner density (again, 110 prisoners per square mile in this sample) is expected to undertake 0.89 fewer activities. This difference represents a 44 percent decline in activity.

With respect to civic engagement more broadly, the results for volunteering are also negative and statistically significant ($p = 0.013$, see table 4.3). The average person living in a neighborhood with no prisoners is expected to volunteer about nine times in a twelve-month period, while the average person living in a neighborhood with the highest prisoner density is expected to volunteer about twice per year. This steep decline is reflected in the graph of the expected level of volunteering for individuals based on the prisoner densities of the block groups in which they live in figure 4.6.

As noted in the introduction and in the table of regression coefficients (table 4.3), the results for group membership are not significant at traditional levels ($p = 0.07$). However, these results are close to statistical significance and are in the expected direction, lending further support to the notion that high spatial concentrations of prisoners diminish participation. Group membership among people living in neighborhoods with the highest levels of prisoners is expected to be

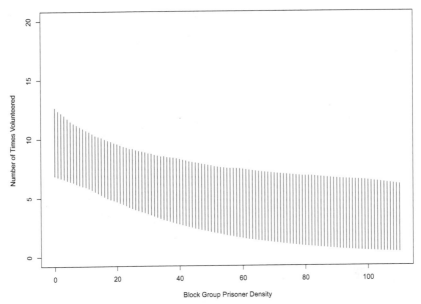

Figure 4.6: Effects of neighborhood imprisonment on individual volunteering. Data from the Charlotte sample of the Social Capital Benchmark Survey.

one-third lower than that of people living in neighborhoods with no prisoners, holding all other factors constant at their means.

DISCUSSION

The individual-level analyses provide consistent evidence that living in a neighborhood with a high spatial concentration of prisoners diminishes political and community participation. For voting and other forms of political participation, the effect sizes are both substantively and statistically significant. The effects on one measure of broader civic engagement, volunteering, are also substantively and statistically significant. For the other measure of civic engagement, group membership, the results are close to traditional statistical significance. As with the aggregate-level analyses, the action appears to be in imprisonment rather than in community supervision.

Conclusion and Implications

As chapter 2 notes, the consensus among anthropologists and sociologists is that the concentration of social ills, including imprisonment, matters for communities with respect to health, crime, poverty, teenage motherhood and other phenomena.[34] This chapter has presented a growing set of evidence that imprisonment also matters for politics—in particular, for individual political participation. The analyses of both individual- and neighborhood-level data, despite using multiple methods and data sources, all point clearly and conclusively in the same direction: that living in a neighborhood with a high spatial concentration of prisoners diminishes political participation. The evidence presented clearly demonstrates the impact of having a high concentration of prisoners in a particular neighborhood: neighborhoods with a higher concentration of prisoners voted at lower rates in the 2008 general election than neighborhoods with lower concentrations of prisoners, all other factors being equal. Moreover, the evidence suggests a strong causal linkage between imprisonment and voter turnout: among neighborhoods that had residents imprisoned in the months surrounding the 2008 election, voter turnout was significantly higher in those neighborhoods where the imprisonment happened after the election than before. While it is possible that in some neighborhoods and under some circumstances sending neighborhood residents to prison might increase political activity, the findings presented here show that, most often, the effect of imprisoning residents is to decrease participation.

Each of the analyses suggests that incarcerating community members has important spillover effects that suppress participation not only of the incarcerated individual but also of those living around him or her. The magnitude of the turnout reduction measured at the neighborhood level is too large to attribute to the removal of only one or two inmates. Likewise, the demonstrated participatory reduction among people who are not themselves in prison also supports the claim that these analyses are capturing spillover effects, rather than the primary effects of imprisonment on felons themselves.

The most frequently raised objection is that of omitted-variable bias. Studying neighborhoods invites bias because it is impossible to know or measure all differences across neighborhoods that are correlated with both the treatment variable and the dependent variable. In response, it is important to note that many of the relevant control variables *are* included in the analysis, and that testing on the full dataset in the section "The First Test" suggests that the model is fully specified. Further, the analysis discussed in the section "The Second Test" takes the added step of preprocessing the data with matching, which makes the treated and control neighborhoods as similar as possible. Moreover, the design of that particular analysis ensures that for bias to occur, the omitted variable has to be correlated not only with voter turnout, but also with the specific timing of the residents' admission to prison. In particular, in the reduced samples the treatment is the *timing* of imprisonment rather than the fact of having residents imprisoned itself; the design assumes that timing of the sentence in the short term is random. Granted, focusing on neighborhoods in which a resident is imprisoned and discarding those that do not experience imprisonment arguably produces a more conservative analysis of the effect of imprisonment. However, this narrower focus also helps limit potential sources of omitted-variable bias.

More important, however, the strength of the evidence presented in this chapter is that it employs multiple tests and multiple datasets to study multiple forms of participation; the objections raised against any one result should not apply to the other analyses. Concerns over omitted variables at the individual level are assuaged by the presence of aggregate-level data that point in the same direction. Objections about election-specific or state-specific effects are made moot by analyzing two states and two election years (2000 and 2008).

Another objection is conceptual—some may wonder whether these results simply reflect the presence in high-imprisonment neighborhoods of ex-felons who do not know of their voting rights. Of course, the first response to this objection is that the analysis does try to control for the presence of ex-felons by including information about the presence of institutions that house or provide services to them for each neighborhood. Moreover, evidence from previous work raises doubts about the claim that large numbers of ex-felons do not vote because they lack knowledge about their rights.[35]

These results do, for the most part, contradict the conventional wisdom that imprisonment unequivocally helps improve neighborhoods and thus raise important issues that deserve further research in future work. The obvious first issue, of course, concerns the difference across states in the effects of imprisonment at low concentrations. The data are unclear with respect to how imprisonment affects voter turnout at lower levels of imprisonment. In North Carolina, the evidence suggests that sending more people to prison when the existing spatial concentration of imprisonment is low might have positive effects on voter turnout. However, the evidence from Georgia suggests that imprisonment hurts voting regardless of the level of spatial concentration of imprisonment.

The next issue concerns the racially disparate impact of imprisonment, which, as chapter 3 shows, falls heavily on black neighborhoods. The data on the concentration of imprisonment in black neighborhoods in Georgia and North Carolina clearly show that these detrimental effects, particularly at the most extreme levels of prisoner density, are almost entirely concentrated in black neighborhoods and thus are experienced by black people to a higher degree than whites and Hispanics. In this way, the criminal justice system produces racial political inequality insidiously: not by the more visible disfranchisement of convicted felons, but by the vicarious disfranchisement of their neighbors.

While these data cannot shed much light on these two issues, these data can be used to shed light on one final issue: mechanisms. Recall from chapter 2 that four mechanisms might operate simultaneously and account for the decrease in political participation: cultural deviance, social disorganization, resource deprivation, and demobilization. Unfortunately, the models tested in this chapter do not give much insight into the relative contribution of these phenomena to decreasing political participation. Further testing is needed to distinguish between mechanisms; this work begins in the next chapter.

5

Exploring Mechanisms

Dear Mr. President I live in the hood
Where people live bad
But say it's all good
And my homies slanging and robbing
Caught a misdemeanor felonies
We can't survive it
— Master P, "Dear Mr. President"

High imprisonment rates lead to political inequality. As shown in the last chapter, people who live in high-imprisonment neighborhoods are less likely to register and vote than are people who live in neighborhoods with fewer prisoners. Moreover, imprisonment decreases the likelihood that people will engage in *any* sort of political activity, including protests, marches, and joining a political group. For most people who tend to live in low-incarceration neighborhoods, imprisonment only slightly affects political participation. However, for people living in neighborhoods with the highest spatial concentrations of imprisonment, the political consequences are dire. High spatial concentrations of imprisonment greatly decrease the likelihood that citizens living in such a neighborhood will attempt to communicate their needs to public officials through traditional means such as voting, joining political groups, and the like. Although recording artists, poets, and activists and others may speak out on behalf of residents of high-imprisonment communities, as Master P does here, those indirect messages may not be as effective as votes or petitions for directly communicating with government officials. Thus, inequalities of political voice,[1] as caused by neighborhood experiences with imprisonment, very likely translate into inequalities of representation or even services, adding to the disadvantages that residents of high-imprisonment neighborhoods already face as a result of living in poor, minority communities.

This chapter probes more deeply into the *how* of the political effects of neighborhood imprisonment. Its goal is to explain the findings of the last chapter by examining the evidence for and against the mechanisms first raised in chapter 2: cultural deviance, social disorganization, resource deprivation, and demobilization. This discussion will not attempt to quantify the relative contributions of the potential mechanisms to decreases in political participation. Rather, the aim of the chapter is to rule out any of the mechanisms that are not supported by the evidence.

To make these claims, the analysis relies on the Charlotte sample of the 2000 Social Capital Benchmark Survey first introduced in the last chapter, combined with evidence from chapters 3 and 4. The findings indicate little support for the cultural deviance explanation: residents of high-imprisonment communities are no more likely to express antigovernment or antipolice attitudes than people in low-imprisonment communities. Certain aspects of resource deprivation also seem to be less viable explanations—people who live in high-imprisonment communities are no more likely to report that lack of time and information prevent them from participating in their communities as they would like.

Instead, the effects of imprisonment most likely operate through social disorganization, demobilization, and economic deprivation. People living in high-imprisonment communities are less likely to trust their neighbors and people in general and are less likely to report feeling a sense of community based on neighborhood ties than people living in neighborhoods with lower concentrations of prisoners. Residents of high-imprisonment communities are also less likely to engage in social and political activities that might get them involved in politics, such as voting, volunteering, and joining groups and churches.

These findings are discussed in detail in the following pages. To simplify the discussion, each mechanism is discussed separately. Each section will first briefly summarize the arguments for each mechanism based on the discussion in chapter 2. A set of expectations with respect to what one should see if the mechanism were operating in the real world will follow this summary. The analysis will present demographic and survey evidence on whether residents in high-imprisonment neighborhoods behave or think in ways that fit these expectations. Finally, the chapter will close with a general discussion of what these patterns mean for solutions.

Cultural Deviance

As noted in chapter 2, cultural deviance theories suggest that the diminished participation seen in high-imprisonment communities stems from nontraditional beliefs about participation that are not shared by the wider society. These beliefs are part of the culture of high-imprisonment neighborhoods, or "modes of behavior learned within the community."[2] The adoption of deviant behaviors may thus be explained as a process of "socialization to subcultural values condoning as right conduct" what the dominant culture thinks of as deviant conduct.[3]

The criminal justice system is perhaps the most visible and coercive manifestation of state power. As a result, one might expect that government actions in this arena would influence social identities and attitudes. The following discussion reviews the two mechanisms by which criminal justice activities might shape the political attitudes and social identities not only of convicted offenders but also of the people living around them: cultural transmission and direct observation.

"Cultural transmission" refers to the idea that individual convicts share their political opinions, beliefs, and attitudes with the people around them, transmitting their experiences with the government to other members of the community. Political attitudes largely are a function of individual social circumstances (such as age and race), attitudes (such as ideology and group consciousness), socialization, political attachments, and the like.[4] However, "external social factors," or neighborhood context, also matter for political behavior.[5] Such neighborhood effects may be contextual effects, which are based on the characteristics of an area's structural or institutional environment, or concentration effects, which result from having a large number people with similar personal characteristics in a single area or demographic group.[6] People who live in high-incarceration neighborhoods may know many people who share the common experience of incarceration and who therefore have similar political attitudes and beliefs. Individuals who live near a high concentration of people who have experienced negative criminal justice outcomes might have been exposed to the higher levels of apathy and perceptions of discrimination that their imprisoned neighbors have.[7] In this sense, one might think of political inefficacy and perceptions of discrimination as contagious.

In contrast to cultural transmission, direct observation refers to the idea that living in proximity to convicted prisoners allows neighborhood residents to observe numerous examples of people having negative experiences with the government. In this explanation, the political attitudes that develop are the result of policy learning, particularly if the negative government experiences are perceived as unfair. The perceived fairness or injustice associated with government actions provides important information to citizens about the workings of government.[8] Thus, the appearance of discrimination against friends and neighbors based on race, class, age, or gender by criminal justice authorities also has important implications for political attitudes. Perceived injustices in the criminal justice system send messages to the broader society about the quality of the social and civil rights enjoyed by targeted groups such as minorities and the poor. Living around people who get sent to prison provides many opportunities to learn about or experience incidents of unfair treatment by police, prosecutors, courts, or even corrections officers. Frequent observations of the criminal justice interactions of others may shape the perceived discrimination and political efficacy of individuals who do not themselves experience incarceration or other forms of punishment.

EVIDENCE FOR THE CULTURAL DEVIANCE MECHANISM

As defined here, the cultural deviance mechanism is marked by the presence of antigovernment sentiments and other attitudes and beliefs that would discourage political participation. The Social Capital Benchmark Survey contains several measures of political trust and efficacy that reflect respondents' views on government and political participation.

Trust in Government

At its core, an individual's degree of trust reveals his or her beliefs about the reliability or faithfulness of other parties. Generalized trust, or trust in strangers and abstracted others, lies at one end of the continuum, while particularized trust, describing trust in specific relationships, lies at the other. The focus here is on particularized trust in the relationship between government and citizens. Scholars have offered a variety of definitions intended to capture the essence of political trust. Hetherington offers a particularly concise definition of political trust: "the degree to which people perceive that government is producing outcomes consistent with their expectations."[9]

What factors shape political trust? Performance and positive governmental results appear to be a crucial ingredient in trust evaluations. Periods of economic growth are also periods when reports of political trust rise.[10] Likewise, individuals with higher incomes report more trust in government than those with lower incomes.[11] Political trust is also affected by politics. The partisan evaluation of incumbents influences trust evaluations; for instance, supporters of losing candidates after an election demonstrate lower political trust than supporters of winning candidates.[12] Political scandals, such as Watergate, have similarly been tied to lower trust levels.[13] Broadly speaking, then, objective and subjective factors that influence beliefs about the ability of government to deliver needed public goods, such as security and well-being, will lead to a decrease in trust either at the individual or at the aggregate level.

Trust in government is also tied to the race of the respondent answering the question, with black respondents typically expressing lower confidence in government, and government institutions, than whites, although descriptive representation may moderate this gap.[14] This gap is especially acute in relation to criminal justice institutions such as the courts and the police.[15] Once again this brings attention to the role performance plays in trust, especially when performance varies across constituency groups.

The standard expression of particularized trust is that X trusts Y to do Z. Not only does the trust occur between particular individuals, but it is also in relation to a particular act or situation. A good many surveys using instruments tapping trust or confidence in government follow the lead of the American National Election Survey and include at least the survey's core item on trust in government, which reads, "How much of the time do you think you can trust the government to do what is right?" The general trend revealed in these questions is that of decline, albeit with peaks and valleys apparent in the time series data.[16]

The Charlotte sample of the Social Capital Benchmark Survey contains measures of the particularized form of trust in government for both the local and national levels, as well as an additional question about trust in police. The question on trust in the national government reads, "How much of the time do you think you can trust the NATIONAL government to do what is right—just about always, most of the time, only some of the time, or hardly ever?" The question on trust in the local government follows the question on trust in the national government and asks, "How about your LOCAL government? How much of the time do you think you can trust the LOCAL government to do what is right? (Would you say just about always, most of the time, only some of the time, or hardly ever?)" For both questions, the four options range from 0, "hardly ever," to 3, "just about always."

The question on trust in police is part of a battery of questions about trust in several groups. It reads, "Next, we'd like to know how much you trust different groups of people. First, think about (GROUP). Generally speaking, would you say that you can trust them a lot, some, only a little, or not at all?" For this question, the group is "the police in your community" and the responses range from 0, "not at all," to 3, "a lot."

Responses to these questions were analyzed using ordered probit regression, because the dependent variables of interest, trust in the police and in local and national governments, are ordinal. As is the case in chapter 4, the models control for several aspects of the individual and neighborhood that might also affect political trust: at the individual level, age, race, gender, ideology, educational attainment, political knowledge, political interest, newspaper reading, Internet access, economic satisfaction, and income; at the neighborhood level, median income, percentage receiving public assistance, poverty rate, unemployment rate, percentage of housing units that are vacant, presence of ex-inmate-serving institutions, homicide rate, median age, citizenship, black percentage of the population, Hispanic percentage, and percentage of the population in group quarters.

The findings lend little support to the cultural deviance hypothesis, as table 5.1 shows. Residents of high-imprisonment communities are not more likely than residents of low- imprisonment communities to hold antigovernment attitudes. In fact, the evidence suggests that residents of high-imprisonment communities are *more* trusting of their local police than are residents of low-imprisonment communities, although this relationship is not statistically significant at the 5 percent level ($p < .1$). Likewise, residents of high-imprisonment communities appear to be more trusting of their local government, although this relationship is not statistically significant at the 5 percent level either ($p = 0.07$). There appears to be no relationship between neighborhood imprisonment and trust in the national government.

Political Efficacy

Morrell concisely captured the essence of political efficacy when he described it as "citizens' perceptions of powerfulness (or powerlessness) in the political realm."[17] Scholars traditionally separate political efficacy along two dimensions: internal political efficacy, which relates to the individual's belief in his or her own ability to influence political outcomes, and external political efficacy, which indicates the

Table 5.1: Ordered probit estimates of the effects of imprisonment on political trust in Charlotte

	Trust Cops	Trust Local Government	Trust National Government
Block group variables:			
Prisoners per square mile	0.008.	0.007.	0.003
	(0.004)	(0.004)	(0.004)
Homicide rate	40.445***	−107.166***	83.241***
	(0.024)	(0.022)	(0.022)
Percentage receiving public	−3.578.	−3.940*	−6.234***
assistance	(1.942)	(1.867)	(1.878)
Median income (in 1,000s)	0.001	0.001	0.001
	(0.002)	(0.002)	(0.002)
Percentage noncitizen	−1.447	−0.556	0.152
	(2.518)	(2.383)	(2.374)
Percentage foreign born	0.423	−0.193	−0.682
	(2.174)	(2.049)	(2.039)
Presence of ex-felon-serving	−0.018	0.349	0.348
institutions	(0.253)	(0.229)	(0.227)
Percentage in group quarters	−0.426	1.026	−0.601
	(0.941)	(0.905)	(0.892)
Percentage vacant	0.678	−0.175	−0.867
	(0.968)	(0.895)	(0.893)
Unemployment rate	0.426	−2.564.	−0.260
	(1.423)	(1.379)	(1.372)
Median age	0.010	0.002	0.011
	(0.009)	(0.008)	(0.008)
Percentage high school graduates	0.307	0.032	0.297
	(0.486)	(0.453)	(0.454)
Poverty rate	0.938	0.935	1.276.
	(0.782)	(0.740)	(0.744)
Percentage black	−0.163	−0.110	0.396
	(0.304)	(0.292)	(0.295)
Percentage Hispanic	0.922	0.223	0.762
	(1.254)	(1.172)	(1.174)
Individual-level variables:			
Hispanic	−0.297	0.466*	0.127
	(0.219)	(0.208)	(0.216)
Black	−0.801***	−0.253*	−0.058
	(0.110)	(0.107)	(0.107)
Citizen	−0.368	−0.084	−0.453*
	(0.236)	(0.219)	(0.225)

(continued)

Table 5.1: *continued*

	Trust Cops	Trust Local Government	Trust National Government
Female	0.241**	0.045	0.053
	(0.075)	(0.070)	(0.070)
Ideology	−0.035	0.018	0.093**
	(0.032)	(0.031)	(0.031)
Educational attainment	0.035	0.014	0.042.
	(0.026)	(0.024)	(0.024)
Income	−0.009	−0.013	−0.048*
	(0.025)	(0.023)	(0.023)
Economic satisfaction	0.096	0.032	−0.030
	(0.083)	(0.078)	(0.078)
Home Internet access	0.117.	0.204***	0.202***
	(0.060)	(0.057)	(0.058)
Age	0.003	0.002	−0.004
	(0.003)	(0.003)	(0.003)
Reads paper	0.026.	0.010	0.008
	(0.014)	(0.013)	(0.013)
Political interest	0.166***	0.236***	0.216***
	(0.043)	(0.041)	(0.041)
Political knowledge	0.028	0.001	0.045.
	(0.029)	(0.026)	(0.026)
Intercepts:			
0|1	−0.310	−0.086	0.532
	(0.627)	(0.574)	(0.581)
1|2	0.401	1.370*	2.084***
	(0.626)	(0.575)	(0.584)
2|3	1.491*	2.870***	3.433***
	(0.627)	(0.673)	(0.750)
3|4		7.067***	6.794
		(0.674)	(0.750)
N	1,067	1,087	1,081

Source: These data rely on the Charlotte sample of the 2000 Social Capital Benchmark Survey.

Note: Standard errors are in parentheses.

. $P < .10$

* $P < .05$

** $P < .01$

*** $P < .001$

individual's perception of how receptive political institutions are to participation. High rates of political efficacy are typically associated with higher rates of participation.[18] The belief that political participation can matter is an important influence on whether political participation is pursued as a mechanism for social change.

The Social Capital Benchmark Survey asks respondents several questions that measure political efficacy. First, respondents are asked, "Overall, how much impact do you think PEOPLE LIKE YOU can have in making your community a better place to live—no impact at all, a small impact, a moderate impact, or a big impact?" Later on, respondents are asked a battery of questions concerning the reasons they do not participate in their communities, including an efficacy question: "Many obstacles keep people from becoming as involved with their community as they would like. Thinking about your own life, are there any obstacles or barriers that make it difficult for you to be as involved with your community as you would like, or not? I'd like you to tell me whether each of the following is a very important obstacle, somewhat important, or not at all important. (Feeling that you can't make a difference)." Based on ordered probit analyses of these dependent variables similar to those above, neighborhood prison density has no effect on internal political efficacy. People living in high-imprisonment communities are neither more likely to say that they can make only a small impact on their communities nor more likely to report that they participate less because they cannot make a difference. These results are reported in table 5.2.

Social Disorganization

As discussed in chapter 2, "social disorganization" refers to the inability of people living in a neighborhood to encourage positive behavior and discourage negative behavior. Communities regulate behavior by rewarding positive behavior and punishing deviant behavior. These punishments are meted out through formal and informal social networks and may include many types of incentives, including money, acclaim, shame, guilt, or even beatings. Communities also socialize members into positive behavior by providing role models. Examples of formal social networks include families as the most basic unit, but also organizations and membership associations.[19] In contrast, examples of informal social networks include friendship, kinship, and other peer networks.[20] Disorganized communities cannot exert control over their

Table 5.2: Ordered probit estimates of the effects of imprisonment on efficacy in Charlotte

	Make a Difference in Community	Efficacy a Barrier
Block group variables:		
Prisoners per square mile	0.004	0.010
	(0.004)	(0.006)
Homicide rate	−60.914***	−130.678***
	(0.023)	(0.034)
Percentage receiving public assistance	1.882	−2.774
	(1.891)	(2.774)
Median income (in 1,000s)	0.000	0.000
	(0.002)	(0.003)
Percentage noncitizen	1.533	−2.897
	(2.380)	(3.497)
Percentage foreign born	−3.334	1.945
	(2.049)	(3.068)
Presence of ex-felon-serving institutions	−0.374.	−0.590.
	(0.224)	(0.309)
Percentage in group quarters	1.595.	0.469
	(0.915)	(1.262)
Percentage vacant	−0.937	0.235
	(0.890)	(1.424)
Unemployment rate	−2.222	−4.327.
	(1.366)	(2.261)
Median age	0.002	−0.006
	(0.009)	(0.013)
Percentage high school graduates	−0.158	−0.354
	(0.456)	(0.710)
Poverty rate	−0.320	1.108
	(0.741)	(1.087)
Percentage black	−0.137	−0.134
	(0.295)	(0.414)
Percentage Hispanic	1.791	0.212
	(1.179)	(1.805)
Individual-level variables:		
Hispanic	−0.340	−0.144
	(0.209)	(0.313)
Black	0.151	−0.093
	(0.108)	(0.155)

(*continued*)

Table 5.2: *continued*

	Make a Difference in Community	Efficacy a Barrier
Citizen	−0.448.	0.172
	(0.230)	(0.340)
Female	0.176*	0.136
	(0.070)	(0.105)
Ideology	−0.009	−0.064
	(0.031)	(0.045)
Educational attainment	0.010	0.061.
	(0.024)	(0.035)
Income	0.051*	−0.011
	(0.024)	(0.036)
Economic satisfaction	0.028	0.043
	(0.079)	(0.117)
Home Internet access	0.196***	−0.340***
	(0.058)	(0.087)
Age	−0.005.	−0.009*
	(0.003)	(0.004)
Reads paper	0.013	0.009
	(0.013)	(0.020)
Political interest	0.232***	0.009
	(0.041)	(0.059)
Political knowledge	−0.001	0.010
	(0.027)	(0.037)
Intercepts:		
0|1	−1.502*	−0.824
	(0.586)	(0.877)
1|2	−0.404	−0.193
	(0.584)	(0.877)
2|3	0.817	0.450
	(.584)	(.8763)
N	1,089	547

Source: These data rely on the Charlotte sample of the 2000 Social Capital Benchmark Survey.

Note: Standard errors are in parentheses.

. $P < .10$

* $P < .05$

** $P < .01$

*** $P < .001$

members, because they lack either or both formal and informal ties such as friendships and stable families that help socialize people into desirable behavior.[21]

Imprisonment affects both formal and informal social networks, thus contributing to neighborhood social disorganization. Incarcerated people are removed from their families and friendship networks, thereby destroying links among neighborhood residents through which social and civic norms are enforced. Imprisonment is a leading cause of family disruption among low-income and minority households.[22] Imprisonment also imposes a stigma on offenders and their families; the shame of convictions might lead families to withdraw from community life and positive influences.[23] Convicted individuals and their families also may be ostracized involuntarily by other neighborhood residents, which removes them from the formal and informal networks that provide political information and encourage voting.

In order for imprisonment to diminish political participation through social disorganization, it should be the case that high-imprisonment neighborhoods exhibit symptoms of social disorganization to a higher degree than low-imprisonment neighborhoods. That is, mechanisms of formal social control (families, associations, and other organizations) and mechanisms of informal social control (friendships and other ties) should be weaker in high-imprisonment neighborhoods than in low-imprisonment neighborhoods.

Several studies have highlighted the link between neighborhood imprisonment and neighborhood social networks. Imprisonment discourages stable families by undermining marriage prospects for single women and breaking up existing family units.[24] Limited evidence also suggests that incarceration leads to diminished informal social networks.[25] For instance, in a study of thirty Baltimore communities, Lynch and Sabol find that incarceration decreases community organization and solidarity.[26]

The Social Capital Benchmark Survey asks several questions related to the formal and informal networks that exist in respondents' communities. First, as a measure of informal social networks, the survey asks respondents how many friends they have. Three additional questions relate to informal social networks more closely. The first question, on generalized interpersonal trust, asks, "Now, I want to ask you some questions about how you view other people. Generally speaking, would you say that most people can be trusted or that you can't be too careful in dealing with people?" Respondents were allowed to give three responses: 0, "You can't be too careful," 1, "It depends," and 2, "People can be trusted." This question mimics the standard question on generalized trust first introduced by Rosenberg,[27] which reads, "Generally speaking, would you say that most people can be trusted or that you can't be too careful dealing with people?" At the individual level, reports of generalized trust are strongly associated with various demographic characteristics. Education, income, and age are all positively related to generalized trust.[28] Outside of socioeconomic status, racial background is perhaps the most noteworthy individual-level demographic influence, with white respondents typically indicating higher degrees of generalized trust than minority respondents.[29] These results should probably be handled with some care, since it is plausible that white respondents are interpreting "most people" as fellow white people, thereby making the measure of generalized trust more a measure of group trust.[30]

The survey also offers a measure of particularized trust—trust of one's neighbors. The question on trust in neighbors is part of the same battery as trusting the police, described in the previous section. This question reads, "Next, we'd like to know how much you trust different groups of people. First, think about (GROUP). Generally speaking, would you say that you can trust them a lot, some, only a little, or not at all?" The relevant group in question is "People in your neighborhood" and the responses range from 0, "not at all," to 3, "a lot." This question gives a sense of respondents' orientations not just toward people in general, but also toward people in their neighborhoods.

Finally, the survey includes a measure of the sense of community respondents feel in their neighborhood. This question is part of a battery that prompts respondents about things that contribute to their sense of community or belonging: "This study is about community, so we'd like to start by asking what gives you a sense of community or a feeling of belonging. I'm going to read a list: For each one, say YES if it gives you a sense of community or feeling of belonging, and NO if it does not." The specific prompt for this question is "The people in your neighborhood." Valid responses include 1, "No," 2, "It depends," and 3, "Yes."

The primary measure of formal social networks is that of family disruption. The Social Capital Benchmark Survey contains questions about marital status. Based on these questions, an indicator for marital breakup was constructed, where divorced or separated respondents were coded as 1. All other respondents were coded as 0. Other measures of formal social networks, including organizational memberships, are discussed in the next section.

As in the previous section, multivariate regression techniques were used to analyze the relationships between these dependent variables and neighborhood prisoner density in order to control for factors that might confound the analysis.[31] With the exception of individual respondents' friendships, the dependent variables are all ordinal responses and are analyzed using ordered probit. The friendships variable is analyzed using ordinary-least-squares.

The results partially support the social disorganization hypothesis. Residents of high-imprisonment neighborhoods report having weaker informal social networks than people in low-imprisonment neighborhoods. First, as shown in table 5.3, residents of high-imprisonment neighborhoods are much less likely to agree that "most people can be trusted" than are residents of low-imprisonment neighborhoods. There is also evidence that neighborhood-specific informal social ties are weaker in high-imprisonment areas. Consistent with the findings of Lynch and Sabol, people living in high-imprisonment neighborhoods are less likely to trust their neighbors than people living in low-imprisonment neighborhoods; however, this relationship is not statistically significant at the traditional level of below 5 percent ($p = 0.055$).[32] Similarly, people living in high-imprisonment neighborhoods are less likely to report that their neighbors give them a sense of community; this relationship is not significant at traditional levels either ($p = 0.078$). The relationship between neighborhood imprisonment and the number of friendships reported by respondents is not statistically significant.

The evidence also suggests that formal social networks are influenced by imprisonment, at least in this limited test of family disruption. As shown in table 5.4, people in high-imprisonment neighborhoods are more likely to be separated or divorced (rather than married, widowed, or single) than people in low-imprisonment neighborhoods. This relationship is statistically significant at the $p < 0.05$ level. Other measures of formal social networks such as organizational membership are discussed below.

Mobilization

As is the case with informal social networks, the strength of ties to formal political and social organizations both within and outside the neighborhood also strengthens individual political participation. As

Table 5.3: Ordered probit estimates of the effects of imprisonment on generalized trust, neighborhood trust, and neighborhood sense of community in Charlotte

	Trust People	Neighbors' Sense of Community	Trust Neighbors
Block group variables:			
Prisoners per square mile	−0.010.	−0.013.	−0.008.
	(0.006)	(0.007)	(0.004)
Homicide rate	6.794***	222.284***	93.082***
	(0.027)	(0.019)	(0.025)
Percentage receiving public assistance	−3.533	−6.401.	−2.790
	(2.333)	(3.586)	(1.920)
Median income (in 1,000s)	−0.001	0.005	0.008**
	(0.002)	(0.004)	(0.003)
Percentage noncitizen	−5.672.	6.563	2.083
	(2.904)	(4.314)	(2.475)
Percentage foreign born	3.753	−7.199.	−3.244
	(2.468)	(3.885)	(2.133)
Presence of ex-felon-serving institutions	0.386	0.314	0.317
	(0.272)	(0.442)	(0.257)
Percentage in group quarters	0.861	−1.100	0.243
	(1.100)	(2.086)	(1.106)
Percentage vacant	−1.451	1.570	0.952
	(1.044)	(1.771)	(1.001)
Unemployment rate	−1.859	−1.133	1.342
	(1.693)	(2.533)	(1.573)
Median age	−0.011	−0.027.	−0.006
	(0.010)	(0.016)	(0.009)
Percentage high school graduates	−0.199	−1.032	0.102
	(0.538)	(0.882)	(0.492)
Poverty rate	0.195	−0.030	1.132
	(0.894)	(1.391)	(0.784)
Percentage black	0.470	0.438	−0.208
	(0.362)	(0.552)	(0.302)
Percentage Hispanic	0.691	0.117	1.428
	(1.422)	(2.390)	(1.241)
Individual-level variables:			
Hispanic	−0.998***	−0.418	−0.546*
	(0.298)	(0.435)	(0.216)
Black	−0.739***	0.151	−0.680***
	(0.131)	(0.199)	(0.108)

(*continued*)

Table 5.3: *continued*

	Trust People	Neighbors' Sense of Community	Trust Neighbors
Citizen	−0.737*	−0.098	−0.007
	(0.293)	(0.394)	(0.229)
Female	0.061	−0.029	−0.026
	(0.082)	(0.136)	(0.075)
Ideology	0.037	−0.054	−0.033
	(0.036)	(0.058)	(0.033)
Educational attainment	0.127***	−0.054	0.049.
	(0.028)	(0.047)	(0.026)
Income	0.040	0.037	0.063*
	(0.028)	(0.043)	(0.025)
Economic satisfaction	0.226*	0.066	0.131
	(0.091)	(0.150)	(0.083)
Home Internet access	0.164*	0.200.	0.107.
	(0.067)	(0.108)	(0.061)
Age	0.011***	0.006	0.014***
	(0.003)	(0.005)	(0.003)
Reads paper	0.010	0.021	0.019
	(0.015)	(0.025)	(0.014)
Political interest	0.065	0.218**	0.099*
	(0.048)	(0.075)	(0.043)
Political knowledge	0.053.	0.010	0.060*
	(0.031)	(0.055)	(0.029)
Intercepts:			
0|1	0.271		−0.189
	(0.698)		(0.622)
1|2	0.419	−1.940.	0.532
	(0.698)	(1.103)	(0.621)
2|3		−1.787	1.723
		(1.102)	(0.622)
N	1,087	536	1,065

Source: These data rely on the Charlotte sample of the 2000 Social Capital Benchmark Survey.

Note: Standard errors are in parentheses.

. $P < .10$

* $P < .05$

** $P < .01$

*** $P < .001$

Table 5.4: Logit estimates of the effects of imprisonment on formal social networks

	Church Membership	Separated or Divorced
Block group variables:		
Prisoners per square mile	−0.010.	0.021*
	(0.005)	(0.010)
Homicide rate	27.504	−396.800
	(139.066)	(301.700)
Percentage receiving public assistance	0.064	3.202
	(2.298)	(4.700)
Median income (in 1,000s)	−0.007**	0.007
	(0.002)	(0.005)
Percentage noncitizen	3.143	−0.861
	(3.069)	(6.400)
Percentage foreign born	−4.886.	0.465
	(2.552)	(5.251)
Presence of ex-felon-serving institutions	0.149	0.554
	(0.285)	(0.518)
Percentage in group quarters	0.611	1.541
	(1.102)	(2.130)
Percentage vacant	−1.194	−0.189
	(1.112)	(2.401)
Unemployment rate	−2.648	−2.411
	(1.690)	(3.312)
Median age	0.030**	0.007
	(0.011)	(0.022)
Percentage high school graduates	0.447	0.149
	(0.561)	(1.166)
Poverty rate	0.859	−3.595.
	(0.946)	(1.991)
Percentage black	0.245	1.109
	(0.372)	(0.725)
Percentage Hispanic	1.937	0.565
	(1.463)	(3.168)
Individual-level variables:		
Hispanic	−0.307	0.297
	(0.256)	(0.554)
Black	0.474***	−0.308
	(0.134)	(0.278)
Citizen	0.198	1.609.
	(0.268)	(0.829)

(continued)

Table 5.4: *continued*

	Church Membership	Separated or Divorced
Female	0.376***	−0.067
	(0.086)	(0.181)
Ideology	−0.177***	0.066
	(0.038)	(0.078)
Educational attainment	0.064*	0.062
	(0.030)	(0.063)
Income	0.014	−0.170**
	(0.029)	(0.060)
Economic satisfaction	−0.083	0.036
	(0.097)	(0.201)
Home Internet access	0.204**	−0.755***
	(0.072)	(0.152)
Age	0.017***	0.022***
	(0.003)	(0.006)
Reads paper	0.019	−0.093**
	(0.016)	(0.034)
Political interest	0.106*	0.003
	(0.050)	(0.104)
Political knowledge	0.042	−0.008
	(0.033)	(0.070)
Intercepts:	−2.531***	−3.623*
	(0.727)	(1.615)
N	1,085	1,087

Source: These data rely on the Charlotte sample of the 2000 Social Capital Benchmark Survey.
Note: Standard errors in parentheses.
. $P < .10$
* $P < .05$
** $P < .01$
*** $P < .001$

was just discussed, these organizations dictate and enforce norms of participation in highly organized neighborhoods. Additionally, however, these organizations also encourage participation by helping citizens overcome collective action problems, information deficiencies, and structural barriers. Organizations mobilize citizens when they undertake activities designed to help citizens in this way.

Many studies confirm the importance of formal social organizations in shaping political participation. These organizations may be explicitly political groups, such as parties and campaign organizations, but also local social or recreational groups. Rosenstone and Hansen attribute the decline of political participation to decreased voter mobilization efforts by political parties.[33] Similarly, Verba, Schlozman, and Brady find that mobilization matters, attributing political activity in part to "isolation from the recruitment networks" that invite people to participate.[34] Organizational membership also helps train citizens for political activity, imparting to them the civic skills necessary to participate.[35] Church membership also encourages political participation by increasing civic skills.[36]

High imprisonment can diminish the strength of formal political and social networks in a neighborhood. As noted previously in chapter 2, imprisonment contributes to the decline of one formal social network, the family, by disrupting marital relationships. Another way imprisonment might disrupt formal social networks is that imprisonment contributes to family, and thus neighborhood, poverty. Poorer neighborhoods do not have the internal financial resources to support churches, businesses, membership associations, and other formal institutions to the degree that neighborhoods with better-off residents do. Likewise, residents left to cover bills and legal fees without the help of incarcerated partners or household members may not have the financial wherewithal to pay membership fees or tithes. Formal social ties might fall victim to the lack of informal social networks in high-imprisonment communities—a lack of a sense of community or trust in other neighborhood residents might make joining formal groups less likely, although Brehm and Rahn argue that the tight relationship between trust and community involvement seems to run from group membership to trust.[37]

If neighborhood imprisonment were diminishing political participation by destroying formal social networks, then there should be some evidence that residents of high-imprisonment neighborhoods are less connected to formal social and political networks than are residents of low-imprisonment neighborhoods. The previous section makes clear that this is the case with respect to family disruption. However, residents of high-imprisonment neighborhoods also should join fewer social and political organizations as well. The logic is similar to that in the previous section on social disorganization: evidence of diminished formal social networks is necessary, but not sufficient, to establish organizational mobilization as a potential mechanism by which imprisonment might shape political participation.

Chapter 4 provides evidence of diminished participation in formal political and social networks. For instance, attachment to political parties is one measure of formal political organization. The evidence presented in chapter 4 shows that residents of high-imprisonment communities are less likely to register and vote than residents of low-imprisonment neighborhoods. Thus, they are less likely to be identified by parties and candidates as politically active supporters. Parties often use registration lists and past turnout patterns to decide whom to contact and are more likely to recruit past voters and volunteers, particularly their primary electorate, to participate.[38] This lack of attachment to partisan organizations may mean a lack of recruitment to political activity later on.

Chapter 4 also demonstrates that participation in nonpolitical social networks also depends on neighborhood imprisonment context. Recall from that chapter that residents of high-imprisonment communities, on average, are members of fewer groups than residents of low-imprisonment communities, all other factors being equal. They also volunteer less frequently than residents of low-imprisonment communities.

A final measure of attachment to formal social networks is provided by the 2000 Social Capital Benchmark Survey, which contains a question about church membership. The question asks respondents, "Are you a member of a local church, synagogue, or other religious or spiritual community?" The responses are coded 1 for "yes" and 0 for "no." Analyzing the relationship between this dichotomous dependent variable and prisoner density using multivariate logit models that control for individual- and neighborhood-level characteristics[39] reveals that people living in high-imprisonment neighborhoods are less likely to be church members than people living in low-imprisonment neighborhoods. However, this relationship is not statistically significant at the $p < 0.05$ level ($p = 0.06$). These results are reported in table 5.4.

Resource Deprivation

As a reminder, "resource deprivation" refers to the notion that sending people to prison often means removing residents who contribute to the economic life of the community.[40] Those residents may hold jobs in the regular economy, or they may contribute to the upkeep of their partners and children through illegal means.[41] For the most part, the families of incarcerated people shoulder much of the economic burden of imprisonment. Having a large number of families with imprisoned members in a community should increase neighborhood poverty, and thus diminish political participation.

The economic impact of imprisonment on neighborhood economic well-being is well established and will not be tested directly here. It is clear from figures 3.3–3.8 that poverty is positively related to neighborhood imprisonment, such that high-poverty neighborhoods send more people to prison than low-poverty neighborhoods. Moreover, ample evidence demonstrates the economic burden that imprisonment places on the families of the incarcerated. These financial disadvantages add to the economic difficulties that are experienced by families who are already poor. In a study of children with incarcerated parents in the Panel Study of Income Dynamics, Johnson finds that family income declines and family poverty increases after a parent is sent to prison.[42] Qualitative research confirms these quantitative results. As already noted in chapter 2, Braman finds that families of prisoners often face financial burdens associated with legal fees, visitation, phone calls, and other hardships due to the incarceration of their loved ones.[43] Toylean Johnson, the 44-year-old single mother mentioned at the beginning of chapter 3, estimates that she has spent more than $50,000 on legal fees and prison costs related to the incarceration of her brother, eldest biological son, and foster son.[44] Such hefty expenditures leave families strapped for cash and leave little money for civic and political engagement.

Money is not the only resource that matters for political participation. As Verba, Schlozman, and Brady note, time and civic skills are important as well.[45] As noted in chapter 2, imprisonment may decrease the availability of these resources to community members, largely by causing them to spend time they might have spent volunteering, paying attention to elections, or voting making up for the absence of their imprisoned friends and neighbors.

The Social Capital Benchmark Survey permits the search for these secondary resource effects. It contains several variables related to the operation of time and civic skills on participation in neighborhood activities. These questions are found in the battery of questions about obstacles to participation. The barriers in question are "An inflexible or demanding work schedule or inadequate childcare" and "Lack of information or not knowing how to begin." These questions help gauge the availability of time and civic skills to respondents. The possible responses are coded from 0 to 3, with 0 representing "no obstacles cited" and 3 representing "a very important obstacle." The relationship between each dependent variable and neighborhood prisoner density was analyzed using multivariate ordered probit regressions.[46] The results, shown in table 5.5, indicate that neighborhood prisoner density is unrelated to responses to either question, suggesting that the resource effects of imprisonment on neighborhood political participation are primarily monetary.

Discussion and Conclusion

This chapter examines more closely the pathways through which imprisonment affects neighborhood political behavior. The strategy employed here is to look for evidence that cultural deviance, social disorganization, demobilization, and resource deprivation vary across neighborhoods based on imprisonment levels. As noted, the social disorganization, demobilization, and resource deprivation arguments were supported, while the cultural deviance mechanism was not. It is important to note that in this type of analysis, differences in cultural deviance, social disorganization, and the like across neighborhoods are necessary to establish the phenomenon as a potential mechanism. However, the variation of phenomena across neighborhoods based on imprisonment is not sufficient to prove that any one phenomenon is the mechanism, or to measure the relative contribution of one mechanism over another.

At first glance, the pattern of results identified here, particularly with respect to efficacy and trust in government, seem to contradict a well-established finding in the policy feedback literature that negative experiences with the government affect trust and efficacy.[47] However, one should note, as in chapter 2, that the original theoretical contribution of this section involves the potential for the *extension* of the policy effects on individual targets to the entire community through cultural transmission or observation.

Unlike Tyler, Mettler, Soss, and others in the policy feedback tradition, this chapter does not test the effects of policies on individual offenders and thus does not contradict their work. This chapter explores whether living near offenders affects people who are not themselves involved with the criminal justice system. The answer, according to the analysis, is no, at least with respect to attitudes toward police and government. Only one other study tests this relationship directly, and

Table 5.5: Ordered probit estimates of the effects of imprisonment on safety, time, and civic skills in Charlotte

	Information a Barrier	Job/Childcare a Barrier	Safety a Barrier
Block group variables:			
Prisoners per square mile	0.006	0.008	0.007
	(0.006)	(0.006)	(0.006)
Homicide rate	16.090***	38.386***	−153.496***
	(0.036)	(0.037)	(0.033)
Percentage receiving	−0.774	−2.815	−1.920
public assistance	(2.790)	(2.937)	(2.787)
Median income (in 1,000s)	0.001	0.000	0.000
	(0.003)	(0.003)	(0.003)
Percentage noncitizen	−5.871.	−5.105	−3.712
	(3.528)	(3.689)	(3.533)
Percentage foreign born	3.336	2.388	2.175
	(3.097)	(3.251)	(3.111)
Presence of ex-felon-serving	−0.398	−0.400	−0.384
institutions	(0.308)	(0.316)	(0.307)
Percentage in group quarters	0.846	−0.075	0.333
	(1.280)	(1.306)	(1.281)
Percentage vacant	−0.663	−1.474	−1.261
	(1.433)	(1.476)	(1.431)
Unemployment rate	−5.335*	−3.899.	−4.562
	(2.310)	(2.339)	(2.354)
Median age	−0.009	0.001	0.004
	(0.013)	(0.014)	(0.013)
Percentage high school	−0.615	−0.684	−0.915
graduates	(0.717)	(0.751)	(0.717)
Poverty rate	0.958	0.958	1.010
	(1.094)	(1.134)	(1.101)
Percentage black	−0.198	−0.018	−0.193
	(0.417)	(0.436)	(0.417)
Percentage Hispanic	0.449	1.657	0.125
	(1.819)	(1.925)	(1.819)
Individual-level variables:			
Hispanic	−0.233	−0.363	−0.066
	(0.327)	(0.333)	(0.315)
Black	−0.169	−0.328*	−0.013
	(0.156)	(0.165)	(0.156)
Citizen	0.057	0.199	0.131
	(0.345)	(0.357)	(0.340)

(continued)

Table 5.5: *continued*

	Information a Barrier	Job/Childcare a Barrier	Safety a Barrier
Female	0.148	0.273*	0.153
	(0.105)	(0.110)	(0.106)
Ideology	−0.064	−0.037	−0.058
	(0.046)	(0.047)	(0.045)
Educational attainment	0.057	0.084*	0.041
	(0.035)	(0.037)	(0.036)
Income	0.006	0.049	0.042
	(0.036)	(0.038)	(0.036)
Economic satisfaction	0.018	0.045	0.058
	(0.118)	(0.123)	(0.119)
Home Internet access	−0.411***	−0.418***	−0.383***
	(0.088)	(0.092)	(0.088)
Age	−0.010*	−0.015***	−0.009*
	(0.004)	(0.004)	(0.004)
Reads paper	0.009	0.005	−0.001
	(0.020)	(0.021)	(0.020)
Political interest	0.041	0.050	0.031
	(0.060)	(0.062)	(0.060)
Political knowledge	−0.011	−0.027	0.006
	(0.038)	(0.039)	(0.038)
Intercepts:			
0|1	−1.344	−0.678	−0.986
	(0.881)	(0.923)	(0.878)
1|2	−0.942	−0.473	−0.482
	(0.881)	(0.923)	(0.878)
2|3	−0.322	−0.143	−0.071
	(0.880)	(0.922)	(0.877)
N	548	548	548

Source: These data rely on the Charlotte sample of the 2000 Social Capital Benchmark Survey.

Note: Standard errors are in parentheses.

. $P < .10$

* $P < .05$

** $P < .01$

*** $P < .001$

it also finds that exposure to criminal offenders does not predict attitudes toward formal political institutions such as police, courts, or the criminal justice system.[48] Instead, previous research shows that other factors such as fear of crime,[49] positive personal experiences with police and courts,[50] and unfair treatment by police[51] have stronger effects on attitudes toward the openness of government.[52]

Thus, the findings in this chapter with respect to the lack of support for the cultural model are in line with this sparse literature: attitudes toward the openness of government held by nonoffenders are not predicted by exposure to offenders at the neighborhood level. Race, gender, and social class at the individual level explain responses on these attitudinal items, as do some aspects of neighborhood context—welfare recipiency in line with Soss's expectations, and homicide rates in line with Sampson and Bartusch's.[53] However, in line with Rose and Clear, neighborhood incarceration rates do not explain responses on items related to the openness of government.[54] With respect to the argument that the large number of control variables might potentially mask the effect, one should note that the same model produces nearly statistically significant effects for items that reflect social disorganization (trust in neighbors, trust in people, institutional presence, and family structure).[55] Collinearity on the nonsignificant items is not a problem. Moreover, it is also the case that the government trust and openness items just are not strongly correlated with neighborhood criminal justice context (for all items, the absolute value of Pearson's R is less than 0.05).

Some might wonder whether the causal direction runs from imprisonment to social disorganization, or the opposite. More important, it could be the case that the apparent relationship between neighborhood imprisonment and political participation in fact reflects the operation of social disorganization. Social disorganization could be causing both high imprisonment and low participation simultaneously, making the causal link between imprisonment and participation shown in chapter 4 spurious. However, further testing of the 2008 turnout model estimated in chapter 4 reveals that the relationship between imprisonment and political participation is not spurious. Including a measure of formal social networks (a count of the number of tax-exempt religious, community improvement, youth development, recreational, sports, leisure, and athletic organizations in each block group) does reduce the magnitude of the estimated relationship between imprisonment and voter turnout, as indicated in table 5.6.[56]

Table 5.6: Beta regression estimates of the effects of imprisonment on voter turnout in Georgia and North Carolina

	Georgia	North Carolina
Intercept	−1.968***	−0.606**
	(0.193)	(0.188)
Prisoner density squared	2.36 ×10⁻⁰⁶.	−3.25 ×10⁻⁰⁵***
	(0.000)	(0.000)
Prisoner density	−0.001*	0.007***
	(0.000)	(0.001)
Vacancy rate	−0.650***	−0.135
	(0.137)	(0.092)
Relative proportion noncitizen	−0.088***	−0.018
	(0.014)	(0.016)
Relative proportion unemployed	−0.035***	−0.034**
	(0.010)	(0.011)
Median income (in 1,000s)	0.007***	0.004***
	(0.000)	(0.001)
Ratio of women to men	0.534.	0.787*
	(0.285)	(0.320)
High school completion rate (female)	1.044***	0.871***
	(0.082)	(0.089)
Proportion of adults under 25	−3.089***	−1.554***
	(0.192)	(0.187)
Homicide rate	55.470***	3.775
	(15.910)	(17.600)
Proportion other minority	−91.710	−47.330
	(103.900)	(122.000)
Proportion black	0.432***	0.218***
	(0.044)	(0.057)
Presence of ex-felon-serving institutions	0.007	0.055.
	(0.026)	(0.028)
Proportion Hispanic	−0.812***	−1.512***
	(0.149)	(0.151)
Proportion in group quarters	−1.457***	−1.485***
	(0.223)	(0.219)
Poverty rate	0.357**	0.276
	(0.116)	(0.135)
Tax-exempt organizations	0.003	0.022***
	(0.004)	(0.006)

(continued)

Table 5.6: *continued*

	Georgia	North Carolina
phi	20.804***	19.255***
	(0.427)	(0.379)
N	4,536	4,948
Pseudo-R^2	0.539	0.650

Source: These data rely on the 2008 Neighborhood Criminal Justice Involvement Data.
Note: Standard errors are in parentheses. County fixed effects are included in the models but are not shown here.

. $P < .10$
* $P < .05$
** $P < .01$
*** $P < .001$

However, a negative, statistically significant relationship between these two phenomena still exists. Prisoner density still has an independent effect on participation even after accounting for this potentially confounding variable. Of course, this analysis cannot fully account for the informal networks that might affect both participation and imprisonment at the block group level. However, testing the relationship for formal social networks should provide some reassurance that the causal link between imprisonment and participation exists.

The same case might be made with respect to resources. As chapter 3 clearly shows, the financial resources available to communities is correlated with imprisonment. However, money also has been shown to affect political participation. The models in chapters 4 and 5 all control for neighborhood and, where applicable, individual socioeconomic status. Even with these controls, the relationship between imprisonment and political participation exists.

The causal arrow probably runs in both directions—there probably is a reciprocal relationship between imprisonment and the economic situation and social disorganization of neighborhoods. However, the fact that imprisonment, poverty, and social disorganization are mutually reinforcing does not affect the main argument in this book, which is that imprisonment demobilizes neighborhoods by contributing to the extent to which neighborhoods experience these social ills. The analyses in this chapter, coupled with those presented in previous chapters, points to the weakening of the formal and informal networks of the community—social disorganization and lack of mobilization—as likely culprits. Imprisonment-related economic decline may be a contributing factor as well.

These results point to a potential remedy: find ways to strengthen the economy and internal social networks in high-imprisonment neighborhoods, or find substitutes that will perform the vital role of incentivizing participation among the residents left behind. The next chapter considers the role that partisan organizations, nonpartisan organizations, and campaigns play in remediating the effects of social disorganization and resource deprivation.

6

Can Mobilization Help?

That's what we really are about, informing the community of the different rights that they have, the different things they should be able to do and get.
— "Morgan," a Grassroots Organizer in Chicago[1]

States, cities, and even the federal government, by exercising their authority to punish and supervise citizens, can have an important effect on local politics. The evidence presented in the previous two chapters documents the power of criminal justice interactions, even vicarious ones, to demobilize and disfranchise entire communities. As chapter 4 shows, independent of their personal characteristics, people who live in high-imprisonment neighborhoods are less likely than people who live in lower-imprisonment neighborhoods to undertake a number of political activities, including voting, marching, and signing petitions. This diminished participation can be seen in the aggregate: communities with a high concentration of prisoners tend to have lower voter turnout than communities that experience less geographically concentrated imprisonment even after controlling for potentially confounding factors such as neighborhood poverty, diversity, and residential mobility. Every new prison admission has a demonstrable causal relationship with voter turnout; sending an individual to prison in the months prior to a general election decreases neighborhood voter turnout by about 1.4 percentage points, on average.

Given the evidence, it is clear that the criminal justice system has a demobilizing effect on disadvantaged communities. As shown in chapter 5, the impact of imprisonment seems to work by weakening the economy and the formal and informal social networks in disadvantaged communities. Thus, it is important to look for potentially mobilizing forces within these communities that can counteract this state-led demobilization by providing the participatory incentives that social disorganization and resource deprivation have taken away. Organizations often invite and encourage people to participate in politics; for this reason, the search for efforts to counterbalance the detrimental effects of the criminal justice system should start there.

This chapter presents fieldwork that was undertaken in 2008 in order to get a sense of the extent to which partisan and nonpartisan organizations attempted to mobilize disadvantaged places. The fieldwork attempted to document and describe the efforts of local campaign offices, county party headquarters, and nonpartisan grassroots organizations to contact, register, and turn out residents of disadvantaged communities in three cities: Atlanta, Charlotte, and Chicago. These three cities are of particular interest given the variation in electoral competitiveness of their states in that election season. The project was designed to get a sense of the standard operating procedures of organizations that engage in voter mobilization efforts in order to see whether, as a matter of practice, they reached out to voters in ways that would engage the communities that were hardest hit by imprisonment. In order to shed light on these procedures, this aspect of the research employs multiple methods, including interviews with directors and staff and participant observation.

The fieldwork gives the impression, as in chapter 5, that disadvantaged communities are detached from the formal and informal political networks that foster political participation. What's more, most formal political organizations such as campaign organizations and parties seem unwilling to reach out to disadvantaged places in the most effective ways. Instead, this work is left to social institutions such as nonpartisan groups and service providers, which many communities lack. For disadvantaged community residents, nonpartisan groups constitute the most significant and visible mobilization force in their communities. Parties and, for the most part, politicians are not inviting residents of disadvantaged communities to get involved in politics; however, as discussed later in this chapter, the Obama campaign and some Chicago aldermen provide interesting exceptions to this generalization.[2] In this way, nonpartisan organizations and other groups that do reach out to disadvantaged neighborhoods provide an important countervailing message to the discouraging one sent out by the state.

The fieldwork brought to light several patterns with respect to whom organizations contacted, why they contacted them, and how they contacted them. For the most part, local county parties, the primary and enduring representative of government in these areas, did not undertake significant efforts to mobilize disadvantaged communities. In all three cities, the Republican county parties reached out to voters according to standard operating procedures that were unlikely to mobilize people in disadvantaged communities. The same is true of the Democratic county parties in Charlotte and Atlanta. For instance, county parties on both sides focused on mobilizing already-registered voters, undertaking get-out-the-vote (GOTV) activities targeting registered citizens closer to election day. Most parties did not begin their mobilization activities until after the registration deadline. With respect to the modes of contact, parties most often relied on traditional methods of contacting individual people at home, like door-to-door canvassing, phone banking, direct mail, and literature distribution rather than reaching out to disadvantaged communities publicly and collectively via registration drives and other events in churches or grocery stores. As the discussion will show, using at-home contacting methods to reach out to registered voters often proves ineffective in mobilizing people in low-income and minority communities— there is a difference in effectiveness between individual-based and neighborhood-based modes of contact based on neighborhood disadvantage.

In contrast, nonpartisan groups, particularly those that were service providers, were more likely to actively target unregistered voters and groups with traditionally low turnout—such as immigrants, ex-felons, and the homeless—than political parties and even candidates. Because of this difference in focus, the purpose of contacting and the outreach strategies employed by nonpartisan groups varied from those of parties and campaigns in ways that were more likely to effectively reach residents of disadvantaged communities. For instance, nonpartisan groups focused more on registration, education, and advocacy for unregistered citizens prior to the registration deadline, leaving parties to mobilize registered voters after the deadline. Nonpartisan groups were more likely to rely on voter registration drives and events at central locations than at-home contacts to reach their targets.

These findings and more are discussed in the following pages. The next section, "The Importance of Mobilization," uses previous literature to develop a clearer understanding of how mobilization works to encourage participation and motivate feelings of belonging. The section after that, "Studying Mobilization in Disadvantaged Communities," describes in greater detail the research design of the fieldwork, the organizations involved, and the data collection. Following that section, the findings of the fieldwork, along with illustrative examples, are presented. The final sections highlights the challenges involved in mobilizing residents of disadvantaged communities and suggests solutions for reincorporating these individuals back into mainstream politics.

The Importance of Mobilization

As noted in chapter 2, the criminal justice system might produce vicarious effects on individual and neighborhood political behavior and attitudes through several mechanisms. First, the criminal justice system deprives communities of bodies and money, leaving fewer people to bear the resource- and time-consuming tasks of childrearing, community organizing, and canvassing. Moreover, having fewer people contributing economically to the tax base and supporting local businesses and civic groups often means fewer opportunities to come together at schools, churches, coffee shops, and other meeting places that sustain civic life. Second, the criminal justice system populates disadvantaged communities with people who have negative experiences with government authorities, producing sources of (understandably) antigovernment attitudes that might discourage participation. Finally, the criminal justice system destroys social capital by destabilizing living situations, removing residents from their communities and their families, and isolating and stigmatizing offenders and their families. Chapter 5 shows that the economic and social effects are more consequential for participation than the attitudinal effects.

In chapter 2, rational choice theory was briefly discussed as a way of thinking about how these phenomena might decrease political participation. To use language consistent with this theory, the criminal justice system changes the calculus of participating in politics for members of disadvantaged communities by reshaping the expected benefits and costs of participating.[3] Having to take up the slack for residents who are absent or unemployable due to criminal convictions decreases the resources—time and money—available for participating in politics, making such activities more costly. With respect to voting in particular, Piven and Cloward note that poll locations and opening hours may not be convenient for people unable to afford childcare, time off from work, or decent transportation; an individual who is now a single parent or working two jobs to fill the gap left by an imprisoned or unemployed partner is likely to feel these added costs of voting.[4] Disorganized communities, by definition, lack the ability to enforce social and political norms of participation; as a result, there is no shame, stigma, or other cost imposed for nonparticipation.[5] The diminished formal and informal ties of disorganized communities also reduce the likelihood that someone will be asked to participate, an important component of activity.[6] Moreover, the criminal justice system often erects barriers to participating. Most obviously, felon disfranchisement is one such barrier, but the residential instability suffered by people living with convicted offenders, as discussed in chapter 2, also imposes the additional burden of reregistering or changing registration.[7] An individual might be kicked off the voter rolls entirely if he or she moves without notifying the board of elections.[8]

Mobilization can work to counteract these effects. Organizations and other institutions can encourage civic engagement primarily by rebalancing the calculus of individual civic participation, making civic engagement and volunteering easier and more beneficial.[9] These groups can encourage participation by taking on the costs of organizing events, learning about the process, and learning about candidates' positions so that the residents of high-imprisonment communities do not have to undertake these costly activities themselves.[10] Organizations also can encourage participation by navigating bureaucracies, solving legal problems, and dispelling rumors for potential voters. Organizations also may provide additional selective benefits to members, such as t-shirts, lunches, discounts, or insurance in order to reward participation.[11] They may impose social pressure to participate or remind people of their duty to participate.[12] Simply the invitation to participate itself has beneficial qualities, making individuals feel like welcome members of the community rather than irrelevant outcasts.[13]

Organizations use many tactics to inspire political participation. Efforts to get out the vote and recruit volunteers mostly involve contacting citizens at home.[14] Door-to-door canvassing is believed to be the most cost-effective way to raise voter turnout in a given election.[15] The evidence on phone calls is mixed; however, upon reanalysis Nickerson argues that high-quality phone calls can increase turnout as well.[16] Direct mail is expensive in comparison to direct mail and phone banking but can be effective, depending on the content. Mail that confronts individuals with their voting records increases turnout.[17] There is very little evidence to show that e-mail or other forms of electronic contacting increase turnout,[18] but Facebook and other social networking sites have been used by activists in several countries to organize rallies.[19] Election day festivals also have been shown to effectively increase voter turnout.[20] Candidate forums and debates are aimed at providing information to registered voters or giving additional selective benefits for turning out, but more work needs to be done to measure the effectiveness of these events.[21]

The overall sense of the literature is that mobilization efforts work, regardless of tactics. According to Rosenstone and Hansen, individual political participation largely reflects the extent to which political organizations mobilize potential supporters.[22] They argue that a key component of mobilization is asking people to vote, often for a particular candidate. As Verba, Schlozman, and Brady put it, when people are not asked, they do not vote.[23] Proponents of this argument point to decreased mobilization as the reason for declining voter turnout over the last quarter of the twentieth century.[24] Avery argues that the major reason for low turnout today is lack of mobilization.[25] Rosenstone and Hansen elaborate: "Had candidates, parties, campaigns, interest groups, and social movements been as active in mobilizing voters in the 1980s as they were in the 1960s, even leaving the social structure and the condition of individual voters unchanged, reported voter participation would have fallen only 2.6%, rather than the 11.3% that it did."[26] In contrast, Goldstein and Ridout contend that levels of mobilization have remained relatively stable from 1966 to 1998, the effectiveness of mobilization has not changed over time, and that changing the targets of mobilization efforts have had no discernible impact on voter turnout.[27] However, regardless of this competing claim, many political scientists, politicians, parties, and other groups still believe that mobilization affects voter registration and turnout.

Do organizations undertake these mobilization activities in disadvantaged communities? Large-scale mobilization efforts are costly, and organizations employ time and resources strategically in order to reach those citizens most likely to participate and participate on behalf of the right side.[28] As shown later in this chapter, nonpartisan groups, service providers, the Obama campaign, and the two Chicago aldermanic offices profiled in this study undertook many of these activities to encourage political participation in low-income and disadvantaged communities. However, county parties and some other candidates did not encourage participation in ways that would reach residents of disadvantaged communities. Why might this scenario be the case?

In theory, political parties and campaigns tend to concentrate their efforts in places where mobilization is more effective and on voters with a record of supporting their side in the past. For instance, parties and campaigns often fail to mobilize communities with low-socioeconomic-status members.[29] Parties are more likely to mobilize whites than ethnic minorities.[30] They tend to contact people who have voted before, especially those who have voted in primaries.[31] Focusing on registered voters enables organizations to focus resources on known supporters rather than wasting efforts mobilizing the competition.[32] Most groups have access to the contact information and participation histories of registered voters, making them easier to contact. However, using voter registration lists to mobilize voters makes it unlikely that people who have never voted will be contacted or mobilized.

Thus, parties and campaigns should focus on the most cost-effective people to reach: their registered supporters.[33] However, nonpartisan groups with a mandate other than winning elections might be willing to go after harder-to-reach unregistered citizens to advance broader goals of civic participation. Often, these nonpartisan groups already provide services to renters, homeless people, immigrants, or other low-participation groups.[34] These groups may not have the money or manpower to contact these potential voters at home, but they have regular contact with them as clients. Often nonpartisan organizations are able to organize voter registration drives or other events to encourage registration among the groups they regularly serve.[35] Such activities reflect the shift of many civil rights and other nonpartisan groups from protest to advocacy.[36]

Thus, one should expect the fieldwork to reveal particular patterns with respect to which citizens groups contact, how the groups contact them, and why. First, as past research has shown, partisan groups are expected first reach out to people they know, especially those who have voted for their side in previous elections, in order to encourage them to participate again. These contacts are expected to occur primarily through at-home contacts like door-to-door canvassing and phone banking, as these methods have been shown to be the most cost-effective ways to increase participation among registered voters. Second, nonpartisan groups should be more likely than partisan groups to reach out to unregistered voters, because in theory these organizations are less invested in electoral outcomes. (Alternatively, one could argue that nonpartisan groups should be more likely to reach out to unregistered voters because such groups are more likely to be lib-eral and unregistered voters are more likely to support the Democratic Party.)[37] Third, if and when they do reach out to unregistered voters, both parties and nonpartisan organizations should be less effective in doing so when they attempt to make contact with these potential voters at home. In fact, nonpartisan groups should be less likely to canvass door-to-door, make phone calls, or do direct mailings not only because these methods are ineffective with unregistered citizens, but also because they are highly resource intensive. Nonpartisan groups should have fewer resources than parties and campaigns to devote to such activities.

Studying Mobilization in Disadvantaged Communities

To explore the role organizations play in mobilizing disadvantaged communities, the research team conducted fieldwork during the 2008 general election cycle beginning in early September and continuing through election day. The interviews and observations were completed by graduate students recruited from local universities in each city. The fieldwork focused on organizations that attempted to contact citizens directly with the intention of getting them to register and vote in the general election. The data are drawn primarily from two sources: in-terviews with directors, staff, and volunteers and observations of the registration and get-out-the-vote activities of these organizations. The field notes and impressions of the researchers, along with their notes on day-to-day operations and conversations with organizational staff and volunteers will be considered in the analysis as well.

The study was conducted in three cities: Charlotte, Chicago, and At-lanta. These three cities are particularly interesting because Charlotte and Atlanta are located in states that were electorally competitive in 2008 (Georgia at various points was considered to be in play throughout the summer and fall by the Obama campaign). Meanwhile, Chicago, while not located in an electorally competitive state, still had the po-tential for high levels of interest and volunteering because it is Obama's home city. This variation in electoral competitiveness allows for the ob-servation of organizations operating in different electoral contexts.

The universe of organizations in each city includes the local field offices of the two major presidential campaigns, the county or city of-fices of the two major parties, and any nonpartisan group or service provider attempting to register or turnout citizens, particularly low-income citizens, in person, by phone, or by mail. In Chicago, a sample of four aldermanic offices—for example, the Forty-ninth Ward Democrats—replaces the overall Chicago or Cook County Democratic Party office. The universe does not include national interest groups without local branches, groups involved in registration and/or GOTV outside the three cities, groups that contact members or voters only for issue advocacy, or groups without offices in the city attempting registration or GOTV. Several sources were used to find organizations in each city that fit these criteria, including the Internet, newspapers, phone books, and word of mouth. Partnerships among local organizations were especially helpful for identifying study respondents.

Eighty potential mobilizing organizations were contacted based on these sources across the three cities. Thirty-two organizations could not be contacted by letter, phone, or e-mail. The ACORN chapters in Charlotte and Chicago initially agreed but then declined to participate amid allegations of voter fraud. An additional thirteen organizations stated that they were not directly contacting voters in those cities; some suggested contacting state-level offices that did host events. The final sample includes thirty-two organizations that were shadowed, observed, or interviewed: ten from Chicago, nine from Atlanta, and fourteen from Charlotte. These organizations are listed in table 6.1. Director interviews were completed with twenty-two of the thirty-two organizations.

Some might worry that the organizations listed in table 6.1 are biased toward liberal or Democratic interests. While it is true that McCain campaign offices and Republican candidates are not as present on the list as Campaign for Change or the Chicago aldermen, this particular feature of the data is the result of the actual on-the-ground organizational capacity of the two parties in these cities. The Republicans ran a more centralized organization, while the Democrats were much more decentralized. For instance, the Chicago/Cook County Democratic Party did not undertake any voter outreach in the city and directed the research team to the city's aldermen to discuss such activities. All but one of Chicago's fifty aldermen are Democrats. Similarly, Campaign for Change had separate headquarters from the county Democrats in all three cities in the study, meaning that the county party and the Obama campaign received separate entries in table 6.1. In contrast, the county Republican parties also tended to be the campaign headquarters for John McCain in the cities as well as for other down-ballot candidates.

Table 6.1: Participating study organizations, by city

Chicago	Charlotte	Atlanta
Target Area Development Corporation	Homeless Helping Homeless	People's Agenda
Southwest Organizing Project	Democracy North Carolina	National Action Network/ SCLC
49th Ward Democrats	Campaign for Change	Georgia League of Women Voters
21st Ward Democrats	Larry Kissel for Congress	Fulton County Republican Party
42nd Ward Democrats	Mecklenburg County Republican Party/	Fulton County Democratic Party
35th Ward Democrats	McCain Campaign	Young Democrats of Georgia
Illinois Coalition for Immigrant and Refugee Rights	Working Families Win	Election Protection of Georgia
Illinois League of Women Voters	Charlotte League of Women Vot ers	Campaign for Change
Chicago League of Women Voters	Democratic Party of Mecklenburg County	Women's Action for New Direction
Chicago/Cook County Republican Party	Charlotte H.E.L.P.	
	Central Piedmont Community College	
	University of North Carolina at Charlotte	
	Planned Parenthood	
	15th Street Church of God	
	El Pueblo	

Note: The table includes organizations that were observed, shadowed, or interviewed during the study period.

Meanwhile, all the remaining nonpartisan organizations must officially be nonpartisan for tax purposes. Whether these organizations advance a "liberal" agenda, however, is in the eye of the beholder. For the majority of nonpartisan organizations on this list, the primary role is that of service provision. Only the National Action Network/ Southern Christian Leadership Conference, Georgia Women's Action for New Directions, Democracy North Carolina, People's Agenda, and Charlotte H.E.L.P. are explicitly political organizations that do not provide services as a primary function, representing five of the nineteen nonpartisan groups on the list. However, even within these organizations, Democracy North Carolina's primary focus is on documenting state-level lobbying dollars, and Charlotte H.E.L.P. is a nondenominational, congregation-based group that encourages activism in local churches. Every attempt to find complementary conservative organizations working to mobilize people in disadvantaged Charlotte, Chicago, and Atlanta communities turned up nothing, including asking the county Republican parties for help in locating such organizations.

INTERVIEWS

Interviews with the outreach directors of local campaigns, parties, and nonpartisan organizations are used to get a sense of the activities organizations undertake to reach voters, as well as the rationale behind these choices. These semistructured interviews were conducted in all three cities by graduate students attending local institutions. The instrument is composed of both multiple-choice and open-ended questions. The interviews cover past and future mobilization drives or canvassing events in an effort to discern the logic behind the locations of these efforts. The outreach directors were asked for schedules of various events and contacts in order to link changes in registration over time to specific activities by mobilizing organizations. The interviews also provide an opportunity to gather information about the organization, such as its relationship to state and national entities, its attempts to collaborate with other organizations, and the structure and resources available to the organization. Apart from the semistructured interviews, the research assistants also noted and recorded several unstructured, informal conversations with staff and volunteers. Most interviewers took between thirty minutes and an hour to get through the questionnaire and finish the interview.

OBSERVATIONAL DATA

As mentioned, the interviews with voter outreach directors also serve as a source of information on the voter outreach activities planned by each organization. From early September through election day, graduate students in each city attended and observed various outreach activities conducted by each organization. The students shadowed staff and volunteers as they conducted voter registration drives, door-to-door canvassing, phone banking, rallies, and other operations. The primary purpose of the shadowing and observations is to document the coverage, preparedness, strategies, and tactics of each organization. These observations give a sense of the kinds of opportunities to participate in campaigns and organizations offered to citizens.

"Coverage" refers to the types of citizens reached by the organizations' outreach activities. Coverage involves the location of activities, such as the addresses of events and the areas in which door-to-door canvasses take place. However, "coverage" might also refer to specific attempts by an organization to target a subset of citizens, such as registered voters, partisan identifiers, young voters, ex-felons, or Latinos. In line with this focus, students documented the locations of canvassing and other operations and took notes on the characteristics of potential voters encountered by the staff and volunteers at canvassing and other events.

"Preparedness" refers to the professionalism by which the outreach activities are carried out. The sense of an organization's preparedness is guided by the "best practices" outlined by Green and Gerber in their guide *Get Out the Vote*.[38] Thus, "preparedness" refers not only to the organization's past history with GOTV activities, but also to the resources it commits to reaching voters in an efficient, professional way. Thus, the experience, training, and appearance of staff and volunteers who encounter potential voters were of interest, as well as the quality of the materials and information presented to potential voters at each contact. Graduate students photographed staff and volunteers at each event, collected copies of materials distributed to voters, and took notes on the appearance, dress, background, and experience of the staff and volunteers they accompanied.

"Strategies and tactics" refers to efforts by organizations to achieve their goals efficiently. In general, organizations try to use their limited resources to contact and turn out as many eligible citizens as possible. In the case of parties and campaigns, this goal might be to contact and turn out as many *supporters* as possible. Into this category fall decisions about the kinds of activities to pursue, as well as the particular considerations of how activities are carried out. The graduate students obtained schedules of the outreach planned by each organization. Moreover, the graduate students observed the different scripts and event formats used by each organization. The observations also were concerned with measures of success, although these objective measures are not the focus of this paper. How many potential voters are reached successfully? What is the attendance at rallies and other events? How many people open the door to canvassers? The students collected data on each of these questions.

Analysis

The interviews and participant observations confirm that, for the most part, parties and campaigns do not seek to mobilize disadvantaged communities. This conclusion is based on the fact that when parties and campaigns undertook outreach activities, they most often did so in ways that were unlikely to reach citizens in disadvantaged communities. With respect to coverage, parties and campaigns were more likely to contact registered voters, particularly past supporters, than unregistered citizens. Regarding tactics, parties and campaigns were more likely to engage in at-home contacting overall, including direct mail, e-mail, and phone banking, than in events. The Obama campaign and several Chicago aldermen are important exceptions to this broader observation: both groups attempted to register unregistered citizens and sponsored events in conjunction with at-home contacts to reach voters. Finally, as expected, parties and campaigns had money, high-quality volunteers, and experienced staff. However, preparedness varied by city, perhaps because of the electoral context.

In contrast, nonpartisan groups explicitly worked to reach voters in disadvantaged communities. With respect to coverage, they specifically targeted immigrants, ethnic minorities, incarcerated felons, the poor, young people, and the homeless. Their strategies focused less on at-home contacts than on voter registration drives, voter training sessions, and rallies. Nonpartisan groups tended to have less money and fewer volunteers than the parties and campaigns, however, meaning that they were able to reach fewer residents of disadvantaged communities than the parties might have if they had used these tactics.

TARGETING DISADVANTAGED CITIZENS

Political parties and most candidates paid more attention to getting out the vote among known partisans, based on the history of voting in party primaries and other characteristics, than people of unknown partisanship, who tended to be unregistered. When asked how they obtained information for the people they contacted, the executive directors of the parties all discussed using voter registration lists and, in some cases, data purchased from private companies to contact potential voters. Within those groups, the directors focused on active as well as inactive voters. For instance, Allen,[39] the director of one Democratic Party organization, says that his group "made sure that people knew that they were running the risk of not being able to vote because their status was listed as inactive" (on the voter registration rolls). In that same county, Mark, the Republican Party director, stated that he contacted people "based on voting history." None of the directors mentioned targeting citizens based on demographic characteristics; partisanship and voting history trumped other factors. For example, Mark mentions picking neighborhoods for canvassing "based on how friendly neighborhoods would be toward Republicans." Allen targeted one mailing to "12,000 likely Democratic voters." Judith, another Republican Party director, wants "to reach out to new populations and new neighborhoods," but admits that "when it comes to trying to maximize our vote for this particular election cycle we probably will go to neighborhoods where we know there are more Republicans and more potential for new Republicans."

Thus, a formal tie to a political party in the form of registering with the party, voting in the party primary, or donating to the party or its candidates is the most important prerequisite for mobilization. However, as noted in chapter 2, households of prisoners, probationers, and parolees are less likely to have these formal ties primarily because of disfranchisement laws, but also because of high residential mobility or economic distress. Moreover, as shown in chapter 4, residents of high-imprisonment neighborhoods more generally are less likely to have these formal ties of registration or past turnout, making it less likely that they will be mobilized as politically active supporters of either party.

The Campaign for Change offices are exceptional among the partisan organizations in that both directors consciously acknowledge reaching out to unregistered voters as well as known Republicans. Although the Obama headquarters in Chicago generated most of the contact lists, the local offices used voter registration lists and knowledge of the city to target outreach to both voters and nonvoters. Karen, a field organizer in one city, notes that the campaign held voter registration drives from the primaries through the general election registration deadline in order to expand the electorate. As she says, "We couldn't just rely on persuading already-registered voters." Norman, another field organizer, points to the Obama campaign as "an all-inclusive campaign" that reaches out to all voters "regardless of historical party affiliation."

Nonpartisan organizations were more likely to focus not only on citizens without a known partisan affiliation, but also on particular demographic subgroups of nonvoters. This finding probably is a function of the types of nonpartisan groups that appeared in this study, many of which were service providers. Many of the traditional groups one would expect to see in a study of voter outreach, such as the NAACP, were not very involved in direct voter mobilization in these three cities, according to our observations. In fact, the few NAACP and National Action Network events we observed in Atlanta were not very well attended (fig. 6.1). Instead, service providers such as the Target Area Development Corporation in Chicago and Homeless Helping Homeless in Charlotte took the lead in conducting voter outreach as part of their general outreach to their clients and neighborhoods. Consequently, many of these groups aimed to empower particular disadvantaged groups such as Latinos, immigrants, ex-felons, renters, students, homeless people, and working parents.

Analyzing the content of the interviews confirms these impressions regarding the difference in focus between partisan and nonpartisan organizations. As shown in table 6.2, partisan interviewees mentioned particular presidential candidates (Obama, Biden, McCain, Palin, Clinton, or Huckabee) or parties (Republican or Democratic) 252 times. Nonpartisan groups, on the other hand, mentioned these people and parties only 19 times. Weighting these mentions by the representation of partisan and nonpartisan organizations in the sample makes these differences even more clear: partisan organizations mention particular parties or candidates nearly 23 times per organization, while nonpartisan organizations make these mentions 2.8 times per organization, about a tenfold difference. With respect to targeting particular groups of citizens, nonpartisan groups mentioned immigrants or immigration 44 times, while partisan organizations mentioned immigrants or immigration only once. Partisan groups made no mention of prison, offenders, or felons, while nonpartisan organizations referred to these terms 81 times.

REASONS FOR CONTACTING

With respect to reasons for contacting potential voters, parties and campaigns tended to focus their efforts on voter turnout, rather than registration. Meanwhile, nonpartisan groups focused almost exclusively on voter registration and advocacy.

County party offices for both major parties focused on GOTV rather than registration. Allen, the Democratic official mentioned previously,

Figure 6.1: NAACP (*top*) and National Action Network (*bottom*) events in Atlanta.

Table 6.2: Results of content analysis of director Interviews

Search String	Partisan Mentions	Nonpartisan Mentions
Obama	43	9
McCain	10	3
Palin	1	0
Biden	0	0
Clinton	1	0
Huckabee	1	0
Candidates total	56	12
Democrat*	94	5
Republican*	102	2
Parties total	196	7
Immigr*	1	44
Prison, offender, or felon	0	81
Register*	87	183
Turnout or GOTV	38	47
Canvass*	189	113
Door to door	169	139

admits that his organization did not make as much effort to register voters in their city this year as they did in the past because "with the Obama campaign on the ground doing so much voter registration, we didn't want to sort of duplicate after them . . . step on toes." Republicans were more explicit about their reasons for avoiding registration efforts. Mark, the Republican Party director mentioned earlier, says:

> We don't focus a lot on registering, we don't, here in [state redacted] 80 percent of people who are eligible to be registered are registered. So you're battling for that extra 20 percent there. If you say that more of that 20 percent are going to be likely Democrat people who are registered, so if its 15 or 5 percent Republican we spend our time and resources trying to get that 5 percent registered. And hope they go vote. . . . Because if you can register someone, it's a double effort. You got to work to get them registered then you got to turn around and get them to turn out.

Judith echoes Mark's sentiments that registration is unlikely to benefit Republicans:

If you're going to put up a voter registration booth anywhere in the city . . . invariably you're going to have more Democrats register than Republicans. . . . It doesn't really do us much good to spend a lot of time and energy and resources to go out and register more Democrats than Republicans. We're not just there to do a public service; we're there to support Republicans.

The party organizations tended to focus much of their voter contact closer to election day. However again, the Obama campaign offices in Charlotte and Atlanta and the Chicago aldermen are exceptions to this generalization, because these groups performed both registration and turnout activities. One Campaign for Change organizer reported holding "several hundred" registration drives in his city.

In contrast to the county parties, nonpartisan groups tended to contact their targets prior to the registration deadline (about thirty days before election day in these three cities). These groups were more focused on registering their clients or target neighborhoods, although some planned events to "kick off" the first day of early voting. Many groups slowed their mobilization efforts dramatically after the final registration deadline passed (in North Carolina, same-day registration continued about a week into the early vote period). In Chicago, two groups—Southwest Organizing Project and the Illinois Coalition for Immigrant and Refugee Rights, did attempt to follow up on the voters they registered in order to make sure they turned out. However, these efforts often were limited by a lack of funding. Mary, a community organizer in Chicago, describes how the denial of funding to update Celltool, which is a database of voter information gathered from door-to-door canvassers, affected her GOTV operation:

The national umbrella groups . . . we did get did get a little shafted because we weren't a battleground state. Celltool is run by CCC, the Center for Community Change, and they made the decision not to update Illinois's voter file, and so the people that we had registered in the field didn't get updated and so . . . we had to take extra steps and like take on a lot more work if we wanted to integrate them into our GOTV because Celltool didn't have them in it. And they decided that battleground states were more important to have that happen.

Such constraints limited the ability of at least this Chicago nonpartisan to pursue GOTV after the registration deadline.

Again, content analysis of the interviews confirms these overall impressions. Returning to table 6.2, partisan organizations mentioned some variant of the word registration 87 times. In contrast, nonpartisan organizations mentioned registration 183 times. Weighting by the differential presence of each type of organization in the study makes this difference even more stark: registration garners only 8 mentions per organization among partisans, but more than 16 mentions per organization among nonpartisan organizations. Nonpartisan organizations were more likely to mention voter turnout or getting out the vote than partisan organizations, although this gap is not nearly as large as that between the two types on registration: nonpartisan organizations recorded 4.3 mentions of these terms per organization, while partisans recorded 3.5 mentions of these terms per organization.

MODES OF CONTACT

Partisan and nonpartisan groups differed with respect to how they reached out to potential voters in consequential ways. To summarize, parties and campaigns tended to reach out to individual people privately at home, while nonpartisan organizations reached out to disadvantaged communities collectively in public places. Parties and campaigns, for the most part, contacted already-registered voters at home through door-to-door canvassing, phone calls, direct mail, and literature distribution. Party directors and campaign managers varied in how they ranked these modes of contact in terms of effectiveness. Conversely, nonpartisan groups relied more extensively on voter registration drives and other events such as candidate forums, voter training, and marches; because of their focus on disadvantaged citizens, at-home contacts were thought to be a less effective form of face-to-face mobilization. These distinct forms of mobilization were a consistent pattern across the research sites. Table 6.3 presents a summary, by organization type, of the types of mobilization activities undertaken.

With respect to door-to-door canvassing, many of the interviewees regarded this tactic as the most effective way to turn out voters. As Martin says, "Nothing beats door-to-door." However, while nearly all campaign and party organizations report going door to door, only half of the nonpartisan groups in this study did so. Many community organizers and party leaders agree that door-to-door canvassing requires many volunteers and thus may not be realistic in certain circumstances. Also, they note that the effectiveness of door-to-door

Table 6.3: Mobilization tactics of partisan and nonpartisan organizations

Activity	Percentage of Partisan Organizations Reporting Activity	Percentage of Nonpartisan Organizations Reporting Activity
Door-to-door canvassing	81.8	54.5
Direct mail	81.8	45.5
E-mail	72.7	36.4
Phone banks	81.8	63.6
Transportation to polls	81.8	54.5
Newspaper, TV, and/or radio advertising	54.5	9.1
Website	72.7	90.9
Providing registration materials	81.8	100.0
Registration events	45.5	90.9

Note: Number of partisan organizations interviewed, 11; number of nonpartisan organizations interviewed, 11.

canvassing is predicated on reaching a person at the door, a task that is increasingly difficult in certain neighborhoods. Allison, an organizer at Southwest Organizing Project, says, "People not being home is often a difficulty. They don't live there anymore, or they are not there during the hours that we're out there. Um, that's difficult." Martin agrees: "The problem now is in our society there is no set time . . . hard to catch people at home on any regular basis any time." Often, door-to-door canvassing works best in moderate-income suburban neighborhoods. Wealthier areas, "where people can afford to have a lot more land and houses are spaced much further apart" are less efficient to canvass, according to Mark. "Is it effective for me to spend three hours walking all that land area and only hitting fifty houses? Probably not, or if I go somewhere less affluent where the houses are closer together I can hit three hundred houses in three hours," he reasons. Likewise, even wealthy apartment communities are hard to access, as Judith points out: "In the city, a lot of areas where there are a lot of Republicans it's a high-rise . . . so it's hard to get access." Another big problem is suspiciousness of strangers. As one director points out, "People are not eager to talk politics to somebody we don't know."

The effectiveness of direct mail was more controversial. Nearly all parties and campaigns mailed literature to citizens, while fewer than half the nonpartisan groups did so. Despite their reliance on this mode of contact, however, the party directors and campaign managers express doubt about its usefulness. One Republican director points out that direct mail is becoming less effective because "rising postage and printing costs make it more expensive." Another Republican director admits that direct mail "is a piece of junk mail" but argues that it is still effective for name recognition: "It may be junk to some but it has to go across their desk; they have to look at it before they throw it in the trash." Martin questions the effectiveness of direct mail because it is expensive, but also because "the average person doesn't check their mail box on the regular because the only thing in there is bills." The Campaign for Change local offices did not themselves conduct direct mail campaigns; all direct mail went out from campaign headquarters.

Nearly all organizations report distributing literature to potential voters either in person or at their homes. Literature distributions were not viewed as the best way to "seal the deal" with voters, Judith says; rather, they "help with name recognition." Mark felt that leaving literature at a person's home was also a good way to "at least let them know that we came, we attempted to visit them at their home." Distributing literature was also used to provide information about candidates, the voting process, and eligibility guidelines. Allen, one of the county Democratic Party directors, says:

> Early voting is a little bit complicated, because we have two different kinds of early voting right now . . . and the days are different and the hours are different. It's just kind of complicated, and so we have to have an easy way to get out a fair amount of information. So that's one of the reasons we distribute literature. And also we can leave literature behind; people can take it with them and put it on their refrigerators. That sort of thing. These are the locations for advance voting, these are the locations for early voting, these are the hours, this is how it works. . . . There's not enough time in the radio spot to give them all of the information that they need.

The nonpartisan groups also provide information about candidates and the process. For instance, groups working with immigrant populations such as Illinois Coalition for Immigrant and Refugee Rights, Southwest Organizing Project, and El Pueblo distribute information about citizenship and eligibility. The League of Women Voters in all

Figure 6.2: Examples of literature distributed by Planned Parenthood of Charlotte.

cities distributed nonpartisan voter guides with information on all candidates. Charlotte's Planned Parenthood distributed issue-related literature along with candidate and voting leaflets from the Mecklenburg County Board of Elections, shown here in figure 6.2.

Nonpartisan groups and partisan groups also differ in their reliance on e-mail for contacting voters. Three-quarters of local party and campaign directors report contacting voters in their areas by e-mail, while just over one-third of the nonpartisan groups did so. However, as with direct mail, most partisan and nonpartisan directors doubted the effectiveness of e-mail for encouraging turnout. E-mail was viewed as a way to communicate with activists and recruit volunteers. As Allen states, "We don't have access to huge amounts of people's e-mail addresses . . . so yeah, our e-mails are targeted to people who have basically signed up to get e-mails from us." Judith agrees, saying that e-mail is designed "more to rally the base and to get people interested and to get volunteers out." Patrick, another community organizer in Chicago, does not use e-mails for registration and GOTV because their target citizens "have limited computer capability." E-mail may be a more effective tool in the future, but for now it is not viewed by organizers as effective for getting people to register and vote.

A final divergence between partisan and nonpartisan groups can be found in holding voter registration drives or other types of face-to-face registration events: nonpartisan groups were twice as likely to report hosting these events as partisan groups. This difference reflects primarily the fact that nonpartisan groups are more likely to focus on registration than the campaigns and parties, but also the fact that nonpartisan groups are recruiting voters from a population for whom traditional at-home contacts are less successful. Although Republican county party leaders did hold some registration events (including the one at the Sandy Springs Festival depicted in fig. 6.3), most found these events ineffective. In fact, one Republican director found "standing on the side of the street or setting up a table in front of the grocery store or something like that" the least effective way of reaching his voters. Another Republican director did not "go places and stand on the corner" because it is "intrusive" in his opinion. "Republicans are more of a private type people. It is possible to turn people off by being too aggressive," he explained. In contrast, a community organizer in Chicago found that tabling at "Ford City Mall has always been, has always brought out big numbers" but described canvassing as "pretty tough" in her neighborhoods because people were so difficult to reach. Similarly, an Obama organizer described holding registration drives in "community centers, public transit stations, night clubs, shopping centers, apartment complexes, and grocery stores" in order to reach disadvantaged citizens. His most successful registration event was tabling at a grocery store over Labor Day weekend, where he and his volunteers collected "hundreds of forms." However, he also reports that some of the target sites in his city such as apartment communities and retail sites discouraged them from canvassing. Events were the most effective way to reach students; the research team observed several events on the campuses of the University of Illinois–Chicago, Central Piedmont Community College, the University of North Carolina–Charlotte, Spelman, Clark Atlanta, Georgia Tech, and Kennesaw State University (fig. 6.4). The Young Democrats of Georgia, despite being a partisan organization, does conduct "bar canvasses," which the Fulton County Democratic Party director thinks is successful with youth voters because it involves "talking to the folks in sort of a more comfortable setting instead of knocking on their doors, and talking when they're out because they're expecting a more social environment and expect to talk to people they don't know."

The increased focus on at-home contacting among partisans is also apparent in the content analysis of the interviews. Partisan organizations mention canvassing 189 times, compared with 113 times for nonpartisan organizations. Per organization, partisans refer to canvassing 17.2 times, while nonpartisan groups refer to canvassing 10.3 times. In particular, the phrase "door to door" occurs 169 times in the partisan interviews and 139 times in the nonpartisan interviews, or 15.4 times per partisan organization and 12.6 times per nonpartisan organization. These data can be found in table 6.2.

PREPAREDNESS

Closely related to the modes of contacting voters are the resources and experience available to organizations for such contacts. At all sites, parties and campaigns had larger staffs and attracted more money and more experienced volunteers than the nonpartisan groups. However, unlike other aspects of the study, the difference in electoral competitiveness across the sites affected the resources available for mobilization. As a result, groups in Charlotte were the best funded and staffed, Chicago groups were the least, and Atlanta groups were somewhere in the middle.

Although party and campaign organizations found it easy to raise money and recruit volunteers, local organizations in Chicago had difficulty obtaining the funds and volunteers they needed to register and turnout disadvantaged local citizens. In Charlotte, organizations such as Project Vote and Blueprint North Carolina provided financial support for the

Figure 6.3: Fulton County Republican Party booth at the Sandy Springs Festival.

Figure 6.4: Central Piedmont Community College campus registration event.

registration and GOTV efforts of Central Piedmont Community College, the University of North Carolina–Charlotte, Democracy North Carolina, and other groups. The experiences of these organizations differ greatly from that of Chicago organizations that, as described in the Celltool incident above, were denied resources on the basis of the electoral map.

Likewise, because so many politically engaged Chicagoans volunteered out of state, local organizations found it difficult to recruit help. Mary, the organizer from Chicago, said, "A lot of my adult volunteers were also very, very pro-Obama and very politically engaged, so it was a struggle just to keep them involved and not to lose them to the Obama campaign, to like lose them on the . . . on the weekend to going to Indiana, and going to Michigan and Wisconsin, but keeping them here and kind of finding that balance." To obtain the help she needed, Mary bargained with her volunteers, telling them, "You can be gone on the weekend but give me one night this week." She also used high school students, who she admits were less effective canvassers.

Interestingly, this same phenomenon was felt in Charlotte, which was much more important electorally. Martin, the community organizer at a Charlotte nonpartisan group, worried that the presidential campaigns were "taking resources away from the local candidates." According to Martin, when he asks local candidates why he rarely encounters their volunteers, they respond, "Martin, it's so hard because I don't have any people. Obama and McCain have them all." Moreover, Martin also acknowledges a lack of public attention to races and issues specific to Charlotte: "Everybody knows who they're going to vote for for president. But they don't know who's running for anything else. There's a lot of things here going on in Charlotte that are important issues that people aren't paying attention to." Martin's observations suggest that the electoral competitiveness of North Carolina at the presidential level helped deprive local organizations of the volunteer base that they would have used to reach disadvantaged citizens. Thus, high-salience elections can be blessings and curses for local organizations. Although groups in competitive environments are better prepared than those in noncompetitive ones, those groups still must compete with local parties and candidates for scarce volunteers and money.

Using Organizations to Reengage Disadvantaged Communities

The findings of the fieldwork point to the potential for nonpartisan organizations to counteract the demobilizing effects of the criminal justice system in disadvantaged communities. It is heartening to note the numerous examples of local nonpartisan political organizations, service providers, and even a few campaigns reaching out specifically to involve residents of disadvantaged communities in politics. However, the barriers these organizations face in mobilizing these communities is monumental. These organizations often are strapped for resources, and mobilizing people in disadvantaged communities even under the best of circumstances is difficult. They are harder to reach and need lots of help, and in the end, the investment of resources still might not produce votes.

Getting registered citizens to vote can be difficult, but reaching unregistered voters and getting them to both register and vote is even more challenging, because doing so requires two successful contacts. Unregistered citizens tend to be younger, have lower socioeconomic status, and have high rates of residential mobility.[40] As a result, attempts to contact these voters at home might be fruitless. Green and Gerber expect that one in six of these low-propensity voters can be reached during a door-to-door canvass and that each nineteen successful contacts will result in only one additional vote.[41] In line with these findings, Ramirez finds that Latino citizens with high levels of residential mobility are less likely to have been contacted by campaigns than those with more stability.[42] Comments in the previous section from nonpartisan groups and service providers confirm that traditional methods often do not work in disadvantaged communities. For instance, one Obama organizer expressed frustration over the difficulty of going door to door in disadvantaged communities because of high residential mobility: "Yeah, a lot of people just aren't home and they're hard to contact or they move, and that's one of the biggest problems, at least in my area, is that we hit a lot of apartments where people are only there for three to six months at a time." One member of the research team also wrote about the particular difficulty of reaching young black males, the group hardest hit by mass incarceration, in her notes on the Cordelia Park block party:

> Most people who had not voted were receptive to being taken to the library to vote with the exception of a few. When I asked the field organizer what population has been harder to persuade to register and/or allow them to take them to the polls, he responded, "African Americans between the ages 18 to 25." While at the block party, I observed that it

was more difficult to persuade young, African American males to vote. Although we were able to persuade some of them to participate in the event, it took more time to do it. When I asked the young African American males why they did not want to go and vote, many responded, "my religion," "don't have the time," or "my vote won't matter."

Considering the fact that even Obama organizers had difficulty mobilizing young black males to vote, it is unclear how other organizations, parties, and candidates might successfully reach out to this group.

Upon successfully reaching people in disadvantaged communities, organizations often found that these residents required a large investment of time and money to help them participate. Most organizations reaching out to people in disadvantaged communities needed to provide services to help these groups overcome several barriers to voting. Several groups in this study acted as advocates for unregistered voters at all stages of the process—registration, voting, and ballot protection.

At the registration stage, organizations often worked to provide information to voters about their rights, eligibility, and the process of voting. Unlike experienced voters, many young voters, immigrants, and first-time registrants do not understand the registration process. As Martin, a Charlotte community organizer observes, "The younger crowd of people don't understand that they had to register to vote. They didn't understand the process. Some 18-year-olds will show up on election day to vote and don't know they have to register." Likewise, Martin observes that several Latinos did not know that they needed to vote again in November even if they had already voted in the primary election earlier in the year. Martin also has to "fight with people to understand that their vote counts; it's not like their vote is provisional" when they vote early. The educational outreach of organizations was particularly important in the 2008 election because each of the states in the study experienced confusing changes in election laws, such as identification requirements, early voting, and one-stop voting.

Eligibility is also an important legal issue, particularly for ex-offenders. Morgan, an organizer for a group that provides services to ex-offenders in Chicago, "found that a lot of our people, me and a woman that had been previously incarcerated did not, don't know if we had the right to vote." She continues:

Some say "Oh no I can't vote because I have a background." And you say no you do. "Oh no I was told that I couldn't." Well not in the state of Illinois. You can vote. So some of them are really surprised. Some know, a few know already, "Yeah I know I can vote," and they're registered. And some you say well have you registered? "Oh yes I've definitely registered, I'm ready, I vote." But it just depends on the individuals. Some of them really know their rights and know that they can, and a lot of them don't. I think somewhere along in this system of our justice system, it has been passed down maybe inadvertently that oh no you have a background, you are a criminal or what have you and you can't vote. And you are no longer a citizen type of attitude that's been given. But I think that that has to be changed, not only with organizations but even in the system. I know there are states where they can't vote, but Illinois is not one of them.

Organizers like Morgan do important work in clarifying the legal status of former offenders, students, immigrants, and others who are not sure whether they have the right to vote. Several groups, including Democracy North Carolina and ElectionProtection.org, maintain eligibility information on their websites and provide hotlines such as 866-OUR-VOTE for voter assistance. In this way, mobilizing organizations provide informal legal advice and education to citizens of disadvantaged communities, facilitating voter registration in circumstances where voters have questions about their eligibility.

Mobilizing organizations also prevented problems with the electoral process that might arise and affect the ability of people living in disadvantaged communities to cast ballots. Several organizations encouraged early voting, worked with boards of elections to ensure proper resources at polling places, and provided transportation to less crowded early voting sites and polling places. For instance, the Obama campaign in Charlotte fought to make early voting more convenient:

> One thing that worries us most right now are the lengths of the lines, they are longer than we anticipated. So . . . we have just rented four vans that we are going to use to transport people from long lines to short lines, to make sure that people don't leave lines. We are also lobbying hard for the board of elections to increase voting sites and the number of machines at each site, so the number of lines are reduced, and there have been a few incidences of erratic behavior . . . there was a fire at a polling location that was probably started by somebody trying to get everybody out of line, so that worries us, but mainly it's the lines. These lines are really long, and we don't want

people, we want the lines too long with people voting, but we don't want them so long that they discourage people to vote.

Many other organizations, such as the League of Women Voters and the Illinois Coalition of Immigrant and Refugee Rights, set up poll-watching operations to protect ballots. The Obama campaign and organizations such as ElectionProtection.org dispatched lawyers to polling places so that they could help resolve disputes on-site on election day (fig. 6.5). Other mobilizing organizations helped prevent and resolve disputes by serving as contact points for citizens and often acting as a liaison between citizens and the board of elections. In one example, in Charlotte, the Homeless Helping Homeless organization registered many homeless citizens using park benches as addresses (fig. 6.6). However, when the board of elections rejected those registrations, Homeless Helping Homeless then had to intercede with the board on behalf of the homeless citizens in order to ensure they were registered. In another example, a mentally disabled youth named Kevin was turned away from the polls because he needed assistance reading the ballot. His guardian, who also was an Obama volunteer, was able to call the board of elections to intercede on Kevin's behalf. The non-partisan groups also spent much of their time dispelling rumors and counteracting intimidation tactics.

Moving toward Solutions?
In light of the finding from previous chapters that the criminal justice system demobilizes citizens in disadvantaged communities, it is clear that some effort to counteract these effects is necessary. This research points to imprisonment's effects on neighborhood social disorganization, defined as the weakness of attachments to formal and informal institutions and networks among neighborhood residents, as a key driver of diminished political participation. For this reason, this chapter focuses on the organizational capacity of disadvantaged neighborhoods, attempting to give the reader a sense of whether and how three different types of local organizations—county parties, campaign offices, and nonpartisan groups—attempt to increase political participation in the disadvantaged communities of their cities. The findings discussed here confirm the impression in the literature that campaigns and parties focus their limited resources on turning out people with established party ties who have supported them in the

Figure 6.5: Election protection training for lawyers, judges, and law students in Atlanta.

Figure 6.6: A participant at the Homeless Helping Homeless voter registration drive.

past. This research provides hope, however, by showing the potential for nonpartisan organizations, particularly service providers, as well as campaigns and partisan organizations, to fill this void by reaching out to people who lack formal relationships with the parties. In order to perform this role better, however, organizations need to change their existing standard operating procedures in ways that enable them to contact and mobilize more people in disadvantaged neighborhoods.

The findings show that party and campaign strategies that focus on turning out registered voters in the days before an election reach different citizens and require different tactics from the strategies focused on recruiting new voters. The partisan and nonpartisan organizations pursued the tactics typically associated with GOTV, such as door-to-door canvassing, phone banking, direct mailing, and literature distribution, albeit at different rates. The research also uncovered variation among the organizations with respect to their beliefs about the effectiveness of these tactics for registering as opposed to turning out voters. Generally, efforts to contact people at their homes work best in moderate-income suburbs filled with older, more stable, already-registered residents. Reaching more mobile unregistered populations, such as young people, ex-felons, renters, poor people, immigrants, and the homeless, requires finding these citizens through service providers, at church, in stores, on campus, or at social events. The research team discovered many other methods for targeting citizens in order to encourage registration and early voting, such as staging free concerts, block parties, and registration drives in high schools and naturalization ceremonies. These on-site contacts seemed most useful for immediate goals, such as filling out a registration form or an early vote ballot, rather than for encouraging more distant activities such as voting on election day several weeks away.

However, organizations vary in the extent to which they can undertake efforts to mobilize residents of disadvantaged communities. In addition to strategic considerations, these differences in tactics we observed across organization type reflect the differential resources available to different types of organizations across electoral contexts. Although the general pattern that parties and campaigns focus on GOTV among registered voters while nonpartisan organizations aim to register new voters holds across sites, organizations do vary in their ability to pursue resource-intensive at-home contacts and to put on events in the three cities. Partisan organizations tend to have more money, more volunteers, and more experience with conducting canvassing, setting up phone banks, and hosting candidate dinners or other events than smaller, nonpartisan organizations.

It is troubling that local parties, as the best-financed and most stable representatives of the government and those most able to overcome these obstacles, do not seem to invest in mobilizing disadvantaged communities in their own cities. During the 2008 campaign, this research found no permanent party apparatus focused on voter registration at the local level in any of the cities in the study. Although the Obama campaign and the Chicago aldermen registered new voters in 2008, candidate-focused activities can continue only as long as that candidate continues to hold or run for office. Local nonpartisan organizations help fill this void to some degree; however, their efforts cannot hope to match the potential for registration held by local parties. If no other campaign or party organization steps up to bring new voters into the electorate, perhaps the expansion of the voter registration rolls that took place in North Carolina, Florida, Virginia, and other states in 2008 will be anomalous.

Parties and campaigns will continue to shift resources based on electoral considerations. For this reason, it makes little sense to rely on them as the sole mobilizing organization within disadvantaged communities. Instead, funding nonpartisan groups and service providers with long-standing commitments to empowering their disadvantaged clients and communities would be a better investment. These organizations, even in noncompetitive national electoral environments, provide important advocacy and legal help to their communities. As Shawn, a Chicago community organizer, said,

> In part we're not looking at the voter registration effort to simply win an election, it's about a larger campaign to build political power among our institutions. We do this every election cycle. It's not about this year's campaign, it's about—it's the building of an ongoing political party. We will be in the same precincts, largely in the same service areas whether it's an alderman election whether there's an open congressional seat, whether there's a contested house seat or state senate seat. . . . That's the big difference between us and political parties.

Moreover, those organizations that primarily act as service providers can best reach disadvantaged neighborhood residents because they already see them as clients. As a result, investing in these grassroots organizations, allowing them to professionalize and expand their staff and put on more events, might be the best way to counteract the demobilizing effects of the criminal justice system.

Obviously, local nonpartisan groups cannot do this work alone. Local political parties still need to be part of the solution. Political parties should begin to experiment with beginning mobilization activities earlier in the season, prior to registration deadlines. The Obama campaign utilized this strategy with great success in North Carolina, adding hundreds of thousands of new Democratic voters to the rolls prior to the 2008 primary and general elections. Another strategy employed by the group Atlanta Campaign for Change involved strategically locating office spaces to attract young voters and volunteers:

> Our particular office is located on the campus of Morris Brown College. And we are within a stone's throw away from the Atlanta University Center, which encompasses Morris Brown College, Morehouse College, Clark College, and Spellman College, the largest collection of African American college students in the country. . . . The location was very strategic in the sense that we were located directly across AUC which I knew was going to be an ideal, robust, and vibrant volunteer base for us. So it was definitely a strategic decision.

Local parties might also pursue different tactics that rely less on at-home contacts.

One other promising development observed throughout the election season was the use of early voting to help get disadvantaged neighborhood residents to the polls. Many nonpartisan groups and the Obama campaign put on special events to promote early voting, encouraging citizens to get to the polls early in order to avoid registration, transportation, and other problems on election day. The Obama campaign sponsored a particularly innovative early voting event: an afternoon rally at Central Piedmont Community College hosted by Usher Raymond, a multiplatinum-selling recording artist, and Hill Harper, an author and actor on the top-rated television series *CSI: NY* (fig. 6.7). This rally was designed to encourage early voting; it was held just across from the campus library, which was also an early voting site. At the end of the rally, both Raymond and Harper walked across the street to mingle with the crowd as they voted early. According to the researcher's field notes, about half the crowd that attended the rally went across to the precinct to vote (fig. 6.8).[43]

Figure 6.7: Hill Harper (*left*) and Usher Raymond (*right*) leaving the Central Piedmont Community College rally.

Figure 6.8: Attendees of the rally hosted by Harper and Raymond, in line for early voting after the event.

Figure 6.9: Cordelia Park block party.

More often, however, the events to encourage early voting were small, such as the Cordelia block party depicted in figure 6.9, which was hosted by Charlotte Campaign for Change. Everyone on foot or in cars near the park and the surrounding neighborhood was approached and asked two questions: (1) Have you voted? and (2) Would you like to be a volunteer for the campaign? They were also offered a free lunch. If the individual had not voted, they were asked if they would like to be driven to the library to vote. If they said yes, they were driven to and from the voting site. Individuals who were stopped were also signed up to volunteer if they were interested. About fifty people were taken to vote during this event.

The advent of one-stop voting in North Carolina, which allows same-day registration and early voting for a short period in October, also produced many innovative tactics for getting disadvantaged neighborhood residents to the polls. Events that focused on the one-stop voting period seemed particularly successful in Charlotte, according to the research team's observations. In one event, "Souls to the Polls," several local churches marched their congregations to one-stop vote after a Sunday sermon on civic participation. In each of these examples, events seem most useful because they reach the people least likely to participate—young people, low-income people, and immigrants—where they shop, worship, and socialize. These events also were geared toward immediate, on-site results—registration and early voting—rather than toward encouraging election day turnout weeks into the future. Such events are reminiscent of the block parties held in the era of old-school machine politics, which were effective in encouraging political participation.

Some might also propose changes to the criminal justice system, such as reducing incarceration and aggressive policing in disadvantaged communities as potential solutions to the problems identified in this book. Criminal justice reform can potentially help reengage the residents of disadvantaged communities with politics. The next and final chapter will engage this subject more fully. However, the certain reality is that criminal justice involvement will continue to be a regular feature of life in disadvantaged and minority communities for the near future. Simply suggesting a reduction in incarceration rates or a change in police practices is not a feasible short- or even medium-term solution to the problem, particularly because doing so is politically impractical and ignores the effects that even community supervision has on political behavior. Instead, mobilization is a lower-cost, less politically contentious way to reengage residents who have been turned off by personal and vicarious experiences with state punishment.

7

State Police Power and Citizen Political Power

Like the political institutions historically preceding it, the state is a relation of men dominating men, a relation supported by means of legitimate (i.e., considered to be legitimate) violence. If the state is to exist, the dominated must obey the authority claimed by the powers that be.
— Max Weber, "Politics as a Vocation," 1921[1]

Authoritarian regimes routinely use police, courts, and prisons to maintain the power of the ruling class through the surveillance, imprisonment, exile, and even execution of the enemies of those in charge. In China and North Korea, for instance, those who dare to challenge the status quo could end up in prison or, worse yet, dead. Where governments openly use the law to quash dissent, the link between punishment and political outcomes is obvious, as the ruling regime blatantly employs the apparatus of state authority to deny particular citizens and groups the right to participate equally in the political life of the nation.

Governments in the United States supervise and imprison a higher proportion of their citizens than any other country in the world, including China and North Korea. Yet the effects of criminal justice on American politics remain largely unrecognized. Unlike the subjects of dictatorships, citizens of the United States are believed to enjoy a fair and impartial justice system. Government officials are not permitted to use legal institutions to punish their political enemies. However, the fact that Americans experience state power through nameless, impersonal bureaucracies does not lessen the impact that the increasing frequency of these interactions has on politics.

This book has explored the repercussions of the criminal justice system for American democracy, arguing that punitive interactions between citizens and the criminal justice system matter for politics. The government, by punishing citizens, affects politics not by deciding who holds office but by shaping the contours of the polity. In the process of administering the law, governments at all levels define who belongs to the political community, specify how and when citizens can participate in politics, redistribute resources among individuals and social groups, and determine the balance of power and influence among citizens. This effect on the political community occurs because criminal convictions destroy the social and human capital of individual offenders and, by extension, that of their families and neighbors as well.

As argued in the second chapter, being convicted of a crime subjects individuals to exclusion from the social, economic, and civic life of their communities. When a person is found guilty of a felony or in some states, a misdemeanor, he or she loses the right to vote and serve on juries. People with criminal histories often are denied access to public assistance, and many employers refuse to hire them. The stigma and shame of being convicted of a crime may lead to greater social isolation; imprisonment further isolates offenders by taking them away from their families. In this way, convicts are denied full membership in the polity, as they no longer have recourse to the civil rights, financial support, and social networks that enable participation in politics.

The effect of convictions on offenders in turn shapes the ability of their families, friends, and neighbors to achieve equal standing in the political community. Being convicted of a crime limits the ability of offenders to contribute positively to family and neighborhood life. People convicted of crimes, to the extent that they do not vote, are not able to encourage participation among their children, friends, or spouses by serving as role models. In fact, their experiences with criminal justice may lead them to express negative views of the government that could be internalized by the people who live around them. The shame and stigma of an individual's convictions may reflect badly not only on the convict, but also on family members, causing them to withdraw from neighborhood life and thus from mobilizing influences as well. The financial strain imposed by convictions prevents offenders from contributing to the maintenance of community institutions; these institutions are thus deprived of the resources they need to continue mobilizing neighborhood residents. Thus, members of communities in which a high number of people are involved with the criminal justice system often experience negative externalities that in turn shape their ability to participate in politics.

Chapter 3 introduces new data on thousands of block groups in order to demonstrate that these neighborhood effects of the criminal justice system are felt unevenly by citizens. While some block groups are fortunate to have none of their residents under correctional supervision, most have some members who are involved with the criminal justice system. An unfortunate few experience shockingly high concentrations of criminal justice supervision; black and poor neighborhoods are most likely to have residents in prison or under community supervision. This phenomenon most likely reflects disparities in criminal activity, arrest, prosecution, and sentencing by race, gender, and class. In several neighborhoods in the sample, imprisonment rates and community supervision rates top 5 percent of the adult population. Distributed over an area as small as a block group, these high rates of prison, probation, and parole translate into spatial concentrations of hundreds of prisoners per square mile in some cases.

While recent scholarship argues that disfranchisement affects elections and that the other consequences of convictions make life worse for offenders, this debate ignores the relationship between prison, probation, and parole and politics. Before this project, advocates, researchers and journalists recognized disfranchisement as the only mechanism by which convictions could shape political outcomes. This preoccupation with disfranchisement comes at the expense of ignoring the more important consequences of convictions that are described in this book. In order to make a compelling case for the repeal of disfranchisement laws, many people argued that repealing these laws would eliminate the role that criminal justice plays in shaping democracy. For instance, Uggen, Manza, and Thompson argue that in Maine and Vermont, the only two states without legal disfranchisement policies, "a felony conviction does not produce social exclusion."[2]

However, as chapter 4 shows, the criminal justice system shapes politics through a different mechanism: by decreasing the political and civic participation of neighborhood residents who are not themselves under criminal justice supervision. Imprisonment has a particularly strong vicarious effect on participation. For instance, a block group with no prisoners has an average voter turnout that is about 6 percentage points higher than that of block groups with a spatial concentration of 250 prisoners per square mile in North Carolina; in Georgia, the figure is 2 percentage points. Other tests show that imprisoning new inmates up to three months prior to the 2008 election decreased voter turnout by 1.4 percentage points from what it would have been had the person been sent to prison within the three months after the election. Even more evidence points toward the detrimental effect of imprisonment for voting: eligible voters who lived in a neighborhood with an average level of prisoner density were less likely to have voted in the 1996 presidential election and less likely to have been registered to vote in 2000 than people living in lower-imprisonment neighborhoods. The effects of imprisonment on other forms of political and civic participation are also clear: people who live in neighborhoods with a prisoner density of 110 prisoners per square mile participate in 43.4 percent fewer political activities, are members of one-third fewer groups, and volunteer almost 78 percent less than people who live in neighborhoods with no prisoners.

The analysis in chapter 5 attributes the diminished participation caused by imprisonment to the economic and social effects of imprisonment. Imprisonment is both caused by and a consequence of poverty, as shown in chapter 3 and in previous research. However, it is also clear from chapter 5 that high-imprisonment neighborhoods lack the formal and informal social ties that encourage political participation. People who live in high-imprisonment neighborhoods are less likely to trust people in general and their neighbors in particular and are less likely to feel a sense of community based on neighborhood ties than people who live in low-imprisonment neighborhoods. Residents of high-imprisonment neighborhoods are also less likely to participate in formal social networks like church and other civic organizations. The evidence suggests that imprisonment decreases participation by taking away the very resources and social networks that foster participation.

Implications

The spatial inequality of criminal justice presented in this book is important because it shapes local politics. Such inequality also leads to racial political inequality and has important implications for political socialization and political representation as well. These four issues are discussed in more detail below.

LOCAL POLITICS

The presence of people with criminal convictions in a neighborhood both positively and negatively affects the weight of the remaining community members' votes and, consequently, the quality of their representation. At the citywide level, people that live in low-conviction neighborhoods tend to benefit from the diminished political participation of people in high-conviction neighborhoods, because, as voters, they have more weight with local politicians than nonvoters. Within communities suffering from high levels of nonvoting, voters benefit from punishment because it augments the power of their votes. Residents who cannot or do not vote fail to communicate their needs to city officials and are less likely to be encouraged to influence government through other channels. If decreased participation in community politics means that influence is shifted toward more advantaged members of the community, then the disadvantaged suffer.[3] Increasing civic engagement in communities where the most disadvantaged members do not participate only leads to greater "unrepresentativeness."[4]

However, even though voters in high-conviction communities enjoy greater advantages at the local level, those benefits are offset by the disadvantages they face at higher levels of aggregation. Because political power is based partly on numeric strength when it comes to votes, low turnout among citizens with certain interests can hurt the ability of other voters who share those same interests to achieve their goals. This dynamic has been shown to operate at the state level: citizens of states with lower levels of mobilization among lower-class voters enjoy fewer social benefits.[5] Disadvantaged communities also suffer from less effective social services, perhaps because they must rely on "altruism, guilt, or fear" rather than electoral threats to achieve their goals.[6] Low participation influences the distribution of resources across localities; Ansolabehere and Snyder also note that "governing parties skew the distribution of funds in favor of voters in areas that provide them with the strongest electoral support."[7] Thus, voters in areas where participation is low often are ignored in favor of areas where participation is higher.

Since the affirmation of the principle of one person, one vote in *Reynolds v. Sims* (1964), it has been a fundamental belief in the United States that the importance of a citizen's vote should not be affected by where he or she lives.[8] As Chief Justice Warren writes:[9]

It would appear extraordinary to suggest that a State could be constitutionally permitted to enact a law providing that certain of the State's voters could vote two, five, or 10 times for their legislative representatives, while voters living elsewhere could vote only once. And it is inconceivable that a state law to the effect that, in counting votes for legislators, the votes of citizens in one part of the State would be multiplied by two, five, or 10, while the votes of persons in another area would be counted only at face value, could be constitutionally sustainable. Of course, the effect of [377 U.S. 533, 563] state legislative districting schemes which give the same number of representatives to unequal numbers of constituents is identical. Overweighting and overvaluation of the votes of those living here has the certain effect of dilution and undervaluation of the votes of those living there.

According to the opinion of the Court, the weight of an individual's vote is affected by the number of other voters present in that voter's district; it is unfair for some votes to have more "weight" simply because the voter happens to live in an area with fewer voters. The criminal justice system does just that: it reduces the importance of votes in neighborhoods with a large number of offenders relative to votes that come from low-conviction neighborhoods.

RACIAL INEQUALITY

The racially disparate impact of punishment, coupled with racial residential segregation, means that these vicarious political effects of imprisonment are felt most strongly by black people and black neighborhoods. The data on the concentration of prison, probation, and parole in black neighborhoods in Georgia and North Carolina presented in chapter 3 clearly show that these effects are almost entirely concentrated in black neighborhoods and thus are experienced by black people to a higher degree than by whites and Hispanics. As noted in that chapter, the average prisoner density in neighborhoods where few blacks live is less than two prisoners per square mile, while the average prisoner density in black neighborhoods is twenty times higher. Mass imprisonment therefore harms the ability of black people and black neighborhoods to participate equally in politics.

The evidence also suggests that the criminal justice system is likely to affect power dynamics within disadvantaged black communities as well. Cohen writes that the worst-off members of marginalized communities may be further marginalized by better-off members of their group, who exercise power by denying group rights and policing behavior.[10] The marginalized members of marginalized groups are least able to communicate their needs to police and other government leaders; in many communities, this dynamic is especially important with respect to crime and other community problems. Skogan writes that the "homeowning, long-term residents of a community" are the ones "who learn about and participate in area-based programs" like community policing; the better-off residents are thus able to exercise power over their more disadvantaged neighbors.[11] Randall Kennedy notes that many members of the Congressional Black Caucus supported the disparate crack-cocaine sentences that have resulted in the mass incarceration of young black men since the 1980s, primarily in response to residents of black neighborhoods who were victims of crack-induced violence and crime.[12]

POLITICAL SOCIALIZATION AND THE FUTURE

In addition to the overall findings from chapter 3, it is also important to note the descriptive finding that a large proportion of young people in black neighborhoods are under criminal justice supervision. In North Carolina and Georgia, this status means that in many black neighborhoods, more than one-fifth of the young adult population is in prison; many more are on probation or parole. In addition to the economic, social, and familial consequences of criminal justice involvement, young people also suffer politically. In Georgia and North Carolina, criminal offenders are barred from voting while they serve their sentences, meaning that a high proportion of young people in many neighborhoods were prevented from voting in the 2008 general election. Although many young people might have stayed home during this election cycle in any case, it is troubling to think about how these early experiences with government supervision, coupled with the lack of experience and training in voting, might affect this cohort's participation in the future. Presently, the high rate of supervision among younger blacks disadvantages them politically relative to both older neighborhood residents and the greater community as a whole. This phenomenon might help explain the growing disaffection of young blacks in the face of noted improvements in material well-being since the civil rights movement.[13]

POLITICAL DEPOPULATION AND REPRESENTATION

There is, of course, the obvious political effect of imprisonment: political depopulation, which erases neighborhood residents from official statistics and from voter registration rolls. Political depopulation is important because federal, state, and local governments apportion voting districts and make decisions about infrastructure and resources based on community population.

Political depopulation first results from disfranchisement laws, which reduce the number of voters, but not necessarily the number of people, in a neighborhood. The growth in the number of people convicted of crimes means that the number of disfranchised felons and misdemeanants in the United States has skyrocketed. Nearly 5 million offenders and ex-offenders were prevented from voting in the 2004 presidential election.[14] Because of the race and gender disparities in convictions, legal disfranchisement disproportionately affects black males. Nearly 13 percent of all adult black men are disfranchised; in Alabama and Florida, 31 percent of all black men are currently disfranchised.[15] In at least ten other states, 15–25 percent of black men are disfranchised, which might explain the persistent gap in voter turnout between black men and black women, white men, and white women.[16] In many states, a growing percentage of Latinos is being disfranchised.[17] Six percent of the Latino voting age population is disfranchised in Washington and Nebraska and 5 percent are disfranchised in Arizona and Florida. Many of these individuals may not be citizens, however, and in most cases, disfranchisement among Latinos is not disproportionate to their presence in the population.[18]

Political depopulation also results from imprisonment, which, again, is distributed unequally across neighborhoods. Imprisonment is particularly problematic for representation and the distribution of resources across communities. The issue results from the census bureau's practice of counting prisoners and other populations in group quarters as residents of the facilities in which they reside, rather than of the neighborhoods from which they came.[19] As a result, more than 2 million incarcerated individuals, many of whom come from a relatively small number of disadvantaged communities, are counted as residents of predominantly rural communities in which they had no rights or representation.[20] Even though many of these individuals return to their communities within a short period of time, official statistics that sample only household population do not recognize their presence in the disadvantaged, mostly urban communities that they leave behind. This administrative decision creates important disparities in the apportionment of state and federal legislative districts, padding the population base in rural areas relative to urban ones. According to the

Prisoners of the Census Project, prisoners imported from other areas of the state added more than 10 percent to the 2000 census population totals in several state legislative districts, including House District 141 in Georgia, Districts 8 and 13 in Texas, and House District 75 Virginia.[21] This statistical relocation of prisoners also results in a massive transfer of resources from predominantly minority, disadvantaged urban communities to predominantly white, rural ones.[22]

Inmates also are erased from official statistics because they are not included in household surveys, the source of census and other information about income, educational attainment, poverty, health, and other data. Such exclusion skews the picture of neighborhood health and resources given by official statistics.[23] According to Western, official statistics underestimate black unemployment and overestimate black median income because these official statistics fail to consider the significant proportion of blacks who are incarcerated.[24] Similarly, the apparent closing of the black-white wage gap since the 1970s can largely be attributed to this statistical anomaly.[25] The high proportion of dropouts in prison also leads to a more positive picture of educational attainment among minority and poor men.[26] Again, these important errors in the measurement of individual and group disadvantage matter for neighborhoods because of the spatial concentration of incarceration; often, the true extent of neighborhood disadvantage cannot be known because many disadvantaged people are obscured from the view of official statistics.

Voting is the most important guarantor of rights in American society. As Hamilton asks in Federalist 35, "Is it not natural that a man who is a candidate for the favor of the people and who is dependent on the suffrages of his fellow-citizens for the continuance of his public honors should take care to inform himself of their dispositions and inclinations?"[27] The political depopulation caused by disfranchisement and imprisonment makes it more difficult for government officials to inform themselves of the needs of the neighborhoods they represent through official statistics; political depopulation also makes it less important for them to consider the needs of particularly disadvantaged neighborhoods, because they are less beholden to them for votes.

Solutions

 These findings point to what appears to be an obvious solution: put fewer people in prison. Advocates have proposed several alternatives to incarceration. Community supervision, which does not seem to depress neighborhoods politically as much, is an obvious alternative to incarceration. Instead of prison, people convicted of crimes might be sentenced to home confinement, drug treatment, intensive probation, or supervision in local halfway houses.

However, it may not be the case that high-imprisonment communities want fewer people in their neighborhoods to be sent to prison, despite the detrimental side effects imprisonment may cause. The evidence in chapter 5 points to an interesting paradox: residents of high-imprisonment neighborhoods are *not* more likely to distrust the local and national governments and in fact seem more likely to trust the police than people in lower-imprisonment neighborhoods. This finding may reflect both the increased likelihood of contact with the police and the tenor of those contacts.[28] Skogan's analysis of results from a Chicago-based survey reveal the importance of timely assistance, cordial and clear communication concerning the case, and helpfulness in eliciting positive attitudes from respondents.[29] Eller et al. report similar results in a study of black and white university students in Britain, where high-quality contact moderated negative attitudes toward the police.[30]

Not surprisingly, dissatisfactory contacts can and frequently do produce negative attitudes, particularly in minority communities.[31] Dissatisfaction can arise from a number of factors. Perceptions of discrimination often cause blacks to rate police lower than whites rate them. For instance, a 2000 Harris Interactive report finds that in the aggregate, most Americans support and trust the police.[32] However, when queried about whether the police "treat all races fairly," there is a marked divergence between white and black respondents: while 69 percent of white respondents answer in the affirmative, only 36 percent of black respondents answer in the same way.[33] The Pew Research Center has more recently surveyed the attitudes of Americans regarding the police, with similar results. Whites in that survey were more likely to have confidence that the police would enforce the law, not use excessive force in doing so, and treat members of all racial groups equally in the pursuit of justice.[34]

Sometimes, however, the negative reaction is not to excessive policing, but to a dearth of attention. One study cites at length a particularly revealing story from a participant in a focus group on the legal system. A middle-aged black woman recounted how calls to the police regarding repeated break-ins at her house failed to elicit police attention.[35] After a third break-in, where the woman confronted and subdued the robber, police finally showed up and arrested the woman for assault and would have potentially harmed her were it not for the efforts of a black officer on the scene.[36] Other, more systematic evidence also shows that, historically, people in minority communities frequently complain more about police neglect than they do about police misconduct.[37]

Still other evidence suggests that residents of high-imprisonment communities might resist alternatives to incarceration that leave offenders in their neighborhoods. In general, the public supports alternatives to prison for nonviolent offenders: 90 percent of Americans support establishing local programs "designed to keep nonviolent and first time offenders active and working in the community."[38] A majority of respondents support using alternative sanctions for nonviolent offenses like burglary or the sale or possession of illegal drugs.[39] However, almost two-thirds of respondents say that alternatives to prison should never be used for violent offenders.[40] The not-in-my-backyard impulse surfaces frequently in local debates about the sites of halfway houses and services for offenders. For instance, 71 percent of respondents to a survey on chronic mental illness responded that they "absolutely would not welcome" the building of a prison in their neighborhood.[41] Respondents to that survey are evenly split on whether they would welcome alternatives such as drug treatment facilities and only narrowly welcome group homes for the mentally ill.[42] Anecdotal evidence also supports the idea that neighborhoods welcome offenders in theory, but not in practice. Residents of Washington, DC, vigorously protest the siting of prisons and halfway houses in their neighborhoods, even establishing a community group, the Capitol East Neighborhood Prison Task Force, to organize against these facilities.[43] In one instance, Representative Eleanor Holmes Norton joined residents in protesting the Federal Bureau of Prisons' efforts to locate a halfway house for women in Southeast DC.[44] Residents primarily cite concerns that such facilities would increase crime and drug activity and decrease property values in their communities.[45]

The disconnect between theory and practice seems to stem from a perceived trade-off between safety on the one hand and the negative externalities of high imprisonment on the other. As one Tallahassee police officer asks, "But if you are trying to clean up these neighborhoods and you don't arrest people who are breaking the law, then what do you do with them?"[46] Todd Clear's examination of attitudes among residents of high-imprisonment neighborhoods in Tallahassee tells a similar story of ambivalence. According to Clear, the residents he interviewed "can describe positive results of incarceration for various aspects of community life, and yet at the same time they see—and can point to—various negative implications of incarceration."[47] Clear documents several instances of neighborhood residents who think that it is good to get drug dealers and prostitutes off the streets, and who acknowledge that a prisoner "may be one of those kind of people that you're kind of glad to get rid of for a while."[48]

Given these practical and political considerations, it seems unlikely that decarceration will emerge as a viable solution to the problems raised in this book in the near future. Hence the solution proposed in chapter 6: encouraging and enabling political parties and campaigns to reach out in new and significant ways to members of low-income and minority communities in order to encourage civic and political involvement. In Charlotte, Chicago, and Atlanta, organizations that already had regular contact with residents of these communities in order to provide services successfully mobilized members of these communities to volunteer and vote during the 2008 election season. Some of the models these organizations developed for their clients might prove useful to parties and campaigns as they try to reach out to new supporters in future elections. While some evidence suggests that the broader political establishment traditionally has lacked the will to mobilize residents of low-income and minority communities, perhaps the success of service providers, some local Chicago aldermen, and the Obama campaign in finding some new voters in these untapped neighborhoods could reverse the trend of neglect in the future.

Nevertheless, it is important to recognize that mobilization undertaken by community outsiders represents only a temporary stop-gap and may not be effective in the long term, particularly given the increasingly dire situation of black youth imprisonment. Chapter 5 points to a more viable long-term solution: ensuring that today's high-imprisonment neighborhoods can rebuild the economic strength and social networks that might increase civic and political activity, and decrease imprisonment, in the future. Several scholars have shown that informal social networks discourage crime and imprisonment.[49] Communities with stable families, strong churches, and flourishing community and civic associations build ties and foster those informal social networks.[50]

Thus, future research on the connection between criminal justice and political behavior should focus on this important relationship between imprisonment and social disorganization, investigating the ways in which prison increases social disorganization and developing models to break this causal pathway.

It might also be useful for political scientists to think more about ways to study and strengthen the formal and informal social networks that operate in low-income and minority neighborhoods today. This work points to the need to revive interest in the new ways in which church and community involvement affect politics in the post-civil-rights era. Likewise, it would be fruitful to note how decreasing attachments to formal and informal networks might affect political involvement among future generations of black youth suffering from disproportionately high rates of criminal justice involvement.

Researchers need to consider the experience of individuals and communities with criminal justice and convictions in future research on political behavior. Scholars of American politics gradually have begun studying the criminal justice system. Recent work highlights political explanations of criminal justice policy changes, measures the effects of public opinion on criminal justice severity, and explores variations in crime policies across states.[51] However, the criminal justice system has been not been given enough attention by scholars of political behavior. This project begins to solve many of the methodological issues surrounding the study of convicted populations, such as data constraints, selection bias, and confounded causal relationships. However, much more work needs to be done in order to understand the relationship between imprisonment and political participation.

Fairness and Democratic Inclusion

To return to a theme raised earlier in this book, the current system of imprisonment as practiced in the United States today undermines political equality and democratic inclusiveness. To many, putting people who commit crimes against society in prison is simply a question of justice, of right and wrong: liberal democratic theory brands an individual who breaks the law "a rebel and a traitor to the homeland" who deserves to be expelled from the community.[52] Reasonable people disagree on the politics of punishment. However, the argument presented in this book is that concerns about individual offenders are not the only factors that matter when thinking about criminal justice policies. It is also important to consider the impact that punishment has on political equality in general. The criminal justice system most heavily affects people in poor and minority neighborhoods, people who already experience significant barriers to political participation and influence. Harsh punishments such as imprisonment exacerbate existing political inequalities and deny disadvantaged citizens the chance to participate fully in politics. Moreover, imprisonment also affects the numerical strength and political resources of disadvantaged neighborhoods and social groups. In this way, imprisonment denies law-abiding citizens the right to participate on an equal footing with people from neighboring communities with lower imprisonment. Is it fair that the votes of people who live in neighborhoods with or share the same social background of convicted offenders count less than those of the more fortunate citizens who live in other, low-imprisonment neighborhoods?

The future of American democracy depends on society's ability to mitigate the impact of thirty years of unprecedented levels of imprisonment on the political behavior of present and coming generations. As was just suggested, the long-term solution lies in improving the conditions of individual convicts and their neighborhoods. If it is correct that social disorganization and economic decline contribute to diminished participation, then problems of disadvantaged neighborhoods might be alleviated by supplementing the informal mechanisms of control in communities. Encouraging home ownership and development of churches, schools, and civic groups may help offset much of the participation that is lost as a result of a community's experience with convictions.

Appendix

Social Capital Benchmark Survey Questions

Number of (Combined) Times Volunteered:
How many times in the past twelve months have you volunteered?
1 Never did this
2 Once
3 A few times
4 2–4 times
5 5–9 times
6 About once a month on average
7 About twice a month on average
8 About once a week on average
9 About twice a week on average
98 Don't know
99 Refused

Registered to Vote:
Are you currently registered to vote?
0 No
1 Yes
3 (VOLUNTEERED) Not eligible to vote
8 Don't know
9 Refused

Belonged to Any Group That Took Local Action For Reform:
Did any of the groups that you are involved with take any LOCAL action for social or political reform in the past 12 months?
0 No
1 Yes
8 Don't Know
9 Refused

Number of Formal Group Involvements including Church:
Now we'd like to ask about other groups and organizations. I am going to read a list: just answer YES if you have been involved in the past 12 months with this kind of group.
Public interest groups, political action groups, political clubs, or party committees.
1 No
2 Yes

8   Don't Know
9   Refused

Worked on a Community Project in the Past Twelve Months:
Which of the following things have you done in the past twelve months?
Have you worked on a community project?
0   No
1   Yes
8   Don't know
9   Refused

Signed a Petition in the Past Twelve Months:
Which of the following things have you done in the past twelve months?
Have you signed a petition?
0   No
1   Yes
8   Don't know
9   Refused

Attended a Political Meeting or Rally in the Past Twelve Months:
Which of the following things have you done in the past twelve months?
Have you attended a political meeting or rally?
0   No
1   Yes
8   Don't know
9   Refused

Participated in Demonstrations, Boycotts, or Marches in the Past Twelve Months:
Which of the following things have you done in the past twelve months?
Have you participated in any demonstrations, boycotts, or marches?
0   No
1   Yes
8   Don't know
9   Refused

Trust Neighbors:
Next, we'd like to know how much you trust different groups of people. First,
think about (GROUP). Generally speaking, would you say that you can trust them
a lot, some, only a little, or not at all?
People in your neighborhood
0   Trust them not at all
1   Trust them only a little
2   Trust them some

3 Trust them a lot
5 (VOLUNTEERED) Does not apply
8 Don't Know
9 Refused

Trust Local Police:
Next, we'd like to know how much you trust different groups of people. First,
think about (GROUP). Generally speaking, would you say that you can trust them
a lot, some, only a little, or not at all?
The Police in your Local Neighborhood
0 Trust them not at all
1 Trust them only a little
2 Trust them some
3 Trust them a lot
5 (VOLUNTEERED) Does not apply
8 Don't know
9 Refused

Can Trust People vs. Be Careful:
Next, we'd like to know how much you trust different groups of people. First,
think about (GROUP). Generally speaking, would you say that you can trust them
a lot, some, only a little, or not at all?
0 Can't be too careful
1 Depends
2 People can be trusted
8 Don't know
9 Refused

Church Membership:
Are you a member of a local church, synagogue, or other religious or spiritual
community?
0 No
1 Yes
8 Don't know
9 Refused

Trust National Government:
How much of the time do you think you can trust the NATIONAL government to
do what is right – just about always, most of the time, only some of the time, or
hardly ever?
0 Hardly ever
1 Some of the time
2 Most of the time

3   Just about always
8   Don't know
9   Refused

Trust Local Government:
How about your LOCAL government? How much of the time do you think you can trust the LOCAL government to do what is right—just about always, most of the time, only some of the time, or hardly ever?
0   Hardly ever
1   Some of the time
2   Most of the time
3   Just about always
8   Don't know
9   Refused

Sense of Community or Feeling of Belonging:
This study is about community, so we'd like to start by asking what gives you a sense of community or a feeling of belonging. Say YES if it gives you a sense of community or feeling of belonging, and NO if it does not.
People in your neighborhood
1   No—does not
2   (VOLUNTEERED) Depends/No strong feelings
3   Yes—does
4   (VOLUNTEERED) Does not apply
8   Don't know
9   Refused

Importance of Obstacle: Concerns for Personal Safety:
Many obstacles keep people from becoming as involved with their community as they would like. We'd like you to tell us whether each of the following is a very important obstacle, somewhat important, or not at all important.
Concerns for your safety
0   Cites no obstacles at all; this obstacle inapplicable
1   Not an important obstacle
2   Somewhat important obstacle
3   Very important obstacle
8   Don't know
9   Refused

Newspaper Readership:
Next we'd like to ask you a few questions about television and newspapers. How many days in the past week did you read a daily newspaper?

VALID RANGE 0–7

8   Don't know
9   Refused

Internet Access:
Do you have access to the Internet in your home?

0   No
1   Yes
8   Don't know
9   Refused

Satisfaction with Current Economic Situation:
We are interested in how people are getting along financially these days. So far as you and your family are concerned, would you say that you are very satisfied, somewhat satisfied, or not at all satisfied with your present financial situation?

0   Not at all satisfied
1   Somewhat satisfied
2   Very satisfied
8   Don't know
9   Refused

Interest in Politics and National Affairs:
Our next questions are about public affairs. How interested are you in politics and national affairs? Are you very interested, somewhat interested, only slightly interested, or not at all interested?

1   Not at all interested
2   Only slightly interested
3   Somewhat interested
4   Very interested
8   Don't know
9   Refused

Political Knowledge:
We'd like to know how well known different governmental leaders are in your area. Could you tell me the names of the two U.S. Senators from your state?

1   Failed to name either
2   One is "close"
3   One is correct or both are "close"
4   One is correct and one is "close"
5   Both are correct
9   Refused

Gender of Respondent
1 Male
2 Female

Ideology of Respondent:
Thinking POLITICALLY AND SOCIALLY, how would you describe your own general outlook—as being very conservative, moderately conservative, middle-of-the-road, moderately liberal or very liberal?
1 Very conservative
2 Moderately conservative
3 Middle-of-the-road
4 Moderately liberal
5 Very liberal
6 (VOLUNTEERED) Something else
8 Don't know
9 Refused

Education of Respondent (including GED follow-up):
What is the highest grade of school or year of college you have completed?
1 Less than high school
2 High school diploma (including GED)
3 Some college
4 Associate's degree (2 year) or specialized technical training
5 Bachelor's degree
6 Some graduate training
7 Graduate or professional degree
8 Don't know
9 Refused

1999 *Total Household Income of Respondent:*
If you added together the yearly incomes, before taxes, of all the members of your household for last year, 1999, would the total be:
0 $20,000 or less
1 Over $20,000 but less than $30,000
2 Less than $30,000 unspecified
3 $30,000 but less than $50,000 (INCLUDES "OVER 30,000 UNSPECIFIED)
4 $50,000 but less than $75,000
5 $75,000 but less than $100,000
6 $100,000 or more
8 Don't know
9 Refused

Hispanic:

To ensure that all types of people are represented in our survey, I would like to ask you whether you are Latino or Hispanic?

0   No

1   Yes

8   Don't know

9   Refused

Non-Hispanic Black:

To ensure that all types of people are represented in our survey, I would like to ask you whether you are African American or Black?

0   No

1   Yes

8   Don't know

9   Refused

Citizenship Status of Respondent:

Are you an American citizen?

0   No

1   Yes

8   Don't know

9   Refused

Survey/Questionnaire for Director Interviews

Thank you for agreeing to speak with me about the activities of [organization]. Before we begin, I just need you to read and sign this form consenting to do the interview. [wait for signature; Review consent form if necessary]. Do you have any questions about the consent form?

Do you mind if I record this interview for accuracy? I will stop the tape at any point if you wish, and we can rewind any comments or thoughts you'd like to take off the record.

Let's get started first with some basic questions about you:

1. How long have you been active in political campaigns? *Months*___

2. And how long have you been with this organization? *Months* ____

3. a. Have you always held this position? *Y*___ *N*___ b. How long? *Months*____

Let's turn now to talking more specifically about [organization].

4. This fall, did your organization have
a. Paid staff? About how many? *(enter 0 if answer is no)*
b. Volunteer staff? About how many? *(enter 0 if answer is no)*____

5. This fall, does your organization *(enter 1 for yes, 0 for no)*:
a. ___Have an office with regular hours?
b. ___Receive money from the state or national organization?
c. ___Receive literature or materials from the state or national organization?
d. ___Maintain a website?

6. For this election, will your organization *(enter 1 for yes, 0 for no)*:
a. ___Provide registration materials to individuals?
b. ___Provide voter information or volunteers to candidates?
c. ___Provide voters transportation to the polls on Election Day?
d. ___Purchase advertisements? Where?
    i. ___In newspapers?
    ii. ___On radio?
    iii. ___On Television?
e. ___Sponsor fundraising events?
f. ___Donate money to candidates?
g. ___Sponsor events in conjunction with other organizations?

7. The following is a list of activities that many political organizations undertake. Please rank them in order of importance to your organization in this past election, with **one being most important** and **four being least important**.

a. ___Registering voters

b. ___Increasing turnout of already-registered voters

c. ___Persuading voters to support particular candidates

d. ___Providing resources to candidates

e. ___Providing information about voting rights, early voting, polling places, etc.

8. Please rank the following types of contests according to their importance to your organization in this election cycle, with **one being most important** and **four being least important**:

a. ___The presidential race

b. ___Statewide races such as governor or senator

c . ___Congressional races

d. ___Local contests

9. For this election, has your organization contacted potential voters through any of the following ways? *(enter 1 for yes, 0 for no)*

a. ___Door-to-door canvassing?

b. ___Voter registration events?

c. ___Other forms of face to face contact?

d. ___Distribute leaflets or literature to voters? (Ask for copies of literature)

e. ___Direct mail to citizens

f. ___Phone calls to citizens?

g. ___Emails to citizens?

h. ___Training staff or volunteers of other organizations?

i. ___Coordinating events and activities among organizations?

10. Did you identify or obtain contact information for potential voters? If so, how? (*PROMPT:* Did you obtain voter registration lists from the county? Did you buy data from private organizations or consultants? Did you receive the information from the national or state *ORGANIZATION* office?)

11. [*IF INTERVIEWEE INDICATES THEY OBTAIN VOTER REGISTRATION LISTS*]

a. How often do you order updated voter registration lists?

b. Do you receive active voters only? Or inactive voters?

c. How do you decide which voters to contact? (*PROMPT: People who voted in the last two elections? Voters in a particular neighborhood?*)

12. Were you trying to contact people with particular characteristics? For instance, non-voters, young voters, or people who had voted before? Voters

with low incomes? Voters in public housing? Soccer moms? (*List all that apply.*) _____

_____

_____

_____

_____

13. *If Yes for any activities in question 9:* I'd like to take a minute to ask you to elaborate on your activities in greater detail. First, let's discuss the . . . [*For transitions between event types: NOW LET'S TALK ABOUT THE . . .*]
a. Door to Door Canvassing events:
    i. Why did you decide to send people out to meet voters?
    ii. How did you decide where to canvass?
    iii. Which streets, blocks, or neighborhoods in [CITY] have you covered so far? Which areas do you plan to cover by the election?
    iv. How did you recruit canvassers? Did you use paid staff or volunteers?
    v. Describe your typical canvasser. How old are they? Are they college students?
    vi. Did you attempt to "match" canvassers to neighborhoods or have them canvass in their own neighborhoods?
    vii. Did you train canvassers? What kind of training do you provide?
    viii. At what times of day or days of the week did you send out canvassers?
    ix. Were you concerned about the safety of canvassers in sending them door to door? What steps did you take to ensure the safety of your canvassers?
    x. Were your canvassers supervised? How?
    xi. Did your canvassers find it difficult to contact/reach the targeted citizens?
b. Voter registration drives and other events
    i. Please tell me in more detail the dates, times, and locations of these events: _____

_____

_____

_____

_____

    ii. Why did you decide to hold these events?
    iii. Did you partner with any other organizations for this event?
    iv. How did you decide on this/these location(s)?
    v. How did you recruit people to staff this event? Did you use paid staff or volunteers?
    vi. Did you train the event staff or volunteers before the event?
    vii. Did you publicize the event? How?
    viii. Did you experience good turnout for these events? Which was your best attended? How many people would you say came to that event?

    ix. What was your least successful event? What would you say happened?

c. Distributing literature (ASK FOR COPIES OF LEAFLETS, FLYERS, DOOR HANGERS, OTHER)

    i. What kind of materials did you distribute?

    ii. Why did you decide to distribute _____?

    iii. Did you distribute these leaflets to people or did you leave them at their homes?

    iv. If in person:

      1. How did you decide where to distribute literature?

      2. Which streets, blocks, or neighborhoods in ___ have you covered so far? Which areas do you plan to cover by the election?

      3. How did you recruit people for these activities? Did you use paid staff or volunteers?

      4. Describe the typical person you sent out to distribute literature.

      5. Did you attempt to "match" the volunteers/staff to neighborhoods or have them work in their own neighborhoods?

      6. Did you train them?

      7. At what times of day or days of the week did these events take place?

      8. Did your workers find it difficult to get people to stop and talk?

      9. How did your workers pick the people they approached?

    v. If lit drop only:

      1. How did you decide where to distribute literature?

      2. Which streets, blocks, or neighborhoods in ___ have you covered so far? Which areas do you plan to cover by the election?

      3. How did you recruit people for these activities? Did you use paid staff or volunteers?

      4. Describe the typical person you sent out to distribute literature.

d. Direct Mail (*get copies of mailings*)

    i. Why did you decide to contact potential voters by mail?

    ii. How did you decide to whom to send mail?

    iii. Did you work with a company to design the mailers? Which company?

    iv. To whom have you sent mail so far? Do you plan to send mail to more potential voters by the election?

e. Telephone calls to citizens

    i. Did you pay an organization to conduct the calls or did your staff and volunteers make the calls? If your staff/volunteers conducted the calls, about how many people would you say worked on this effort?

    ii. Do you have office space for phone banking?

    iii. Did most of the calls take place from your office or from volunteers' homes?

    iv. About how many people would you say you contacted?

     v. How did you find contact information for the people you called? From voter registration lists? From a private company? Random digit dialing? Another source?

     vi. Were you trying to contact a particular group of voters with these calls—say, a particular demographic group or people living in a particular part of the city?

    vii. Now I'd like to ask about the content of the calls:

       1. Did you use a pre-recorded message? Who recorded the message?

       2. Did the callers have scripts?

       3. About how long does each call last?

f. Emails

     i. Did you pay an organization to write the emails or did your staff and volunteers send them?

     ii. About how many people would you say you contacted?

    iii. How did you find email addresses for the people you contacted?

    iv. Were you trying to contact a particular group of voters with these emails—say, college students, a particular demographic group or people living in a particular part of the city?

     v. About how often did you send emails?

     vi. May I have copies of the emails for the project records?

14. *For all "no" responses on Question 9: Open-ended:* Why didn't your organization pursue [activity]? Was cost a factor? Did not you believe this strategy was effective?

a. Canvassing

b. Other face to face outreach

c. Distributing literature

d. Direct mail

e. Phone calls

f. Emails

g. Voter registration drives

15. Have you tried any other activities to encourage people to vote? (Open ended)

For these last few questions, I'd like to get a sense of your experiences and observations as your organization conducted these events.

16. Are you worried about any factors that might depress turnout this year? What is your organization doing to address this (these)?

17. Which strategies did you find most effective in reaching potential voters?

18. Which strategies were least effective for contacting potential voters?

19. Have you noticed differences in which strategies are most effective across different neighborhoods or groups of people? For instance, does canvassing work better in certain kinds of neighborhoods?

That concludes the formal interview. I have no questions left, but if there's anything I left out or anything you'd like to clarify, please feel free to let me know now, or to contact me at [email] or [phone]. Do you mind if I photograph your offices, just to document your neighborhood location, before I leave?

Thank you very much for agreeing to participate in this process.

Table A.1: Descriptive statistics for 2008 Neighborhood Criminal Justice Involvement Data

	Minimum	Median	Mean	Standard Deviation	Maximum	N
North Carolina:						
Voter turnout 2008	0.010	0.628	0.614	0.165	0.998	4,948
Prisoners per square mile, squared	0.000	0.853	402.484	2,553.138	67,600.000	4,948
Prisoners per square mile	0.000	0.924	7.344	18.671	260.000	4,948
Proportion vacant housing units	0.021	0.122	0.142	0.091	0.895	4,948
Relative proportion noncitizen	0.000	0.240	0.529	0.795	6.260	4,948
Relative proportion unemployed	0.000	0.750	0.909	0.751	10.000	4,948
Median income (in 1,000s)	4.999	44.596	48.279	21.911	500.001	4,948
Ratio of females to males	0.331	0.513	0.516	0.027	0.652	4,948
Female high school completion rate	0.189	0.773	0.770	0.126	1.009	4,948
Proportion of adults under 25	0.024	0.110	0.115	0.046	0.663	4,948
Homicide rate	0.000	0.000	0.000	0.000	0.006	4,948
Proportion other minorities	0.000	0.000	0.000	0.000	0.001	4,948
Proportion black	0.000	0.141	0.225	0.229	0.995	4,948
Presence of ex-felon-serving institutions	0.000	0.000	0.072	0.258	1.000	4,948
Proportion Hispanic	0.000	0.039	0.069	0.092	0.861	4,948
Proportion in group quarters	0.000	0.000	0.012	0.031	0.199	4,948
Poverty rate	0.000	0.080	0.098	0.079	0.647	4,948
Georgia:						
Voter turnout 2008	0.011	0.486	0.489	0.152	0.992	4,536
Prisoners per square mile, squared	0.000	13.297	2,455.818	11,711.159	220,900.000	4,536
Prisoners per square mile	0.000	3.647	21.131	44.830	470.000	4,536

Proportion vacant housing units	0.006	0.132	0.142	0.068	0.763	4,536
Relative proportion noncitizen	0.000	0.210	0.571	0.951	6.830	4,536
Relative proportion unemployed	0.000	0.810	0.998	0.826	7.980	4,536
Median income (in 1,000s)	4.999	45.329	51.722	29.395	500.001	4,536
Ratio of females to males	0.308	0.514	0.517	0.031	0.658	4,536
Female high school completion rate	0.061	0.762	0.756	0.148	1.017	4,536
Proportion of adults under 25	0.009	0.122	0.129	0.049	0.764	4,536
Homicide rate	0.000	0.000	0.000	0.000	0.006	4,536
Proportion other minorities	0.000	0.000	0.000	0.000	0.003	4,536
Proportion black	0.000	0.238	0.340	0.291	0.997	4,536
Presence of ex-felon-serving institutions	0.000	0.000	0.083	0.276	1.000	4,536
Proportion Hispanic	0.000	0.032	0.067	0.100	0.881	4,536
Proportion in group quarters	0.000	0.000	0.011	0.031	0.196	4,536
Poverty rate	0.000	0.077	0.105	0.097	0.815	4,536

Table A.2: Means and standard deviations for original and matched data for models 1–6

	Means Treated	Means Control	Standard Deviation
Model 1:			
Summary of balance for all data:			
Distance	0.7205	0.2011	0.2282
Number of inmates sent to prison	2.6417	0.4291	0.7712
Proportion black	0.4321	0.2745	0.2577
Incarceration rate	0.0176	0.0094	0.012
Homicide rate	0.0001	0.0001	0.0004
Median income (in 1,000s)	46.4314	55.5278	33.0206
Proportion ages 18–25	0.1347	0.1246	0.0552
Summary of balance for matched data:			
Distance	0.9734	0.4911	0.2275
Number of inmates sent to prison	4.299	1.4183	0.7521
Proportion black	0.5259	0.3373	0.2927
Incarceration rate	0.0227	0.0133	0.0152
Homicide rate	0.0002	0.0001	0.0005
Median income (in 1,000s)	42.7892	49.4146	23.401
Proportion ages 18–25	0.1401	0.1304	0.0444
Model 2:			
Summary of balance for all data:			
Distance	0.7467	0.6018	0.1255
Number of inmates sent to prison	2.6417	1.4168	0.7511
Proportion black	0.4321	0.3376	0.2922
Incarceration rate	0.0176	0.0133	0.0153
Homicide rate	0.0001	0.0001	0.0005
Median income (in 1,000s)	46.4314	49.3514	23.3933
Proportion ages 18–25	0.1347	0.1311	0.046
Summary of balance for matched data:			
Distance	0.9202	0.6027	0.1248
Number of inmates sent to prison	4.299	1.4183	0.7521
Proportion black	0.5261	0.3373	0.2927
Incarceration rate	0.0226	0.0133	0.0152
Homicide rate	0.0002	0.0001	0.0005
Median income (in 1,000s)	42.9525	49.4146	23.401
Proportion ages 18–25	0.1399	0.1304	0.0444

(*continued*)

Table A.2: *continued*

	Means Treated	Means Control	Standard Deviation
Model 3:			
Summary of balance for all data:			
Distance	0.5864	0.194	0.1975
Number of inmates sent to prison	2.8508	0.6535	1.0228
Proportion black	0.4485	0.2898	0.2669
Incarceration rate	0.0182	0.0103	0.0128
Homicide rate	0.0002	0.0001	0.0004
Median income (in 1,000s)	46.1031	54.3562	32.0143
Proportion ages 18–25	0.1351	0.1259	0.0534
Summary of balance for matched Ddata:			
Distance	0.6507	0.3656	0.2181
Number of inmates sent to prison	3.1595	1.6197	1.0178
Proportion black	0.501	0.3534	0.2963
Incarceration rate	0.0201	0.0142	0.0156
Homicide rate	0.0002	0.0001	0.0004
Median income (in 1,000s)	43.6558	48.7405	23.7625
Proportion ages 18–25	0.137	0.1308	0.0415
Model 4:			
Summary of balance for all data:			
Distance	0.7838	0.2151	0.2406
Number of inmates sent to prison	3.0219	0.4343	0.7651
Proportion black	0.2744	0.1756	0.1928
Incarceration rate	0.0078	0.0035	0.0045
Homicide rate	0.0001	0.0001	0.0003
Median income (in 1,000s)	43.834	52.7028	25.9215
Proportion ages 18–25	0.1219	0.1091	0.0484
Summary of balance for matched data:			
Distance	0.9977	0.5231	0.2243
Number of inmates sent to prison	5.6118	1.4065	0.7277
Proportion black	0.3732	0.2186	0.2218
Incarceration rate	0.0121	0.005	0.0059
Homicide rate	0.0002	0.0001	0.0004
Median income (in 1,000s)	39.1349	46.5256	16.3185
Proportion ages 18–25	0.1302	0.1183	0.0443

(continued)

	Means Treated	Means Control	Standard Deviation
Model 5:			
Summary of balance for all data:			
Distance	0.8093	0.6465	0.1241
Number of inmates sent to prison	3.0219	1.4258	0.7399
Proportion black	0.2744	0.2153	0.22
Incarceration rate	0.0078	0.0049	0.0057
Homicide rate	0.0001	0.0001	0.0004
Median income (in 1,000s)	43.834	46.6604	16.101
Proportion ages 18–25	0.1219	0.1178	0.0439
Summary of balance for matched data:			
Distance	0.9827	0.6465	0.1241
Number of inmates sent to prison	5.728	1.4258	0.7399
Proportion black	0.3705	0.2153	0.22
Incarceration rate	0.0118	0.0049	0.0057
Homicide rate	0.0002	0.0001	0.0004
Median income (in 1,000s)	39.4642	46.6604	16.101
Proportion ages 18–25	0.1296	0.1178	0.0439
Model 6:			
Summary of balance for all data:			
Distance	0.6425	0.2296	0.2124
Number of inmates sent to prison	3.2558	0.7418	1.124
Proportion black	0.2823	0.188	0.2036
Incarceration rate	0.0082	0.004	0.005
Homicide rate	0.0001	0.0001	0.0003
Median income (in 1,000s)	43.5462	51.3187	24.6972
Proportion ages 18–25	0.1231	0.1105	0.0482
Summary of balance for matched data:			
Distance	0.8036	0.4069	0.2239
Number of inmates sent to prison	4.2184	1.725	1.1183
Proportion black	0.3137	0.2265	0.2258
Incarceration rate	0.0101	0.0056	0.0061
Homicide rate	0.0002	0.0001	0.0004
Median income (in 1,000s)	40.5916	45.9514	16.3819
Proportion ages 18–25	0.1284	0.1179	0.0453

Table A.3: Descriptive statistics for Charlotte sample of the 2000 Social Capital Benchmark Survey

Descriptive Statistic	Minimum	Median	Mean	Standard Deviation	Maximum	N
Dependent variables:						
Sense of community from neighbors	2	4	3.6384	0.747087	4	625
Divorced or separated	0	0	0.156473	0.363448	1	1,259
Political activity scale	0	3	2.676936	1.712856	8	1,201
Trust neighbors	1	3	3.246954	0.894848	4	1,231
Trust cops	1	4	3.348706	0.841585	4	1,236
Trust local government	1	1	1.532153	0.61476	3	1,073
Trust national government	1	1	1.372864	0.567981	3	995
Safety a barrier	1	1	1.996759	1.189779	4	617
Church membership	0	1	0.647059	0.478075	1	1,258
Trust people	1	1	1.890389	0.965573	3	1,259
Voter turnout	0	1	0.67101	0.470038	1	1,228
Times volunteered	0	2	9.166	16.021	60	1,262
Neighborhood-level:						
Prison density	0	1.111111	5.618963	11.86712	110	1,266
Percentage public assistance	0	0.012945	0.020418	0.026204	0.157525	1,266
Percentage foreign born	0	0.041477	0.062683	0.06737	0.448736	1,266
Homicide rate	0	0	0.000109	0.000358	0.002211	1,266
Poverty rate	0	0.060594	0.089026	0.083555	0.592391	1,266
Percentage unemployed	0	0.026504	0.03259	0.03615	0.488688	1,266
Median income (in 1,000s)	11.429	45.419	50.36809	24.28636	200.001	1,266

(continued)

Table A.3: *continued*

Descriptive Statistic	Minimum	Median	Mean	Standard Deviation	Maximum	N
Percentage noncitizen	0	0.026386	0.045336	0.057967	0.412874	1,266
Presence of ex-felon-serving institutions	0	0	0.029226	0.168506	1	1,266
Percentage in group quarters	0	0	0.017209	0.050289	0.596324	1,266
Percentage vacant	0.006803	0.057751	0.06678	0.039956	0.299663	1,266
Median age	16.2	35.7	35.94526	5.050439	54.9	1,266
Percentage high school grads	0.40625	0.824627	0.807712	0.126766	1	1,266
Percentage black	0	0.104793	0.184654	0.208521	0.96596	1,266
Individual-level:						
Gender	1	2	1.592417	0.491579	2	1,266
Ideology	1	3	2.684211	1.146781	6	1,235
Educational attainment	1	3	3.440826	1.745843	7	1,259
Income	0	3	3.187719	1.823615	6	1,140
Age	18	41	43.48519	15.98858	118	1,249
Hispanic	0	0	0.049719	0.217452	1	1,247
Black	0	0	0.182839	0.386689	1	1,247
Internet access	0	1	0.556962	0.496941	1	1,264
Political knowledge	1	1	2.085191	1.45856	5	1,256
Economic satisfaction	0	1	1.097056	0.637321	2	1,257
Days per week reading paper	0	3	3.441805	2.898094	7	1,263
Political interest	1	3	2.863492	0.96997	4	1,260

Notes

Chapter 1

1 X 1965: 186.
2 Abu-Jamal 2000: 21.
3 Dennis v. United States, 341 U.S. 494 (1951).
4 FBI involvement in the civil rights movement possessed both a passive and an active aspect. On the one hand, J. Edgar Hoover's directives forestalled investigations of abuses of civil rights workers. On the active front, the FBI's resources were bent toward the goal of surveillance of civil rights workers and, as the 1960s wore on, the infiltration of black militant groups (O'Reilly 1989).This effort included the infamous attempt to undermine the reputation of Martin Luther King and thereby damage the civil rights movement.
5 Bunche 1973.
6 *The Long Shadow of Jim Crow* 2005: 15.
7 *The Long Shadow of Jim Crow* 2005.
8 Conyers 2002.
9 Mauer 2006.
10 For the most part, this book focuses on punishment as supervision by authorities as a result of felony convictions—that is, on people sentenced to serve time in prison, on probation, or on parole under federal or state jurisdiction.
11 Travis 2004: 252.
12 Western, Pattillo, and Weiman 2004: 7.
13 Bonczar 2003.
14 Throughout this book, neighborhoods are defined as census block groups.
15 The national average incarceration rate is about 1 percent, but the average imprisonment rate is about 0.5 percent (author's calculations). The remainder are incarcerated in local and county jails and other facilities.
16 Verba, Schlozman, and Brady 1995.
17 Lynch and Sabol 2004b; Lynch et al. 2002.
18 Hannerz [1969] 2004; Kornhauser 1978; Verba and Nie 1972.
19 Bursik and Grasmick 1993; Sampson 1988; Sampson and Groves 1989; Shaw and McKay 1942.
20 Braman 2002; Huckfeldt and Sprague 1992; Rose and Clear 1998; Skocpol 1999.
21 Huckfeldt and Sprague 1992; Rosenstone and Hansen 1993.
22 Braman 2002; Edin, Nelson, and Paranal 2004; Foreman 2002; Holzer, Rafael, and Stoll 2004; Sampson and Groves 1989.
23 Guerino, Harrison, and Sabol 2011.
24 Glaze, 2011.
25 Glaze, 2011.
26 Glaze, 2011; Pettit 2012.

27 Bonczar 2003.

28 Evans, Rueschemeyer, and Skocpol 1985; Schneider and Ingram 1990; Skocpol 1992.

29 Bobo and Johnson 2004; Brown-Dean 2003; see also Gottschalk (2002) for a more extensive review; Peffley and Hurwitz 2010; Zimring 2001.

30 Manza and Uggen 2006.

31 Burch 2011.

32 Studies of the urban riots of the 1960s explicitly considered the role of the criminal justice system, most often law enforcement, in political mobilization. Efforts to understand the genesis of these events soon turned up a mixture of background causes and a common trigger. The background causes were (1) a general background of racial discrimination and housing and educational segregation, which led to economic and social inequality; (2) tense relationships with the police, which were often characterized by brutality and disrespect; and (3) a lack of political voice, such that complaints over 1 and 2 often fell on deaf ears. The triggering cause was often a relatively routine example of policing (Fogelson 1968; Kerner and Lindsay 1968). This pattern was largely followed in the Miami riot of 1980 (Porter and Dunn 1984) and in the Los Angeles riot following the failure to convict the police officers who had beaten Rodney King (Kennedy 1997). Based upon his analysis of the attributes of rioters, Paige (1971, 819) characterized the 1960s riots as "a form of disorganized political protest engaged in by those who have become highly distrustful of existing political institutions."

33 Kerner and Lindsay 1968; Sigelman et al. 1997; Tuch and Weitzer 1997.

34 But see Peffley and Hurwitz (2010) for a notable exception.

35 For instance, Skogan's (2005) analysis of results from a Chicago-based survey reveal the importance of timely assistance, cordial and clear communication concerning the case, and helpfulness in eliciting positive reviews of police by respondents. Eller et al. (2007) report similar results in a study of black and white university students in Britain, where high-quality contact moderated negative attitudes toward the police. Studies by Dean (1980) and Fairdosi (2009) find that dissatisfactory contacts with police produce negative attitudes.

36 Nozick 1974; Weber 1921.

37 Honig 1993.

38 Mauer 2006; B. Walker 2003.

39 Zimring 2001.

40 Farmer 2002; Baillargeon et al. 2004.

41 Sampson and Groves 1989; Rose and Clear 1998.

42 Western, Lopoo, and McClanahan 2004.

Chapter 2

1 Pateman 1970.

2 Pateman 1970; Rousseau 1987.

3 Rosenstone and Hansen 1993; Skocpol 1992; Verba, Schlozman, and Brady 1995; Wolfinger and Rosenstone 1980.

4 Almond and Verba 1963.

5 Skocpol 1992; Verba, Schlozman, and Brady 1995.

6 Almond and Verba 1963.

7 Pateman 1970.

8 Putnam 2000; Skocpol 1992.

9 Andrea Campbell 2003; Mettler 2005; Skocpol 1992.

10 Foucault 1999; Holzer, Rafael, and Stoll 2004; Manza and Uggen 2006; Pager and Quillian 2005; Wacquant 2001.

11 Mayer and Jencks 1989.

12 Harlow 2003.

13 Beck et al. 1993.

14 Guerino, Harrison, and Sabol 2011

15 Guerino, Harrison, and Sabol 2011.

16 Baillargeon et al. 2004; Krebs 2006; Massoglia 2008.

17 Ditton 1999.

18 *Correctional Populations in the United States* 2000.

19 Mumola 1999.

20 Mumola 1999.

21 Hochschild 1981.

22 Rousseau 1987: 159.

23 D. King and Waldron 1988.

24 Shklar 1991: 27.

25 Tocqueville 2000: 260.

26 Richardson v. Ramirez, 418 U.S. 24 (1974), Justice Marshall, dissenting.

27 Shklar 1991: 39.

28 Pateman 1970.

29 Tocqueville 2000: 228.

30 D. King and Waldron 1988: 440.

31 D. King and Waldron 1988: 419.

32 Mettler 2005: 119.

33 Wacquant 2001.

34 Holzer, Rafael, and Stoll 2004.

35 "The Disenfranchisement of Ex-Felons" 1989.

36 In Re E. L. Reid and E. O . Curtis 1896 (N.C. 1896), Justice Avery, dissenting.

37 Silber 2000.

38 In Re E. L. Reid and E. O . Curtis 1896, Justice Avery, dissenting.

39 Downs 1957.

40 Downs 1957; Verba and Nie 1972; Verba, Schlozman, and Brady 1995.

41 Downs 1957.

42 Uhlaner 1995.

43 Rosenstone and Hansen 1993.

44 Apart from posing a barrier to voting, periods of disfranchisement also impede the development of the "habit" of voting, which increases turnout. See Plutzer 2002; and Gerber, Green, and Shachar 2003.

45 Behrens, Uggen, and Manza 2003; Keyssar 2000.

46 Keyssar 2000.

47 Keyssar 2000.

48 Pettit 2012: 73.

49 Rosenstone and Hansen 1993; Wolfinger and Rosenstone 1980.

50 Fleisher and Decker 2001; Rosenstone and Hansen 1993; Squire, Wolfinger, and Glass 1987.

51 Piven and Cloward 2000.

52 Verba, Schlozman, and Brady 1995.

53 Rosenstone and Hansen 1993; Verba, Schlozman, and Brady 1995.

54 Verba, Schlozman, and Brady 1995. While educational attainment and other resources are correlated with most forms of participation, Verba, Schlozman, and Brady (1995, 359) note that "with the exception of vocabulary skill and family income, which have weak effects, resources play virtually no role for voting." Other turnout studies in the United States and other countries have found relationships between education and voting; however the models have little power to predict voter turnout any "more accurately than random guessing" See Matsusaka and Palda 1999.

55 Verba, Schlozman, and Brady 1995.

56 Holzer, Rafael, and Stoll 2004.

57 Holzer, Rafael, and Stoll 2004.

58 Pager and Quillian 2005.

59 21 U.S.C. § 862.

60 Western, Lopoo, and McLanahan 2004; see also 42 U.S.C. § 1437(d).

61 Abu-Jamal 1995: 12.

62 Holzer, Rafael, and Stoll 2004.

63 Fleisher and Decker 2001.

64 Soss 1999: 364.

65 Mettler 2005: 13.

66 Soss 1999: 366.

67 Soss 1999: 366.

68 Soss 1999: 366.

69 Wacquant 2001.

70 Mettler 2005: 110.

71 Abu-Jamal 1995: 105.

72 Manza and Uggen 2006.

73 Kerner and Lindsay 1968; Manza and Uggen 2006.

74 Hochschild 1981.

75 Davis 2003: 71.

76 Mauer 2006.

77 Bonczar 2003.

78 *Sourcebook of Criminal Justice Statistics Online* 2009.

79 Bonczar 2003.

80 Durose and Langan 2007.

81 Lundman and Kaufman 2003; Schmitt and Durose 2006.

82 Correll et al. 2007.

83 Whren v. United States, 517 U.S. 806 (1996).

84 Bates 2010; Lundman and Kaufman 2003; Schmitt, Langan, and Durose 2002; Schmitt and Durose 2006.

85 Powell 2006.

86 The federal law concerning crack cocaine sentencing has just been modified. Whereas, previously, possession of just 5 grams of crack would trigger criminal penalties similar to those for possession of 500 grams of powder cocaine, this figure has now been raised to 28 grams (Bazinet 2010).

87 Mauer 2006.

88 Herbert 2010.

89 D. Harris 1997.

90 Vitello 2006.

91 Kofman 2007.

92 Maricopa County Sheriff's Office 2011.

93 "Illegal Checkpoints?" 2010.

94 D. Harris 1999.

95 Albonetti 1997; Barnes and Kingsnorth 1996; Beaulieu and Messner 1999; Boerner and Lieb 2001; Bushway and Morrison 2001; Crawford, Chiricos, and Kleck 1998; Engen et al. 2003; Foley, Adams, and Goodson 1996; Free 1997; Gross and Mauro 1984; Hebert 1997; Kautt and Spohn 2002; Klepper, Nagin, and Tierney 1983; J. Kramer and Steffensmeir 1993; Kupchik and Harvey 2007; Mazzella and Feingold 1994; Petersilia 1985; Pfeifer and Ogloff 1991; Radelet 1981; Schwartz and Milovanovic 1996; Sommers and Ellsworth 2000; Spohn 1990; Spohn, DeLone, and Spears 1998; Spohn and Holleran 2000; Spohn and Spears 1996; Steffensmeier and Demuth 2001; Steffensmeier, Ulmer, and Kramer 1998; Tinker, Quiring, and Pimentel 1985; Tonry 1995; Urbina 2003; Walsh 1985; Weitzer 1996; Zatz 1987.

96 Albonetti 1997.

97 Steffensmeier and Demuth 2000.

98 Bushway and Morrison 2001; Humphrey and Fogarty 1987; Paternoster et al. 2003; Rodriguez 2003; Thomson and Zingraff 1981. For more extensive reviews, see Sweeney and Haney 1992; Pratt 1998; and McDougall et al. 2003.

99 Verba and Nie 1972.

100 Burbank 1997; Angus Campbell et al. 1960; Foldare 1968; Huckfeldt 1979.

101 Verba and Nie 1972: 229.

102 Nagler 1991; Piven and Cloward 2000; Wolfinger and Rosenstone 1980.

103 Gimpel, Dyck, and Shaw 2004; Huckfeldt 1979; Lazarsfeld, Berelson, and Gaudet [1944] 1968; Tam-Cho, Gimpel, and Dyck 2006.

104 Verba and Nie 1972: 229.

105 Huckfeldt 1979: 581.

106 Fagan, West, and Holland 2004.

107 Travis 2004: 252.

108 Travis 2004: 252.

109 Travis 2004: 252.

110 Lynch and Sabol 2004a; Lynch et al. 2002.

111 Mayer and Jencks 1989: 1442.

112 M. Johnson, Shively, and Stein 2002.

113 Hannerz [1969] 2004: 384.

114 Mayer and Jencks 1989.

115 Alexander 2011; Burch 2007.

116 Angus Campbell et al. 1960; Tam-Cho, Gimpel, and Dyck 2006: 156.

117 Angus Campbell et al. 1960; Straits 1990.

118 Tyler and Huo 2002.

119 Rose and Clear 1998.

120 Rose and Clear 1998.

121 Edin, Nelson, and Paranal 2004.

122 Braman 2002.

123 Cohen and Dawson find that living in an impoverished neighborhood decreases the probability that a person will belong to a church or other voluntary organization. Residence in a high-poverty neighborhood (where more than 20 percent of residents live below the poverty line) decreases the likelihood that an individual will talk about politics, attend public meetings, or give money to candidates.

124 Huckfeldt and Sprague 1992.

125 Bursik and Grasmick 1993; Kornhauser 1978; Sampson 1988; Shaw and McKay 1942.

126 Hannerz [1969] 2004: 180. As used here, the term "deviant" seems to connote irrationality. However, "deviant," as used in this context, is less loaded and refers mostly to attitudes that are not mainstream, regardless of their rationality or source (Kornhauser 1978). The term "cultural deviance" is used not to cause controversy, but merely to remain consistent with a long sociological literature that describes the processes at hand.

127 Kornhauser 1978.

128 Lewis 1969: 188.

129 Massey and Denton 1993.

130 Verba and Nie 1972: 229.

131 Kornhauser 1978.

132 Hannerz [1969] 2004: 185.

133 W. Wilson 1987: 61.

134 Cohen 1999; Dawson 2001; Harris-Lacewell 2004.

135 Clark [1965] 1989: 13.

136 Clark [1965] 1989: 13.

137 As more and more community members experience hostile interactions with police, for instance, "a level of hostility between police and communities of color that undermines community support for crime fighting" develops (Foreman 2002: 158–59).

138 Angus Campbell et al. 1960; Verba and Nie 1972; Verba, Schlozman, and Brady 1995.

139 Skogan 2005; Tyler 2006.

140 Tyler 2006; Tyler and Huo 2002.

141 Abu-Jamal 1995; Manza and Uggen 2006.

142 Mettler 2005.

143 Andrea Campbell 2003.

144 W. Wilson 1996: 75.

145 Foreman 2002: 63; W. Wilson 1996.

146 Angus Campbell et al. 1960; Tam-Cho, Gimpel, and Dyck 2006: 156.

147 Angus Campbell et al. 1960; Straits 1990.

148 D. Johnson 2008.

149 Bobo and Thompson 2006; Eller et al. 2007; Skogan 2005; Tyler 2006; Tyler and Huo 2002.

150 Peffley and Hurwitz 2010.

151 Kornhauser 1978; Morenoff, Sampson, and Raudenbush 2001; J. Wilson and Kelling 1982.

152 Bursik and Grasmick 1993; Kornhauser 1978; Sampson 1988; Shaw and McKay 1942.

153 W. Wilson 1996: 61–62.

154 Sampson 1988.

155 Richie 2002.

156 Rose and Clear 1998.

157 Austin 2004.

158 Braman 2002.

159 Foreman 2002.

160 W. Wilson 1996: 63.

161 Skocpol 1992; Skogan 1990.

162 Skogan 1990: 24.

163 Morenoff and Sampson 1997.

164 Wacquant and Wilson 1989.

165 Stoloff, Glanville, and Bienenstock 1999.

166 W. Wilson 1987: 144.

167 W. Wilson 1987: 144.

168 Putnam 2000; Skocpol 1992, 1999; Skogan 1989; Tocqueville 2000; Verba, Schlozman, and Brady 1995; W. Wilson 1987, 1996.

169 Rose and Clear 1998.

170 Rose and Clear 1998: 450.

171 Travis 2004: 253.

172 Braman 2002.

173 Holzer, Rafael, and Stoll 2004; Pager and Quillian 2005; Western, Kling, and Weiman 2001.

174 W. Wilson 1996: 113.

175 W. Wilson 1996.

176 W. Wilson 1996.

177 Putnam 2000; W. Wilson 1996.

178 Braman 2002.

179 Western, Lopoo, and McLanahan 2004.

180 Edin, Nelson, and Paranal 2004.

181 Richie 2002.

182 Rubenstein and Mukamal 2002.

183 Angus Campbell et al. 1960; Huckfeldt, Plutzer, and Sprague 1993; Verba and Nie 1972; Verba, Schlozman, and Brady 1995; W. Wilson 1987: 56.

184 Alex-Assensoh 2001; Harris-Lacewell 2004; F. Harris 1994.

185 Cohen and Dawson 1993.

186 Alex-Assensoh 1997; Cohen and Dawson 1993.

187 Huckfeldt and Sprague 1992.

188 Huckfeldt and Sprague 1992.

189 Gerber and Green 2000; Green, Gerber, and Nickerson 2003; Rosenstone and Hansen 1993.

190 Huckfeldt and Sprague 1987.

191 Huckfeldt and Sprague 1992.

192 Burbank 1997; Foldare 1968; Huckfeldt and Sprague 1987.

193 Mayhew 1974.

194 Mendelberg 2001.

195 Schneider and Ingram 1997.

196 Cassidy 1998.

197 Cassidy 1998.

198 Putnam 2000; J. Wilson and Kelling 1982.

199 Putnam 2000; Rosenfeld, Messner, and Baumer 2001.

200 Foreman 2002; Putnam 2000; Rosenfeld, Messner, and Baumer 2001.

201 M. Johnson, Shively, and Stein 2002.

202 Massey and Denton 1993: 149.

203 See Fagan, West, and Holland (2004) for a notable exception.

204 Austin 2004.

Chapter 3

1 Moore 2007.

2 "General Social Survey" 2006.

3 "General Social Survey" 2006.

4 "African American Men Survey" 2006.

5 Cose et al. 2000.

6 Cose et al. 2000.

7 Cose et al. 2000.

8 Block groups are the smallest level of aggregation for which data on population size were available for 2008 and thus represent "communities" in this analysis. According to the Census Bureau, block groups typically contain 300 to 3,000 people, with an optimum size of 1,500 ("Glossary of Geographic Terms" 2007). The choice of block groups as the unit of analysis matters in spatial analysis because of three well-known problems: boundary, scale, and modifiable area units (Chou 1997). The boundary problem refers to how different choices with respect to boundaries (block groups instead of blocks) can lead to different statistical relationships depending on the data. For instance, a pattern of imprisonment may appear dispersed if one is looking at one block, but clustered if one enlarges the picture to include four other blocks in which no one is imprisoned. The scale problem refers to the fact that spatial descriptive statistics can vary as increasingly aggregated units are used. Thus, the community supervision rate for an area may be different when measured at the census tract level as opposed to the block group level. The problem of modifiable are units refers to the fact that units may be aggregated differently (for instance, the assignment of census blocks to block groups may be arbitrary, although they are contiguous) and that different patterns of aggregation may result in different statistical results.

9 The data used for the analysis of the 2000 Social Capital Benchmark Survey presented in chap. 5 come from the 2000 census.

10 U.S. Census Bureau 2010.

11 Scan/US 2008.

12 Geolytics 2011.

13 In 2008, federal courts commenced 2,437 cases against criminal defendants in North Carolina and 2,271 in Georgia (Administrative Office of the United States Courts 2008). Although comparable data on the number of felony cases commenced by state authorities are not available, similar data on admissions to supervision show that in 2006, more than 90,000 people were admitted to state prison or probation in GA and more than 80,000 in North Carolina (*Sourcebook of Criminal Justice Statistics Online* 2009, "Table 6.3.2006," "Table 6.0009.2008").

14 These data were also obtained for 2000 and are used in the analysis of the 2000 Social Capital Benchmark Survey presented in chap. 5.

15 Levitt 2004. The Georgia Department of Public Health also provided a measure of emergency room discharges resulting from intentional nonfatal injuries.

16 Holzer, Rafael, and Stoll 2004; Pager and Quillian 2005.

17 *Bureau of Justice Statistics (BJS) Total Correctional Population* 2011; *USA Quick Facts from the US Census Bureau* 2011.

18 West, Sabol, and Greenman 2010.

19 Glaze, Bonczar, and Zhang 2010.

20 D. Harris 1997, 1999; Herbert 2010.

21 Kleck 1981; Peterson and Hagan 1984; Tucker 2002.

22 Again, see Sweeney and Haney (1992); Pratt (1998); and McDougall et al. (2003) for more extensive reviews.

23 Demuth and Steffensmeier 2004.

24 It is unlikely that this relationship differs in states with larger Latino populations. The 2008 Neighborhood Criminal Justice Involvement Data contain information on inmate releases and community supervision in Florida. The correlations between the Hispanic percentage of the population and probationers and parolees per square mile and inmate releases per square mile are quite low (Pearson's R = 0.0706 and 0.0039, respectively).

25 "Estimated Number and Rate . . . of Sentenced Prisoners" 2009.

26 Fagan, West, and Holland 2004; Lynch and Sabol 2004b; Lynch et al. 2002; Travis 2004.

27 Alesina, Baqir, and Hoxby 2004: 360.

Chapter 4

1 Gonzalez 1997.

2 Flynn 1994.

3 Hierarchical linear models yield similar predictions.

4 Further testing supports the claim that these relationships are not the result of bias from outliers, spatial autocorrelation, or omitted variables.

5 Some addresses were masked in the data at the voters' request, while some cast absentee ballots from locations outside their respective states.

6 Defined here as the percent percentage of households with incomes under $10,000.

7 Cohen and Dawson 1993; Foldare 1968; G. King, Keohane, and Verba 1994; Mayer and Jencks 1989; Morenoff, Sampson, and Raudenbush 2001; Plutzer 2002; Sampson and Groves 1989; Straits 1990; Verba, Schlozman, and Brady 1995; Campbell, 1960.

8 Angus Campbell et al. 1960; Verba and Nie 1972; Verba, Schlozman, and Brady 1995.

9 These proportions do not sum to 1; they represent the proportions that are US born, naturalized, and noncitizen relative to the national average for each block group.

10 There are sex differences in voter turnout, and imprisonment helps shape the sex ratio of a block group (Braman 2002). For these reasons, it is important to include the male-to-female ratio in the models.

11 The analysis uses the R package "betareg."

12 Coefficients predicted using a hierarchical linear model with random intercepts demonstrate the same sign and statistical significance, although the effect sizes change. For Georgia, the coefficient on prisoner density is -7.892×10^{-5}, $t = -1.620$. For North Carolina, the coefficient of prisoner density is 4.567×10^{-4}, $t = 4.353$.

13 Coefficients predicted using a hierarchical linear model with random intercepts demonstrate the same sign and statistical significance, although the effect sizes change. For Georgia, the coefficient of prisoner density squared is 7.864×10^{-7}, $t = 2.435$, and prisoner density is -3.052×10^{-4}, $t = -2.91$. For North Carolina, the coefficient of prisoner density squared is -6.161×10^{-6}, $t = 4.846$, and prisoner density is 1.359×10^{-3}, $t = 6.362$.

14 For North Carolina, the curvilinear model improves on the linear model: the log-likelihood increases from 4300.11 for the linear model to 4315.32 for the curvilinear model, while the AIC declines from −8368.22 for the linear model to −8396.637 for the curvilinear model. In Georgia, the curvilinear model offers only a slight improvement: the log-likelihood increases from 3860.66 to 3862.14, while the AIC declines from −7375.33 for the linear model to −7376.28 for the curvilinear model.

15 G. King, Tomz, and Wittenberg 2000. Predicted probabilities and expected values for this section were simulated using the author's own code.

16 The prisoner density was set at 250 prisoners per square mile in order to present the data for the two states in a comparable way.

17 Community supervision seems to have little effect on turnout in North Carolina; much of the effect seems to be driven by imprisonment. For instance, in a model that replaces the prisoner density and prisoner density squared with the total supervision density and total supervision density squared (total supervision density = prisoners + probationers + parolees per square mile), going from a block group with no supervised offenders to a block group with 250 offenders per square mile decreases expected voter turnout by 11.6 percent.

18 Moran's I = 0.00463 in Georgia, and Moran's I = .0070 in North Carolina for the curvilinear models; however, both are statistically significantly different from the expected value of 0 at $p < .001$. Typically, Moran's I ranges from −1 to +1, with negative values representing dispersion and positive values indicating clustering.

19 Typically, these neighborhoods have some demographic oddity with respect to voting—they have abnormally high vacancy or group quarters rates or a large number of ineligible noncitizens. While the analysis does exclude neighborhoods with the highest levels of these phenomena, the criteria for exclusion are not so strict as to exclude them all. This decision avoids the issue of cherry-picking the data to skew the results in favor of the hypothesis.

20 Ramsey 1969; W. Kramer and Sonnberger 1986.

21 Hahn, Todd, and Klaauw 2001; Thistlethwaite and Campbell 1960.

22 One potential problem with this research design concerns discerning intent-to-treat effects from the average treatment effect. To take an extreme example, neighborhoods that have had individuals sentenced to prison the day before election day have received the treatment in theory, but if the effects take longer than twenty-four hours to manifest themselves, then there will be no measurable treatment effect. In this analysis, 6 percent of block groups in the sample had prisoners who were convicted less than a week before the election.

23 The introduction of early voting may bias the estimates of the treatment effect toward zero. Both Georgia and North Carolina allowed early voting for the 2008 general election—Georgia in late September and North Carolina beginning in mid-October. Early voting does not affect control groups that did not experience an imprisonment prior to election day. However, early voting may affect the treated groups, causing this analysis to *underestimate* the extent to which imprisonment affects neighborhood voter turnout. If an imprisonment occurred after the beginning of early voting, it may have taken place after some individuals in the surrounding community had already voted. Thus, people who might have been prevented from voting on election day due to imprisonment appear in the data as having voted because they cast their ballots early. In this sense, the full treatment effect is masked by early voting and cannot be expressed; because of early voting, the estimates of the treatment effects are biased toward zero.

24 Verba, Schlozman, and Brady 1995.

25 Fishman 1990.

26 Austin 2004; Fleisher and Decker 2001.

27 Peffley and Hurwitz 2010.

28 Ho, Imai, and King 2007.

29 Morgan and Harding 2006.

30 Ho, Imai, and King 2007; G. King and Zeng 2006.

31 The sample was drawn using Random Digit Dialing of area codes and exchanges in the area. The survey's response rate for this area is reported as 25 percent.

32 Individual-level information on criminal justice involvement is not available in this data set. Although we know that respondents are not in prison at the time of the survey, they may be on probation or parole or even disfranchised. This phenomenon has the potential to bias estimates of registration and turnout downward. However, factors such as group membership, volunteering, or other forms of political activity should be less affected by the status of the individual respondent. With respect to the presence of ex-felons more generally, at the neighborhood level, the presence of residential reentry facilities, halfway houses, shelters, and other ex-felon-serving organizations are meant to account for the potential bias that might result from an unusually high ex-felon presence at the neighborhood level. Also, it is important to remember that the analysis in the previous section helps alleviate this concern by comparing neighborhoods with similar imprisonment profiles to one another.

33 Verba, Schlozman, and Brady 1995; Morenoff, Sampson, and Raudenbush 2001; Plutzer 2002; Angus Campbell et al. 1960; Straits 1990.

34 Clear 2007, 2002.

35 Burch 2011.

Chapter 5

1 Verba, Schlozman, and Brady 1995.

2 Hannerz [1969] 2004: 180.

3 Kornhauser 1978.
4 Angus Campbell et al. 1960.
5 Huckfeldt 1979.
6 M. Johnson, Shively, and Stein 2002.
7 Abu-Jamal 1995; Manza and Uggen 2006.
8 Hochschild 1981.
9 Hetherington 2005: 9.
10 Citrin and Green 1986; Hetherington 1998; Mishler and Rose 1997; Weatherford 1987.
11 Hetherington 2005.
12 Abramson and Finifter 1981; Citrin 1974; Levi and Stoker 2000.
13 Orren 1997.
14 J. Avery 2007; Howell and Fagan 1988; Mansbridge 1999; Rahn and Rudolph 2005.
15 Bayley and Mendelsohn 1968; Gabbidon and Higgins 2009; Hurwitz and Peffley 2005; Tuch and Weitzer 1997.
16 Chanely, Rudolph, and Rahn 2000; Hetherington 2005; Levi and Stoker 2000.
17 Morrell 2003: 589.
18 Angus Campbell et al. 1960; Rosenstone and Hansen 1993.
19 Sampson and Groves 1989.
20 Sampson and Groves 1989.
21 Bursik and Grasmick 1993; Kornhauser 1978; Shaw and McKay 1942.
22 Edin, Nelson, and Paranal 2004.
23 Austin 2004.
24 Western 2006; Western, Lopoo, and McLanahan 2004.
25 Lynch and Sabol 2004a.
26 Lynch and Sabol 2004b.
27 Rosenberg 1956.
28 Leigh 2006; Ross, Mirowsky, and Pribesh 2001; P. Taylor, Funk, and Clark 2007.
29 Brehm and Rahn 1997; Rahn et al. 2009; Smith 2010; P. Taylor, Funk, and Clark 2007; Uslaner 2002.
30 B. Simpson, McGrimmon, and Irwin 2007.
31 The models control at the individual level: age, race, gender, ideology, educational attainment, political knowledge, political interest, newspaper reading, Internet access, economic satisfaction, and income; at the neighborhood level: median income, percent receiving public assistance, poverty rate, unemployment rate, percent vacant housing units, ex-inmate serving institutions, homicide rate, median age, citizenship, percent black black percentage of the population, Hispanic percentage, and percentage of the population in group quarters.
32 Lynch and Sabol 2004a.
33 Rosenstone and Hansen 1993.
34 Brady, Verba, and Schlozman 1995.

35 Brady, Verba, and Schlozman 1995.
36 Brady, Verba, and Schlozman 1995.
37 Brehm and Rahn 1997.
38 Huckfeldt and Sprague 1992.
39 The models control at the individual level age, race, gender, ideology, educational attainment, political knowledge, political interest, newspaper reading, Internet access, economic satisfaction, and income; and at the neighborhood level, median income, percentage receiving public assistance, poverty rate, unemployment rate, percentage of housing units that are vacant, presence of ex-inmate-serving institutions, homicide rate, median age, citizenship, black percentage of the population, Hispanic percentage, and percentage of the population in group quarters.
40 Rose and Clear 1998.
41 Rose and Clear 1998.
42 R. Johnson 2009.
43 Braman 2002.
44 Cose et al. 2000.
45 Verba, Schlozman, and Brady 1995.
46 The models control at the individual level age, race, gender, ideology, educational attainment, political knowledge, political interest, newspaper reading, Internet access, economic satisfaction, and income; and at the neighborhood level, median income, percent receiving public assistance, poverty rate, unemployment rate, percentage of housing units that are vacant, ex-inmate-serving institutions, homicide rate, median age, citizenship, black percentage of the population, Hispanic percentage, and percentage of the population in group quarters.
47 Mettler 2005; Mettler and Soss 2004; Soss 1999; Tyler and Huo 2002.
48 Rose and Clear 2004.
49 D. Johnson 2008.
50 Bobo and Thompson 2006; Eller et al. 2007; Skogan 2005; Tyler 2006; Tyler and Huo 2002.
51 Peffley and Hurwitz 2010.
52 Some might argue that the relevant explanatory factor is safety: people in high-imprisonment communities might feel less safe than people in low-imprisonment communities. Controlling for crime rates and the presence of ex-felons in the models helps alleviate some concerns that this is in fact the mechanism at work. However, the Social Capital Benchmark Survey also provides evidence that imprisonment does not decrease political participation by creating safety concerns. In the battery of questions on barriers to community participation, respondents are asked whether "concerns for your safety" are "a very important obstacle, somewhat important, or not at all important" to being as involved in their communities as they would like. As shown in table 5.5, neighborhood prisoner density was not a significant predictor of responses to this question.

53 Soss 1999; Sampson and Bartusch 1998.
54 Rose and Clear 2004.
55 One should also note that lack of statistical significance of particular control variables in my models of attitudes should not be taken to mean that those individual or neighborhood characteristics have no effect. Ascertaining the effects of education on political trust, for instance, requires a different model with different variables. The lack of statistical significance of the control variables merely signals that there is no direct effect of that control variable once others are included (G. King 1986).
56 Variable constructed by geocoding valid street addresses or nine-digit zip codes for organizations with National Taxonomy of Exempt Organizations codes N, O, S, and X from the Internal Revenue Service list of tax-exempt organizations.

Chapter 6

1 The names have been changed for confidentiality.
2 As Galvin (2009) notes, this may reflect a tendency of parties out of power to mobilize new voters.
3 Riker and Ordeshook 1968; Uhlaner 1995: 70–71.
4 Piven and Cloward 2000.
5 See Gerber, Green, and Larimer (2008) for a discussion of the effectiveness of shame in promoting turnout.
6 Rosenstone and Hansen 1993; Verba, Schlozman, and Brady 1995.
7 Squire, Wolfinger, and Glass 1987.
8 For instance, in North Carolina, the law requires the board of elections to periodically send confirmation mailings to voters that, if not returned, may result in purging from the voter registration rolls (North Carolina State Board of Elections 2008).
9 Skocpol and Fiorina 1999.
10 Hansen 1985; Skocpol 1992.
11 Hansen 1985; Olson 1965.
12 Aldrich 1993.
13 Verba, Schlozman, and Brady 1995.
14 Green and Gerber 2008.
15 Gerber and Green 2000; Green and Gerber 2008; Green, Gerber, and Nickerson 2003; Michelson 2003.
16 Nickerson 2007.
17 Nickerson 2007.
18 Green and Gerber 2008; however, see Dale and Strauss (2009) for evidence that text messaging increases voter turnout.
19 Etling, Faris, and Palfrey 2010.
20 Addonizio, Green, and Glaser 2007.
21 Green and Gerber 2008.
22 Rosenstone and Hansen 1993.

23 Verba, Schlozman, and Brady 1995.

24 M. Avery 1989; Kernell and Jacobson 2000; Rosenstone and Hansen 1993.

25 M. Avery 1989: 13.

26 Rosenstone and Hansen 1993: 218.

27 Goldstein and Ridout 2002: 21–22.

28 See Weilhouwer and Lockerbie (1994) for a contrasting view.

29 Huckfeldt 1979; Leighley 2001.

30 Frymer 1999; Leighley 2001.

31 Huckfeldt 1979.

32 Anderson 2008.

33 Huckfeldt 1979; Leighley 2001.

34 Anderson 2008.

35 Green and Gerber 2008.

36 Sampson et al. 2005.

37 Piven and Cloward 2000.

38 Green and Gerber 2008.

39 The names have been changed to protect anonymity.

40 Verba and Nie 1972; Verba, Schlozman, and Brady 1995; Wolfinger and Rosenstone 1980.

41 Green and Gerber 2008: 37.

42 Ramirez 2005.

43 The Mecklenburg County Republicans also held celebrity events. However, for them, events in Charlotte were less successful. Rallies with surrogates from out of state like Mike Huckabee were well attended, but useful only "for exciting the activists to work harder . . . generally we didn't find it a good way to attract new people" according to the party interviewee from that city.

Chapter 7

1 Weber 1921.

2 Uggen, Manza, and Thompson 2006: 313.

3 Verba, Schlozman, and Brady 1995.

4 Fiorina 1999.

5 Hill and Leighley 1992.

6 Clark [1965] 1989; Massey and Denton 1993.

7 Ansolabehere and Snyder 2003.

8 Reynolds v. Sims, 377 U.S. 533 (1964).

9 Reynolds v. Sims, 377 U.S. 533 (1964) (opinion of the court).

10 Cohen 1999.

11 Skogan 1990.

12 Kennedy 1998.

13 Cohen 2009. But see also Pettit (2012), which questions that these improvements even exist.

14 Manza and Uggen 2004.

15 Fellner and Mauer 1998.
16 Fellner and Mauer 1998.
17 Demeo and Ochoa 2003.
18 Demeo and Ochoa 2003.
19 "U.S. Census Bureau Report" 2006.
20 Huling 2002: 210.
21 Prison Policy Initiative 2011.
22 Huling 2002: 210.
23 Pettit 2012.
24 Western 2006.
25 Western 2006.
26 Western 2006.
27 Hamilton, Madison, and Jay [1787] 1982.
28 Bayley and Mendelsohn 1968; Dean 1980; Jacob 1971; D. Walker et al. 1972.
29 Skogan 2005.
30 Eller et al. 2007.
31 Dean 1980.
32 H. Taylor 2000.
33 Hispanic respondents, in this survey, have response patterns similar to white respondents.
34 Pew Research 2010.
35 Bobo and Thompson 2006, 457.
36 Bobo and Thompson 2006, 457.
37 United States National Advisory Commission on Civil Disorders 1968.
38 "Crime in America" 1995.
39 "NCSC Sentencing Attitudes Survey" 2006.
40 "NCSC Sentencing Attitudes Survey" 2006.
41 "Chronic Mental Illness" 1989.
42 "Chronic Mental Illness" 1989.
43 A. Simpson 1987.
44 Wolfe 1992. For another example, see Shear and Santana (1996).
45 Shear and Santana 1996; Wolfe 1992.
46 Fletcher 1999.
47 Clear 2007: 124.
48 Clear 2007: 124.
49 Sampson and Groves 1989.
50 Brehm and Rahn 1997.
51 Bobo and Johnson 2004; Brown-Dean 2003; Zimring 2001; see Gottschalk (2002) for a more extensive review.
52 Rousseau 1987.

References

Abramson, Paul R., and Ada W. Finifter. 1981. "On the Meaning of Political Trust: New Evidence from Items Introduced in 1978." *American Journal of Political Science* 25:297–307.

Abu-Jamal, Mumia. 1995. *Live from Death Row*. Reading, PA: Addison-Wesley.

———. 2000. *All Things Censored*. Edited by N. Hanrahan. New York: Seven Stories Press.

Addonizio, Elizabeth M., Donald P. Green, and James M. Glaser. 2007. "Putting the Party Back into Politics." *PS: Political Science and Politics* 40:721–27.

Administrative Office of the United States Courts. 2008. "Table E-2, Persons under Supervision." Accessed June 21, 2010. http://www.uscourts.gov/uscourts/Statistics/FederalJudicialCaseloadStatistics/2008/tables/E02Mar08.pdf.

"African American Men Survey." 2006. Dataset, Henry J. Kaiser Family Foundation, Harvard University, and the Washington Post.

Albonetti, Celesta A. 1997. "Sentencing under the Federal Sentencing Guidelines: Effects of Defendant Characteristics, Guilty Pleas, and Departures on Sentence Outcomes for Drug Offenses, 1991–1992." *Law and Society Review* 31:789–822.

Aldrich, John H. 1993. "Rational Choice and Turnout." *American Journal of Political Science* 37:246–78.

Alesina, Alberto, Reza Baqir, and Caroline Hoxby. 2004. "Political Jurisdictions in Heterogeneous Communities." *Journal of Political Economy* 112:348–96.

Alexander, Michelle. 2011. *The New Jim Crow*. New York: New Press.

Alex-Assensoh, Yvette. 1997. "Race, Concentrated Poverty, Social Isolation, and Political Behavior." *Urban Affairs Review* 33:209–27.

———. 2001. "Inner-City Contexts, Church Attendance, and African-American Political Participation." *Journal of Politics* 63:886–901.

Almond, Gabriel, and Sidney Verba. 1963. *The Civic Culture*. Princeton: Princeton University Press.

Anderson, Kristi. 2008. "In Whose Interest? Political Parties, Context, and the Incorporation of Immigrants." Pp. 17–38 in *New Race Politics in America*, edited by J. Junn and K. L. Haynie. New York: Cambridge University Press.

Ansolabehere, Stephen, and James M. Snyder. 2003. "Party Control of State Government and the Distribution of Public Expenditures." Massachusetts Institute of Technology Department of Economics Working Paper Series. http://dspace.mit.edu/bitstream/handle/1721.1/64050/partycontrolofstooanso.pdf?sequence=1

Austin, Regina. 2004. "The Shame of It All: Stigma and the Political Disenfranchisement of Formerly Convicted and Incarcerated Persons." *Columbia Human Rights Law Review* 36:173–92.

Avery, James M. 2007. "Race, Partisanship, and Political Trust Following Bush versus Gore (2000)." *Political Behavior* 29:327–42.

Avery, Michael J. 1989. *The Demobilization of American Voters: A Comprehensive Theory of Voter Turnout.* New York: Greenwood.

Baillargeon, Jacques, Sandra A. Black, Charles T. Leach, Hal Jenson, John Pulvino, Patrick Bradshaw, and Owen Murray. 2004. "The Infectious Disease Profile of Texas Prison Inmates." *Preventive Medicine* 38:607–12.

Barnes, Carole Wolff, and Rodney Kingsnorth. 1996. "Race, Drugs, and Criminal Sentencing: Hidden Effects of the Criminal Law." *Journal of Criminal Justice* 24:39–55.

Bates, Timothy. 2010. "Driving While Black in Suburban Detroit." *Du Bois Review* 7, no. 1 (2010): 133–50.

Bayley, David H., and Harold Mendelsohn. 1968. *Minorities and the Police: Confrontation in America.* New York: Free Press.

Bazinet, Kenneth R. 2010. "President Obama Signs Bill Reducing Gap in Cocaine Sentences." *New York Daily News,* August 4.

Beaulieu, Mark, and Steven F. Messner. 1999. "Race, Gender, and Outcomes in First Degree Murder Cases." *Journal of Poverty* 3:47–68.

Beck, Allen, Darrell Gilliard, Lawrence Greenfeld, Caroline Harlow, Thomas Hester, Louis Jankowski, Tracy Snell, James Stephan, and Danielle Morton. 1993. *Survey of State Prison Inmates, 1991.* Washington, DC: Bureau of Justice Statistics. http://bjs.ojp.usdoj.gov/content/pub/pdf/SOSPI91.pdf.

Behrens, Angela, Christopher Uggen, and Jeff Manza. 2003. "Ballot Manipulation and the 'Menace of Negro Domination': Racial Threat and Felon Disenfranchisement in the United States 1850–2002." *American Journal of Sociology* 109:559–605.

Bobo, Lawrence D., and Devon Johnson. 2004. "A Taste for Punishment: Black and White Americans' Views on the Death Penalty and the War on Drugs." *Du Bois Review: Social Science Research on Race* 1:151–80.

Bobo, Lawrence D., and Victor Thompson. 2006. "Unfair by Design: The War on Drugs, Race, and the Legitimacy of the Criminal Justice System." *Social Research* 73, no. 2 (Summer 2006): 445–72.

Boerner, David, and Roxanne Lieb. 2001. "Sentencing Reform in the Other Washington." *Crime and Justice* 28:71–136.

Bonczar, Thomas P. 2003. *Prevalence of Imprisonment in the U.S. Population, 1974–2001.* Washington, DC: Bureau of Justice Statistics. http://bjs.ojp.usdoj.gov/content/pub/pdf/piuspo1.pdf.

Brady, Henry E., Sidney Verba, and Kay Lehman Schlozman. 1995. "Beyond SES: A Resource Model of Political Participation." *American Political Science Review* 89:271–94.

Braman, Donald. 2002. "Families and Incarceration." In *Invisible Punishment,* edited by M. Mauer and M. Chesney-Lind. New York: New Press.

Brehm, John, and Wendy Rahn. 1997. "Individual-Level Evidence for the Causes and Consequences of Social Capital." *American Journal of Political Science* 41:999–1023.

Brown-Dean, Khalilah L. 2003. "Culture, Context, and Competition: Explaining State-Level Variation in Felon Disenfranchisement Laws." Paper presented at the Annual Meeting of the Midwest Political Science Association, Chicago.

Bunche, Ralph J. 1973. *The Political Status of the Negro in the Age of FDR.* Chicago: University of Chicago Press.

Burbank, Matthew J. 1997. "Explaining Contextual Effects on Vote Choice." *Political Behavior* 19:113–32.

Burch, Traci. 2007. "Punishment and Participation: How Criminal Convictions Threaten American Democracy." PhD diss., Harvard University.

———. 2011. "Turnout and Party Registration among Convicted Offenders in the 2008 General Elections." *Law and Society Review* 45:699–730.

Bureau of Justice Statistics (BJS) Total Correctional Population. 2011. Washington, DC: Bureau of Justice Statistics.

Bursik, Robert J., and Harold G. Grasmick. 1993. *Neighborhoods and Crime.* New York: Lexington.

Bushway, Shawn D., and Piehl Anne Morrison. 2001. "Judging Judicial Discretion: Legal Factors and Racial Discrimination in Sentencing." *Law and Society Review* 35:733–64.

Campbell, Andrea Louise. 2003. *How Policies Make Citizens: Senior Political Activism and the American Welfare State.* Princeton: Princeton Univ Press.

Campbell, Angus, Philip E. Converse, Warren E. Miller, and Donald E. Stokes. 1960. *The American Voter.* Chicago: University of Chicago Press.

Cassidy, Tina. 1998. "Lawmakers Act to Rescind Voting Rights of Prisoners." *Boston Globe,* July 30.

Chanely, Virginia A., Thomas J. Rudolph, and Wendy M. Rahn. 2000. "The Origins and Consequences of Public Trust in Government." *Public Opinion Quarterly* 64, no. 3:239–56.

Chou, Yue Hong. 1997. *Exploring Spatial Analysis in Geographic Information Systems.* Santa Fe, NM: OnWord.

"Chronic Mental Illness, Dec, 1989." 1989. Dataset, iPOLL Databank, Roper Center for Public Opinion Research, University of Connecticut. Retrieved July 21, 2011. http://www.ropercenter.uconn.edu.turing.library.northwestern.edu/data_access/ipoll/ipoll.html.

Citrin, Jack. 1974. "Comment: The Political Relevance of Trust in Government." *American Political Science Review* 68:973–88.

Citrin, Jack, and Donald P. Green. 1986. "Presidential Leadership and the Resurgence of Trust in Government." *British Journal of Political Science* 16:431–53.

Clark, Kenneth B. (1965) 1989. *Dark Ghetto: Dilemmas of Social Power.* Hanover, NH: Wesleyan University Press. Page references are to the 1989 edition.

Clear, Todd R. 2002. "The Problem with 'Addition by Subtraction': The Prison-

Crime Relationship in Low-Income Communities." In *Invisible Punishment*, edited by M. Mauer and M. Chesney-Lind. New York: New Press.

———. 2007. *Imprisoning Communities*. New York: Oxford University Press.

Cohen, Cathy J. 1999. *The Boundaries of Blackness*. Chicago: University of Chicago Press.

———. 2009. "From Kanye West to Barack Obama: Black Youth, the State, and Political Alienation." In *The Unsustainable American State*, edited by L. Jacobs and D. Kind: Oxford University Press.

Cohen, Cathy J., and Michael C. Dawson. 1993. "Neighborhood Poverty and African-American Politics." *American Political Science Review* 87:286–302.

Conyers, John, Jr. 2002. Letter to Attorney General John Aschcroft, December 17. NAME AND PHYSICAL LOCATION OF COLLECTION.

Correctional Populations in the United States, 1997. 2000. Washington, DC: Bureau of Justice Statistics. http://bjs.ojp.usdoj.gov/content/pub/pdf/cpus97.pdf.

Correll, Joshua, Bernadette Park, Charles M. Judd, Bernd Wittenbrink, Melody S. Sadler, and Traci Keesee. 2007. "Across the Thin Blue Line: Police Officers and Racial Bias in the Decision to Shoot." *Journal of Personality and Social Psychology* 92, no. 6 (June 2007): 1006–23.

Cose, Ellis, Vern E. Smith, Ana Figueroa, Victoria Scanlan Stefanakos, and Joseph Contreras 2000. "The Prison Paradox." *Newsweek*, November 13, p. 40.

Crawford, Charles, T. E. D. Chiricos, and Gary Kleck. 1998. "Race, Racial Threat, and Sentencing of Habitual Offenders." *Criminology* 36:481–512.

"Crime in America, Jun, 1995." 1995. iPOLL Databank, Roper Center for Public Opinion Research, University of Connecticut. Retrieved July 21, 2011. http://www.ropercenter.uconn.edu.turing.library.northwestern.edu/data_access/ipoll/ipoll.html.

Dale, Allison, and Aaron Strauss. 2009. "Don't Forget to Vote: Text Message Reminders as a Mobilization Tool." *American Journal of Political Science* 53:787–804.

Davis, Angela Y. 2003. "Political Prisoners, Prisons, and Black Liberation." Pp. 64–77 in *Imprisoned Intellectuals*, edited by J. James. New York: Roman and Littlefield.

Dawson, Michael C. 2001. *Black Visions*. Chicago: University of Chicago Press.

Dean, Deby. 1980. "Citizen Ratings of the Police: The Difference Contact Makes." *Law and Policy Quarterly* 2, no. 4 (October 1980): 445–71.

Demeo, M., and S. A. Ochoa. 2003. *Diminished Voting Power in the Latino Community*. Mexican American Legal Defense and Education Fund.

Demuth, Stephen, and Darrell Steffensmeier. 2004. "Ethnicity Effects on Sentence Outcomes in Large Urban Courts: Comparisons among White, Black, and Hispanic Defendants." *Social Science Quarterly* 85:994–1011.

"The Disenfranchisement of Ex-Felons: Citizenship, Criminality, and 'The Purity of the Ballot Box.'" 1989. *Harvard Law Review* 102:1300–1317.

Ditton, P. M. 1999. *Mental Health and Treatment of Inmates and Probationers.* Washington, DC: Bureau of Justice Statistics. http://bjs.ojp.usdoj.gov/content/pub/pdf/mhtip.pdf.

Downs, Anthony. 1957. *An Economic Theory of Democracy.* New York: Harper and Row.

Durose, Matthew R., and Patrick A. Langan. 2007. *Felony Convictions in State Courts, 2004.* Washington, DC: Bureau of Justice Statistics. http://bjs.ojp.usdoj.gov/content/pub/pdf/fssc04.pdf.

Edin, Kathryn, Timothy J. Nelson, and Rechelle Paranal. 2004. "Fatherhood and Incarceration as Potential Turning Points in the Criminal Careers of Unskilled Men." Pp. 46–75 in *Imprisoning America: The Social Effects of Mass Incarceration,* edited by M. Pattillo, D. Weiman, and B. Western. New York: Sage.

Eller, Anja, Dominic Abrams, G. Tendayi Viki, Dionne A. Imara, and Shafick Peerbux. 2007. "Stay Cool, Hang Loose, Admit Nothing: Race, Intergroup Contact, and Public-Police Relations." *Basic and Applied Social Psychology* 29, no. 3:213–24.

Engen, Rodney L., Randy R. Gainey, Robert D. Crutchfield, and Joseph G. Weis. 2003. "Discretion and Disparity under Sentencing Guidelines: The Role of Departures and Structured Sentencing Alternatives." *Criminology* 41:99–130.

"Estimated Number and Rate (per 100,000 U.S. Resident Population in Each Group) of Sentenced Prisoners under Jurisdiction of State and Federal Correctional Authorities, 2008." 2009. In *Sourcebook of Criminal Justice Statistics Online.* Washington, DC: U.S. Department of Justice.

Etling, Bruce, Robert Faris, and John Palfrey. 2010. "Political Change in the Digital Age: The Fragility and Promise of Online Organizing." *SAIS Review* 30:37–49.

Evans, Peter B., Dietrich Rueschemeyer, and Theda Skocpol. 1985. *Bringing the State Back In.* Cambridge: Cambridge University Press.

Fagan, Jeffrey, Valerie West, and Jan Holland. 2004. "Neighborhood, Crime, and Incarceration in New York City." *Columbia Human Rights Law Review* 36:71–107.

Fairdosi, Amir. 2009. "Arrested Development: The Effects of Criminal Justice Supervision on Political Efficacy." University of Chicago, Center for the Study of Race, Politics and Culture, Black Youth Project. http://www.blackyouthproject.com/wp-content/uploads/2009/06/Arrested-Development-FINAL.pdf.

Farmer, Paul. 2002. "The House of the Dead: Tuberculosis and Incarceration." In *Invisible Punishment,* edited by M. Mauer and M. Chesney-Lind. New York: New Press.

Fellner, J., and Marc Mauer. 1998. *Losing the Vote: The Impact of Felony Disfranchisement Laws in the United States.* Washington, DC: Sentencing Project, Washington.

Fiorina, Morris. 1999. "Extreme Voices: A Dark Side of Civic Engagement." Pp. 395–426 in *Civic Engagement in American Democracy,* edited by T. Skocpol and M. P. Fiorina. Washington, DC: Brookings Institution.

Fishman, Laura. 1990. *Women at the Wall.* Albany, NY: SUNY Press.

Fleisher, M. S., and S. H. Decker. 2001. "Going Home, Staying Home: Integrating Prison Gang Members into the Community." *Corrections Management Quarterly* 5:65–77.

Fletcher, Michael A. 1999. "High Imprisonment Rates Could Fuel Crime." *Washington Post,* July 12.

Flynn, Adrianne. 1994. "Prison 'Alumni' Lock Up the Ex-Con Vote for Barry: D.C. Law Lets Felons Cast Ballots Once They're Released." *Washington Times,* October 18.

Fogelson, Robert. 1968. "From Resentment to Confrontation: The Police, the Negroes, and the Outbreak of the Nineteen Sixties Riots." *Political Science Quarterly* 83, no. 2 (June 1968): 217–47.

Foldare, Irving S. 1968. "The Effect of Neighborhood on Voting Behavior." *Political Science Quarterly* 83:516–29.

Foley, Linda A., Afesa M. Adams, and James L. Goodson. 1996. "The Effect of Race on Decisions by Judges and Other Officers of the Court." *Journal of Applied Social Psychology* 26:1190–1212.

Foreman, James, Jr. 2002. "Children, Cops, and Citizenship: Why Conservatives Should Oppose Racial Profiling." In *Invisible Punishment,* edited by M. Mauer and M. Chesney-Lind. New York: New Press.

Foucault, Michel. 1999. *Discipline and Punish: The Birth of the Prison.* New York: Vintage Books.

Free, Marvin D., Jr. 1997. "The Impact of Federal Sentencing Reforms on African Americans." *Journal of Black Studies* 28:268–86.

Frymer, Paul. 1999. *Uneasy Alliances.* Princeton: Princeton University Press.

Gabbidon, Shaun L., and George E. Higgins. 2009. "The Role of Race/Ethnicity and Race Relations on Public Opinion Related to the Treatment of Blacks by the Police." *Police Quarterly* 12, no. 1 (March 2009): 102–15.

Galvin, Daniel J. 2009. *Presidential Party Building: Dwight D. Eisenhower to George W. Bush.* Princeton: Princeton University Press.

"General Social Survey." 2006. Dataset, National Opinion Research Center.

Geolytics. 2011. "Annual Estimates for 2001–2007: Methodology." Geolytics. http://www.geolytics.com/USCensus,Estimates-Projections,Data,Methodology,Products.asp.

Gerber, Alan S., and Donald P. Green. 2000. "The Effects of Canvassing, Telephone Calls, and Direct Mail on Voter Turnout." *American Political Science Review* 94:653–63.

Gerber, Alan S., Donald P. Green, and Christopher W. Larimer. 2008. "Social Pressure and Voter Turnout: Evidence from a Largescale Field Experiment." *American Political Science Review* 102:33–48.

Gerber, Alan S., Donald P. Green, and Ron Shachar. 2003. "Voting May Be Habit-Forming: Evidence from a Randomized Field Experiment." *American Journal of Political Science* 47:540–50.

Gimpel, James G., Joshua J. Dyck, and Daron R. Shaw. 2004. "Registrants, Voters, and Turnout Variability across Neighborhoods." *Political Behavior* 26:343–75.

Glaze, Lauren E. 2011. *Correctional Populations in the United States, 2010.* Washington, DC: Bureau of Justice Statistics. http://www.bjs.gov/content/pub/pdf/cpus10.pdf.

Glaze, Lauren E., Thomas P. Bonczar, and Fan Zhang. 2010. *Probation and Parole in the United States, 2009.* Washington, DC: Bureau of Justice Statistics. http://bjs.ojp.usdoj.gov/content/pub/pdf/ppus09.pdf.

"Glossary of Geographic Terms." 2007. U.S. Census Bureau. Retrieved April 6, 2007. http://www.census.gov/geo/www/tiger/glossary.html#glossary.

Goldstein, Kenneth M., and Travis N. Ridout. 2002. "The Politics of Participation: Mobilization and Turnout over Time." *Political Behavior* 24:3–29.

Gonzalez, David. 1997. "About New York; The Election That Failed to Electrify." *New York Times*, November 5.

Gottschalk, Marie. 2002. "Review: Black Flower; Prisons and the Future of Incarceration." *Annals of the American Academy of Political and Social Science* 582:195–227.

Green, Donald P., and Alan S. Gerber. 2008. *Get Out the Vote: How to Increase Voter Turnout.* 2nd ed. Washington, DC: Brookings Institution.

Green, Donald P., Alan S. Gerber, and David W. Nickerson. 2003. "Getting Out the Vote in Local Elections: Results from Six Door-to-Door Canvassing Experiments." *Journal of Politics* 65:1083–96.

Gross, Samuel R., and Robert Mauro. 1984. "Patterns of Death: An Analysis of Racial Disparities in Capital Sentencing and Homicide Victimization." *Stanford Law Review* 37:27–153.

Guerino, Paul, Paige M. Harrison, and William J. Sabol. 2011. *Prisoners in 2010.* Washington, DC: Bureau of Justice Statistics. http://bjs.ojp.usdoj.gov/content/pub/pdf/ppus09.pdf.

Hahn, Jinyong, Petra Todd, and Wilbert Van der Klaauw. 2001. "Identification and Estimation of Treatment Effects with a Regression Discontinuity Design." *Econometrica* 69:201–9.

Hamilton, Alexander, James Madison, and John Jay. (1787) 1982. *The Federalist Papers.* Edited by G. Wills. New York: Bantam.

Hannerz, Ulf. (1969) 2004. *SoulSide: Inquiries into Ghetto Culture and Community.* Chicago: University of Chicago Press.

Hansen, John Mark. 1985. "The Political Economy of Group Membership." *American Political Science Review* 79:79–96.

Harlow, Caroline Wolf. 2003. *Education and Correctional Populations.* Washington, DC: Bureau of Justice Statistics. bjs.ojp.usdoj.gov/content/pub/pdf/ecp.pdf.

Harris, David A. 1997. "'Driving While Black' and All Other Traffic Offenses: The Supreme Court and Pretextual Traffic Stops." *Journal of Criminal Law and Criminology* 87, no. 2 (Winter 1997): 544–82.

————. 1999. "The Stories, the Statistics, and the Law: Why Driving While Black Matters." *Minnesota Law Review* 84:265.

Harris, Frederick C. 1994. "Something Within: Religion as Mobilizer of African-American Political Activism." *Journal of Politics* 56:42–68.

Harris-Lacewell, Melissa. 2004. *Barbershops, Bibles, and BET.* Princeton: Princeton University Press.

Hebert, Christopher. 1997. "Sentencing Outcomes of Black, Hispanic, and White Males Convicted under Federal Sentencing Guidelines." *Criminal Justice Review* 22:133–56.

Herbert, Bob. 2010. "Jim Crow Policing." *New York Times*, February 1.

Hetherington, Marc J. 1998. "The Political Relevance of Political Trust." *American Political Science Review* 92:791–808.

————. 2005. *Why Trust Matters: Declining Political Trust and the Demise of Political Liberalism.* Princeton: Princeton University Press.

Hill, Kim Quaile, and Jan E. Leighley. 1992. "The Policy Consequences of Class Bias in State Electorates." *American Journal of Political Science* 36:351–65.

Ho, Daniel E., Kosuke Imai, and Gary King. 2007. "Matching as Nonparametric Preprocessing for Reducing Model Dependence in Parametric Causal Inference." *Political Analysis* 15:199–236.

Hochschild, Jennifer L. 1981. *What's Fair?* Cambridge, MA: Harvard University Press.

Holzer, Harry, Stephen Rafael, and Michael J. Stoll. 2004. "Will Employers Hire Ex Offenders? Employer Preferences, Background Checks, and Their Determinants." Pp. 205–46 in *Imprisoning America: The Social Effects of Mass Incarceration*, edited by M. Pattillo, D. Weiman, and B. Western. New York: Sage.

Honig, Bonnie. 1993. "Rawls on Politics and Punishment." *Political Research Quarterly* 46:99–125.

Howell, Susan E., and Deborah Fagan. 1988. "Race and Trust in Government: Testing the Political Reality Model." *Public Opinion Quarterly* 52, no. 3 (Autumn 1988): 343–50.

Huckfeldt, R. Robert. 1979. "Political Participation and the Neighborhood Social Context." *American Journal of Political Science* 23:579–92.

Huckfeldt, Robert, Eric Plutzer, and John Sprague. 1993. "Alternative Contexts of Political Behavior: Churches, Neighborhoods, and Individuals." *Journal of Politics* 55:365–81.

Huckfeldt, Robert, and John Sprague. 1987. "Networks in Context: The Social Flow of Political Information." *American Political Science Review* 81:1197–1216.

————. 1992. "Political Parties and Electoral Mobilization: Political Structure, Social Structure, and the Party Canvass." *American Political Science Review* 86:70–86.

Huling, Tracy. 2002. "Building a Prison Economy in Rural America." In *Invisible Punishment*, edited by M. Mauer and M. Chesney-Lind. New York: New Press.

Humphrey, John A., and Timothy J. Fogarty. 1987. "Race and Plea Bargained Outcomes: A Research Note." *Social Forces* 66:176–82.

Hurwitz, Jon, and Mark Peffley. 2005. "Explaining the Great Racial Divide: Perceptions of Fairness in the U.S. Criminal Justice System." *Journal of Politics* 67, no. 3 (August 2005): 762–83.

"Illegal Checkpoints? Escondido's Traffic Stops May Violate State Vehicle Code." 2010. *San Diego Union-Tribune*, January 4.

Jacob, Herbert. 1971. "Black and White Perceptions of Justice in the City." *Law and Society Review* 6, no. 1 (August 1971): 69–90.

Johnson, Devon. 2008. "Racial Prejudice, Perceived Injustice, and the Black-White Gap in Punitive Attitudes." *Journal of Criminal Justice* 36:198–206.

Johnson, M., W. Phillips Shively, and R. M. Stein. 2002. "Contextual Data and the Study of Elections and Voting Behavior: Connecting Individuals to Environments." *Electoral Studies* 21:219–33.

Johnson, Rucker C. 2009. "Ever-Increasing Levels of Parental Incarceration and the Consequences for Children." Pp. 177–206 in *Do Prisons Make Us Safer?*, edited by S. Rafael and M. A. Stoll. New York: Sage.

Kautt, Paula, and Cassia Spohn. 2002. "Cracking Down on Black Drug Offenders? Testing for Interactions among Offenders' Race, Drug Type, and Sentencing Strategy in Federal Drug Sentences." *Justice Quarterly* 19:1–35.

Kennedy, Randall. 1997. *Race, Crime and the Law*. New York: Vintage Books.

———. 1998. *Race, Crime and the Law*. New York: Vintage Books.

Kernell, Samuel, and Gary Jacobson. 2000. *Logic of American Politics*. Washington, DC: Congressional Quarterly.

Kerner, Otto, and John V. Lindsay. 1968. *Report of the National Advisory Commission on Civil Disorders*. Washington, DC: National Advisory Commission on Civil Disorders.

Keyssar, Alexander. 2000. *The Right to Vote*. New York: Basic Books.

King, Desmond S., and Jeremy Waldron. 1988. "Citizenship, Social Citizenship and the Defence of Welfare Provision." *British Journal of Political Science* 18:415–43.

King, Gary. 1986. "How Not to Lie with Statistics: Avoiding Common Mistakes in Quantitative Political Science." *American Journal of Political Science* 30:666–87.

King, Gary, Robert O. Keohane, and Sidney Verba. 1994. *Designing Social Inquiry*. Princeton: Princeton University Press.

King, Gary, Michael Tomz, and Jason Wittenberg. 2000. "Making the Most of Statistical Analyses: Improving Interpretation and Presentation." *American Journal of Political Science* 44:314–55.

King, Gary, and Lanche Zeng. 2006. "The Dangers of Extreme Counterfactuals." *Political Analysis* 14:131–59.

Kleck, Gary. 1981. "Racial Discrimination in Criminal Sentencing: A Critical Evaluation of the Evidence with Additional Evidence on the Death Penalty." *American Sociological Review* 46:783–805.

Klepper, Steven, Daniel Nagin, and Luke I. Tierney. 1983. "Discrimination in the Criminal Justice System: A Critical Appraisal of the Literature." Pp. 55–128 in *Research on Sentencing: The Search for Reform*, edited by A. Blumenstein, J. Cohen, S. E. Martin, and M. A. Tonry. Washington, D.C.: National Academies Press.

Kofman, Jeffrey. 2007. "'America's Toughest Sheriff' Takes on Illegals." *ABC News*, October 18. http://abcnews.go.com/Nightline/story?id=3735938&page=1.

Kornhauser, Ruth Rosner. 1978. *Social Sources of Delinquency*. Chicago: University of Chicago Press.

Kramer, John, and Darrell Steffensmeir. 1993. "Race and Imprisonment Decisions." *Sociological Quarterly* 34:357–76.

Kramer, Walter, and Harald Sonnberger. 1986. *The Linear Regression Model under Test*. Heidelberg: Physica.

Krebs, Christopher P. 2006. "Inmate Factors Associated with HIV Transmission in Prison." *Criminology and Public Policy* 5:113–35.

Kupchik, Aaron, and Angela Harvey. 2007. "Court Context and Discrimination: Exploring Biases across Juvenile and Criminal Courts." *Sociological Perspectives* 50:417–44.

Lazarsfeld, Paul F., Bernard Berelson, and Hazel Gaudet. (1944) 1968. *The People's Choice*. New York: Columbia University Press.

Leigh, Andrew. 2006. "Trust, Inequality and Ethnic Heterogeneity." *Economic Record* 82:268–80.

Leighley, Jan E. 2001. *Strength in Numbers*. Princeton: Princeton University Press.

Levi, Margaret, and Laura Stoker. 2000. "Political Trust and Trustworthiness." *Annual Review of Political Science* 3:475–507.

Levitt, Steven D. 2004. "Understanding Why Crime Fell in the 1990s: Four Factors That Explain the Decline and Six That Do Not." *Journal of Economic Perspectives* 18:163–90.

Lewis, Oscar. 1969. "The Culture of Poverty." In *On Understanding Poverty: Perspectives from the Social Sciences*, edited by Daniel Patrick Moynihan. New York: Basic Books.

The Long Shadow of Jim Crow: Voter Intimidation and Suppression in America Today. 2005. Washington, DC: People for the American Way; Baltimore: National Association for the Advancement of Colored People.

Lundman, Richard J., and Robert L. Kaufman. 2003. "Driving While Black: Effects of Race, Ethnicity, and Gender on Citizen Self-Reports of Traffic Stops." *Criminology* 41:195–220.

Lynch, James P., and William J. Sabol. 2004a. "Assessing the Effects of Mass Incarceration on Informal Social Control in Communities." *Criminology and Public Policy* 3:267–94.

———. 2004b. "Effects of Incarceration on Informal Social Control in Communities." In *Imprisoning Communities*, edited by B. Western, M. Pattillo, and D. Weiman. New York: Russell Sage.

Lynch, James P., William J. Sabol, Michael Planty, and Mary Shelly. 2002. "Crime, Coercion and Community: The Effects of Arrest and Incarceration Policies on Informal Social Control in Neighborhoods, Executive Summary." National Criminal Justice Reference Service. https://www.ncjrs.gov/App/abstractdb/AbstractDBDetails.aspx?id=195170.

Mansbridge, Jane. 1999. "Should Blacks Represent Blacks and Women Represent Women? A Contingent 'yes.'" *Journal of Politics* 61:628–57.

Manza, Jeff, and Christopher Uggen. 2004. "Punishment and Democracy: Disenfranchisement of Nonincarcerated Felons in the United States." *Perspectives on Politics* 2:491–506.

———. 2006. *Locked Out: Felon Disenfranchisement and American Democracy.* Oxford: Oxford University Press.

Maricopa County Sheriff's Office. 2011. "Illegal Immigration." Maricopa County Sheriff's Office website. http://www.mcso.org.

Massey, Douglas S., and Nancy A. Denton. 1993. *American Apartheid.* Cambridge. MA: Harvard University Press.

Massoglia, Michael. 2008. "Incarceration as Exposure: The Prison, Infectious Disease, and Other Stress-Related Illnesses." *Journal of Health and Social Behavior* 49:56–71.

Matsusaka, John G., and Filip Palda. 1999. "Voter Turnout: How Much Can We Explain?" *Public Choice* 98:431–46.

Mauer, Marc. 2006. *Race to Incarcerate: Revised and Updated.* New York: New Press.

Mayer, Susan E., and Christopher Jencks. 1989. "Growing Up in Poor Neighborhoods: How Much Does It Matter?" *Science* 243:1441–45.

Mayhew, David. 1974. *Congress: The Electoral Connection.* New Haven: Yale University Press.

Mazzella, Ronald, and Alan Feingold. 1994. "The Effects of Physical Attractiveness, Race, Socioeconomic Status, and Gender of Defendants and Victims on Judgments of Mock Jurors: A Meta-analysis." *Journal of Applied Social Psychology* 24:1315–38.

McDougall, Cynthia, Mark A. Cohen, Raymond Swaray, and Amanda Perry. 2003. "The Costs and Benefits of Sentencing: A Systematic Review." *Annals of the American Academy of Political and Social Science* 587:160–77.

Mendelberg, Tali. 2001. *The Race Card: Campaign Strategy, Implicit Messages, and the Norm of Equality.* Princeton: Princeton University Press.

Mettler, Suzanne. 2005. *Soldiers to Citizens: The G.I. Bill and the Making of the Greatest Generation.* Oxford: Oxford University Press.

Mettler, Suzanne, and Joe Soss. 2004. "The Consequences of Public Policy for Democratic Citizenship: Bridging Policy Studies and Mass Politics." *Perspectives on Politics* 2:55–73.

Michelson, Melissa R. 2003. "Getting Out the Latino Vote: How Door to Door Canvassing Influences Voter Turnout in Rural Central California." *Political Behavior* 25:247–63.

Mishler, William, and Richard Rose. 1997. "Trust, Distrust, and Skepticism: Popular Evaluations of Civil and Political Institutions in Post-communist Societies." *Journal of Politics* 59:418–51.

Moore, Solomon. 2007. "Texas Seeks to Break Prison Recidivism Cycle." *New York Times*.

Morenoff, Jeffrey D., and Robert J. Sampson. 1997. "Violent Crime and the Spatial Dynamics of Neighborhood Transition: Chicago, 1970–1990." *Social Forces* 76:31–64.

Morenoff, Jeffrey D., Robert J. Sampson, and Stephen W. Raudenbush. 2001. "Neighborhood Inequality, Collective Efficacy, and the Spatial Dynamics of Urban Violence." *Criminology* 39:517–60.

Morgan, Stephen L., and David J. Harding. 2006. "Matching Estimators of Causal Effects: Prospects and Pitfalls in Theory and Practice." *Sociological Methods and Research* 35:3–60.

Morrell, Michael E. 2003. "Survey and Experimental Evidence for a Reliable and Valid Measure of Internal Political Efficacy." *Public Opinion Quarterly* 67:589–602.

Mumola, C. J. 1999. *Substance Abuse and Treatment, State and Federal Offenders, 1997.* Washington, DC: Bureau of Justice Statistics.

Nagler, Jonathan 1991. "The Effect of Registration Laws and Education on US Voter Turnout." *American Political Science Review* 85:1393–1405.

"NCSC Sentencing Attitudes Survey, Mar, 2006." 2006. iPOLL Databank, Roper Center for Public Opinion Research, University of Connecticut. Retrieved July 21, 2011. http://www.ropercenter.uconn.edu.turing.library.northwestern.edu/data_access/ipoll/ipoll.html.

Nickerson, David W. 2007. "Quality Is Job One: Professional and Volunteer Voter Mobilization Calls." *American Journal of Political Science* 51:269–82.

North Carolina State Board of Elections. 2008. "NGCA General Statutes: Chapter 163: Elections and Election Laws." Accessed March 4, 2011. http://www.app.sboe.state.nc.us/erc/Documents/Documents_for_Linking/Governing_Documents/GOVERNING%20DOCUMENTS%20-%20NC%20Election%20Laws.pdf.

Nozick, Robert. 1974. *Anarchy, State, and Utopia.* New York: Basic Books.

Olson, Mancur. 1965. *The Logic of Collective Action.* Cambridge, MA: Harvard University Press.

O'Reilly, Kenneth. 1989. *"Racial Matters": The FBI's Secret File on Black America, 1960–1972.* New York: Free Press.

Orren, Gary. 1997. "Fall from Grace: The Public's Loss of Faith in Government." In *Why People Don't Trust Government*, edited by J. S. Nye, P. D. Zelikow, and D. C. King. Cambridge, MA: Havard University Press.

Pager, Devah, and Lincoln Quillian. 2005. "What Employers Say vs. What They Do." *American Sociological Review* 70:355–80.

Paige, Jeffrey M. 1971. "Political Orientation and Riot Participation." *American Sociological Review* 36, no. 5 (October 1971): 810–20.

Pateman, Carole. 1970. *Participation and Democratic Theory*. Cambridge: Cambridge University Press.

Paternoster, Raymond, Robert Brame, Sarah Bacon, Andrew Ditchfield, David Biere, Karen Beckman, Deanna Perez, Michael Strauch, Nadine Frederique, Kristin Gawkoski, Daniel Zeigler, and Katheryn Murphy. 2003. "An Empirical Analysis of Maryland's Death Sentencing System with Respect to the Influence of Race and Legal Jursidiction." University of Maryland. http://www .newsdesk.umd.edu/pdf/finalrep.pdf.

Peffley, Mark, and Jon Hurwitz. 2010. *Justice in America: The Separate Realities of Blacks and Whites*. Cambridge: Cambridge University Press.

Petersilia, Joan. 1985. "Racial Disparities in the Criminal Justice System: A Summary." *Crime Delinquency* 31:15–34.

Peterson, Ruth D., and John Hagan. 1984. "Changing Conceptions of Race: Towards an Account of Anomalous Findings of Sentencing Research." *American Sociological Review* 49:56–70.

Pettit, Becky. 2012. *Invisible Men : Mass Incarceration and the Myth of Black Progress*. New York: Russell Sage Foundation.

Pew Research. 2010. "A Year after Obama's Election: Blacks Upbeat about Black Progress, Prospects." Pew Research Social and Demographic Trends. http://www .pewsocialtrends.org/2010/01/12/blacks-upbeat-about-black-progress-prospects/.

Pfeifer, Jeffrey E., and James R. P. Ogloff. 1991. "Ambiguity and Guilt Determinations: A Modern Racism Perspective." *Journal of Applied Social Psychology* 21:1713–25.

Piven, Frances Fox, and Richard A. Cloward. 2000. *Why Americans Still Don't Vote*. Boston: Beacon Press.

Plutzer, Eric. 2002. "Becoming a Habitual Voter: Inertia, Resources, and Growth in Young Adulthood." *American Political Science Review* 96:41–56.

Porter, Bruce, and Marvin Dunn. 1984. *The Miami Riot of 1980: Crossing the Bounds*. Lexington, MA: Lexington Books.

Powell, Michael. 2006. "Profiles of Men Who 'Fit the Description.'" *Washington Post*, December 14.

Pratt, Travis C. 1998. "Race and Sentencing: A Meta-analysis of Conflicting Empirical Research Results." *Journal of Criminal Justice* 26:513–23.

Prison Policy Initiative. 2011. Prisoners of the Census. http://www.prisonersof thecensus.org/problem/state.html.

Putnam, Robert. 2000. *Bowling Alone: The Collapse and Revival of American Community*. New York: Simon and Schuster Paperbacks.

Radelet, Michael L. 1981. "Racial Characteristics and the Imposition of the Death Penalty." *American Sociological Review* 46:918–27.

Rahn, Wendy M., and Thomas J. Rudolph. 2005. "A Tale of Political Trust in American Cities." *Public Opinion Quarterly* 69, no. 4 (Winter 2005): 530–60.

Rahn, Wendy M., Kwang Suk Yoon, Michael Garet, Steven Lipson, and Katherine Loflin. 2009. "Geographies of Trust." *American Behavioral Scientist* 52:1646–63.

Ramirez, Ricardo. 2005. "Residential Mobility and Latino Political Mobilization." Berkeley: Institute of Governmental Studies.

Ramsey, J. B. 1969. "Tests for Specification Error in Classical Linear Least Squares Regression Analysis." *Journal of the Royal Statistical Society, Series B* 31:350–71.

Richie, Beth. 2002. "The Social Impact of Mass Incarceration on Women." In *Invisible Punishment*, edited by M. Mauer and M. Chesney-Lind. New York: New Press.

Riker, William H., and Peter C. Ordeshook. 1968. "A Theory of the Calculus of Voting." *American Political Science Review* 62:25–42.

Rodriguez, N. 2003. "The Impact of 'Strikes' in Sentencing Decisions: Punishment for Only Some Habitual Offenders." *Criminal Justice Policy Review* 14:106.

Rose, Dina R., and Todd R. Clear. 1998. "Incarceration, Social Capital, and Crime: Implications for Social Disorganization Theory." *Criminology* 36:441–80.

———. 2004. "Who Doesn't Know Someone in Jail? The Impact of Exposure to Prison on Attitudes toward Formal and Informal Controls." *Prison Journal* 84:228–47.

Rosenberg, Morris. 1956. "Misantrhopy and Political Ideology." *American Sociological Review* 21:690–95.

Rosenfeld, Richard, Steven F. Messner, and Eric P. Baumer. 2001. "Social Capital and Homicide." *Social Forces* 80:283–309.

Rosenstone, Steven J., and John Mark Hansen. 1993. *Mobilization, Participation, and Democracy in America.* New York: MacMillan.

Ross, Catherine E., John Mirowsky, and Shana Pribesh. 2001. "Powerlessness and the Amplification of Threat: Neighborhood Disadvantage, Disorder, and Mistrust." *American Sociological Review* 66:568–91.

Rousseau, Jean Jacques. 1987. "The Social Contract." In *The Basic Political Writings of Jean-Jacques Rousseau*, edited by D. A. Cress. Indianapolis: Hackett.

Rubenstein, Gwen, and Debbie Mukamal. 2002. "Welfare and Housing: Denial of Benefits to Drug Offenders." In *Invisible Punishment*, edited by M. Mauer and M. Chesney-Lind. New York: New Press.

Sampson, Robert J. 1988. "Local Friendship Ties and Community Attachment in Mass Society: A Multilevel Systemic Model." *American Sociological Review* 53:766–79.

Sampson, Robert J., and Dawn Jeglum Bartusch. 1998. "Legal Cynicism and (Subcultural?) Tolerance of Deviance: The Neighborhood Context of Racial Differences." *Law and Society Review* 32:777–804.

Sampson, Robert J., and W. Byron Groves. 1989. "Community Structure and Crime: Testing Social-Disorganization Theory." *American Journal of Sociology* 94:774–802.

Sampson, Robert J., Doug McAdam, Heather MacIndoe, and Simon Weffer-Elizondo. 2005. "Civil Society Reconsidered: The Durable Nature and Community Structure of Collective Civic Action." *American Journal of Sociology* 111:673–714.

Scan/US. 2008. "Scan/US Methodology White Paper." http://www.scanus.com/pdfs/mwp2004.pdf.

Schmitt, Erica Leah, and Matthew Durose. 2006. "Characteristics of Drivers Stopped by Police, 2002." United States Department of Justice, Washington, D.C.

Schmitt, Erica L., Patrick A. Langan, and Matthew Durose. 2002. "Characteristics of Drivers Stopped by the Police, 1999." United States Department of Justice, Washington, DC.

Schneider, Anne, and Helen Ingram. 1990. "Behavioral Assumptions of Policy Tools." *Journal of Politics* 52:510–29.

———. 1997. *Policy Design for Democracy*. Lawrence: University Press of Kansas.

Schwartz, Marin D., and Dragan Milovanovic. 1996. *Race, Gender, and Class in Criminology: The Intersection*. New York: Garland Publications.

Shaw, Clifford R., and Henry D. McKay. 1942. *Juvenile Delinquency and Urban Areas*. Chicago: University of Chicago Press.

Shear, Michael D., and Arthur Santana. 1996. "Communities Learn Where Parolees Live: Manassas, Alexandria Head the List in N. Va." *Washington Post*.

Shklar, Judith. 1991. *American Citizenship: The Quest for Inclusion*. Cambridge, MA: Harvard University Press.

Sigelman, Lee, Susan Welch, Timothy Bledsoe, and Michael Combs. 1997. "Police Brutality and Public Perceptions of Racial Discrimination: A Tale of Two Beatings." *Political Research Quarterly* 50, no. 4 (December 1997): 777–91.

Silber, John. 2000. "Mass Inmates Shouldn't Vote." *Boston Herald*, October 24.

Simpson, Anne. 1987. "Capitol East Neighbors to Rally against Prison." *Washington Post*, March 19.

Simpson, Brent, Tucker McGrimmon, and Kyle Irwin. 2007. "Are Blacks Really Less Trusting Than Whites? Revisiting the Race and Trust Question." *Social Forces* 98 (December 2007): 525–52.

Skocpol, Theda. 1992. *Protecting Mothers and Soldiers*. Cambridge, MA: Harvard University Press.

———. 1999. "How America Became Civic." In *Civic Engagement in American Democracy*, edited by T. Skocpol and M. Fiorina. Washington, DC: Brookings Institution.

Skocpol, Theda, and Morris Fiorina. 1999. "Making Sense of the Civic Engagement Debate." Pp. 1–25 in *Civic Engagement in American Democracy*, edited by T. Skocpol and M. Fiorina. Washington, DC: Brookings Institution.

Skogan, Wesley G. 1989. "Communities, Crime, and Neighborhood Organization." *Crime and Delinquency* 35:437–57.

———. 1990. *Disorder and Decline*. New York: Free Press.

———. 2005. "Citizen Satisfaction with Police Encounters." *Police Quarterly* 8, no. 3:298–321.

Smith, Sandra Susan. 2010. "Race and Trust." *Annual Review of Sociology* 36: 453–75.

Sommers, Samuel R., and Phoebe C. Ellsworth. 2000. "Race in the Courtroom: Perceptions of Guilt and Dispositional Attributions." *Personality and Social Psychology Bulletin* 26:1367–79.

Soss, Joe. 1999. "Lessons of Welfare: Policy Design, Political Learning, and Political Action." *American Political Science Review* 93:363–80.

Sourcebook of Criminal Justice Statistics Online. 2009. Washington, DC: U.S. Department of Justice.

Spohn, Cassia. 1990. "The Sentencing Decisions of Black and White Judges: Expected and Unexpected Similarities." *Law and Society Review* 24:1197–1216.

Spohn, Cassia, M. DeLone, and J. Spears. 1998. "Race/Ethnicity, Gender and Sentence Severity in Dade County, Florida: An Examination of the Decision to Withhold Adjudication." *Journal of Crime and Justice* 21:111–38.

Spohn, Cassia, and David Holleran. 2000. "The Imprisonment Penalty Paid by Young, Unemployed Black and Hispanic Male Offenders." *Criminology* 38, no. 1 (2000): 281–306.

Spohn, Cassia, and Jeffrey Spears. 1996. "The Effect of Offender and Victim Characteristics on Sexual Assault Case Processing Decisions." *Justice Quarterly* 13:649–79.

Squire, Peverill, Raymond E. Wolfinger, and David P. Glass. 1987. "Residential Mobility and Voter Turnout." *American Political Science Review* 81:45–65.

Steffensmeier, Darrell, and Stephen Demuth. 2000. "Ethnicity and Sentencing Outcomes in U.S. Federal Courts: Who Is Punished More Harshly?" *American Sociological Review* 65:705–29.

———. 2001. "Ethnicity and Judges' Sentencing Decisions: Hispanic-Black-White Comparisons." *Criminology* 39:145–78.

Steffensmeier, Darrell, Jeffery Ulmer, and John Kramer. 1998. "The Interaction of Race, Gender, and Age in Criminal Sentencing: The Punishment Cost of Being Young, Black, and Male." *Criminology* 36:763–98.

Stoloff, Jennifer A., Jennifer L. Glanville, and Elisa Jayne Bienenstock. 1999. "Women's Participation in the Labor Force: The Role of Social Networks." *Social Networks* 21:91–108.

Straits, Bruce C. 1990. "The Social Context of Voter Turnout." *Public Opinion Quarterly* 54:64–73.

Sweeney, Laura T., and Craig Haney. 1992. "The Influence of Race on Sentencing: A Meta-analytic Review of Experimental Studies." *Behavioral Sciences and the Law* 10:179–95.

Tam-Cho, Wendy K., James G. Gimpel, and Joshua J. Dyck. 2006. "Residential Concentration, Political Socialization, and Voter Turnout." *Journal of Politics* 68:156–67.

Taylor, Humphrey. 2000. "In Spite of Amadou Diallo, Public Perceptions of Police Show Marked Improvements." PR Newswire. http://www.thefreelibrary.com/In+Spite+Of+Amadou+Diallo,+Public+Perceptions+of+Police+Show+Marked . . . -a061400728.

Taylor, Paul, Cary Funk, and April Clark. 2007. "Americans and Social Trust: Who, Where, and Why." Pew Research Center. http://www.pewsocialtrends.org/files/2010/10/SocialTrust.pdf.

Thistlethwaite, Donand L., and Donald T. Campbell. 1960. "Regression-Discontinuity Analysis: An Alternative to the Ex Post Facto Experiment." *Journal of Educational Psychology* 51:309–17.

Thomson, Randall J., and Matthew T. Zingraff. 1981. "Detecting Sentencing Disparity: Some Problems and Evidence." *American Journal of Sociology* 86:869–80.

Tinker, John N., John Quiring, and Yvonne Pimentel. 1985. "Ethnic Bias in California Courts: A Case Study of Chicano and Anglo Felony Defendants." *Sociological Inquiry* 55:83–96.

Tocqueville, Alexis de. 2000. *Democracy in America.* Edited by H. C. Mansfield and D. Winthrop. Chicago: University of Chicago Press.

Tonry, Michael A. 1995. *Malign Neglect: Race, Crime, and Punishment in America.* New York: Oxford University Press.

Travis, Jeremy. 2004. "Reentry and Reintegration: New Perspectives on the Challenges of Mass Incarceration." Pp. 247–68 in *Imprisoning America: The Social Effects of Mass Incarceration,* edited by M. Pattillo, D. Weiman, and B. Western. New York: Sage.

Tuch, Steven A., and Ronald Weitzer. 1997. "Trends: Racial Differences in Attitudes toward the Police." *Public Opinion Quarterly* 61, no. 4 (Winter 1997): 642–63.

Tucker, William. 2002. "Crime, Race, and Capital Punishment." *Human Events,* May.

Tyler, Tom. 2006. *Why People Obey the Law.* Princeton: Princeton University Press.

Tyler, Tom, and Yuen J. Huo. 2002c. *Trust in the Law: Encouraging Public Cooperation with the Police and Courts.* New York: Russell Sage Foundation Publications.

Uggen, Christopher, Jeff Manza, and Melissa Thompson. 2006. "Citizenship, Democracy, and the Civic Reintegration of Criminal Offenders." *Annals of the American Academy of Political and Social Science* 605:281–310.

Uhlaner, Carole Jean. 1995. "What the Downsian Voter Weighs: A Reassessment of the Costs and Benefits of Action." In *Information, Participation, and Choice: An Economic Theory of Participation,* edited by B. Grofman. Ann Arbor: University of Michigan Press.

United States National Advisory Commission on Civil Disorders. 1968. *Report of the National Advisory Commission on Civil Disorders.* New York: Bantam.

Urbina, Martin G. 2003. *Capital Punishment and Latino Offenders: Racial and Ethnic Differences in Death Sentences.* New York: LFB Scholarly Publications.

USA Quick Facts from the US Census Bureau. 2011. Washington, DC: U.S. Census Bureau. http://quickfacts.census.gov/qfd/index.html.

U.S. Census Bureau. 2010. "Table 7: Cumulative Estimates of Population Change for Metropolitan Statistical Areas and Rankings: April 1, 2000 to July 1, 2009."

Retrieved July 29, 2010. http://www.census.gov/popest/metro/tables/2009/CBSA-EST2009-07.xls.

"U.S. Census Bureau Report: Tabulating Prisoners at Their 'Permanent Home of Record' Address." 2006. U.S Census Bureau. http://www.census.gov/newsroom/releases/pdf/2006-02-21_tabulating_prisoners.pdf.

Uslaner, Eric M. 2002. *The Moral Foundations of Trust*. Cambridge: Cambridge University Press.

Verba, Sidney, and Norman H. Nie. 1972. *Participation in America*. New York: Harper and Row.

Verba, Sidney, Kay Lehman Schlozman, and Henry Brady. 1995. *Voice and Equality: Civic Voluntarism in American Politics*. Cambridge, MA: Harvard University Press.

Vitello, Paul. 2006. "Path to Deportation Can Start with a Traffic Stop." *New York Times*, April 14, 2006.

Wacquant, Loïc. 2001. "Deadly Symbiosis." *Punishment and Society* 3:95–134.

Wacquant, Loïc J. D., and William Julius Wilson. 1989. "The Cost of Racial and Class Exclusion in the Inner City." *Annals of the American Academy of Political and Social Science* 501:8–25.

Walker, Bela August. 2003. "The Color of Crime: The Case against Race-Based Suspect Descriptions." *Columbia Law Review* 103:662–88.

Walker, Darlene, Richard J. Richardson, Thomas Denyer, Oliver Williams, and Skip McGaughey. 1972. "Contact and Support: An Empirical Assessment of Public Attitudes toward the Police and the Courts." *North Carolina Law Review* 51:43–79.

Walsh, Anthony. 1985. "Extralegal Factors in Felony Sentencing: Classes of Behavior or Classes of People?" *Sociological Inquiry* 55:62–82.

Weatherford, M. Stephen. 1987. "How Does Government Performance Influence Political Support?" *Political Behavior* 9:5–28.

Weber, Max. 1921. "Politics as a Vocation." Anthropological Research on the Contemporary. http://anthropos-lab.net/wp/wp-content/uploads/2011/12/Weber-Politics-as-a-Vocation.pdf.

Weilhouwer, Peter W., and Brad Lockerbie. 1994. "Party Contacting and Political Participation, 1952–1990." *American Journal of Political Science* 38:211–29.

Weitzer, Ronald. 1996. "Racial Discrimination in the Criminal Justice System: Findings and Problems in the Literature." *Journal of Criminal Justice* 24:309–22.

West, Heather C., William J. Sabol, and Sarah Greenman. 2010. *Prisoners in 2009*. Washington, DC: Bureau of Justice Statistics. http://bjs.ojp.usdoj.gov/content/pub/pdf/p09.pdf.

Western, Bruce. 2006. *Punishment and Inequality in America*. New York: Russell Sage Foundation.

Western, Bruce, Jeffrey R. Kling, and David F. Weiman. 2001. "The Labor Market Consequences of Incarceration." *Crime and Delinquency* 47:410–27.

Western, Bruce, Leonard Lopoo, and Sara McLanahan. 2004. "Incarceration and the Bonds between Parents in Fragile Families." Pp. 21–45 in *Imprisoning*

America: The Social Effects of Mass Incarceration, edited by M. Pattillo, D. Weiman, and B. Western. New York: Sage.

Western, Bruce, Mary Pattillo, and David Weiman. 2004. "Introduction." Pp. 1–20 in *Imprisoning America: The Social Effects of Mass Incarceration*, edited by M. Pattillo, D. Wiman, and B. Western. New York: Sage.

Wilson, James Q., and George L. Kelling 1982. "Broken Windows." *Atlantic Monthly*, March, pp. 29–38.

Wilson, William Julius. 1987. *The Truly Disadvantaged*. Chicago: University of Chicago Press.

———. 1996. *When Work Disappears*. New York: Knopf.

Wolfe, Frank. 1992. "Neighbors Protest SE Halfway House." *Washington Times*, March 1.

Wolfinger, Raymond E., and Steven J. Rosenstone. 1980. *Who Votes?* New Haven: Yale University Press.

X, Malcolm. 1965. *The Autobiography of Malcolm X, as Told to Alex Haley*. New York: Ballantyne.

Zatz, Marjorie S. 1987. "The Changing Forms of Racial/Ethnic Biases in Sentencing." *Journal of Research in Crime and Delinquency* 24:69–92.

Zimring, Franklin E. 2001. "Imprisonment Rates and the New Politics of Criminal Punishment." In *Mass Imprisonment: Social Causes and Consequences*, edited by D. Garland. Thousand Oaks, CA: Sage.

Index

Page numbers in italics refer to figures and tables.

Abu-Jamal, Mumia, 25
ACLU (American Civil Liberties
    Union), 24
ACORN, 141
AFDC (Aid to Families with Dependent
    Children), 25
African American Men Survey, 44
African Americans (blacks). *See* blacks
    (African Americans); black youth
Aid to Families with Dependent Chil-
    dren (AFDC), 25
alcohol abuse data, 18
Almond, Gabriel, 15
already-registered voters, 135
American Civil Liberties Union
    (ACLU), 24
American National Election Survey,
    109
ArcGIS, 50, 78
Arpaio, Joe, 28
Atlanta, Georgia, and fieldwork,
    140–47, *142*, *148*, 149–56, *157*, 158.
    See also Georgia
authority or power, of criminal justice
    system, 1–3, 170, 179–81

Barber, Kenneth, 44
belonging to political community, 3–4,
    15, 117, 135–40
beta regression models, 76, 81, *82–83*,
    129, *130–31*
blacks (African Americans): com-
    munity supervision data and, 46;
    employment opportunities, 24;
    financial resources and, 178; impris-
    onment data for, 4, 17–18, 26, 44–46,
    56–58, *57–59*, 68; male imprison-
    ment data and, 4; political attitudes
    of, 26; political participation for, 78;
    political trust and, 109, 179, 221n33;
    punishment effects on felons and,
    17–18; resource deprivation effects
    on, 39; selective enforcement and,
    27–28, 179–80; sentencing discrimi-
    nation and, 28–29, 56, 172; women
    imprisonment data, 26. *See also*
    whites
black youth: felony disfranchisement
    for, 176; imprisonment of, 4, 68, *72*,
    74, 176, 181, 182, 205n15; mobiliza-
    tion of, 159–60; political attitudes
    of, 176; political trust and, 179;
    selective enforcement and, 27; social
    networks and, 182; voter turnout for,
    176. *See also* blacks (African Ameri-
    cans); youth
block groups, 45–47, 63, 66, *66*,
    205n14, 216n8. *See also* community
    supervision data
Brady, Henry E., 23, 87, 123, 125, 138,
    208nn54
Braman, Donald, 125, 214n10

Census Bureau (U.S. Census Bureau),
    5, 8, 47, 93, 177–78, 205n14, 213n8,
    213n9
Charlotte, North Carolina, and field-
    work, 140–47, *142*, 149–56, *154*, *157*,
    158, 220n43
Charlotte sample of 2000 Social Capital
    Benchmark Survey: individual-level
    analyses and, 94, 95, *97–98*, 99, *99*,
    100, *100*, *101*; mechanisms evidence
    of effects for political participation

Charlotte sample of 2000 Social Capital Benchmark Survey (*continued*) and, 106, 109–10, *111–12, 114–15, 119–22*, 126, *127–28, 203–4*, 213n9, 213n14; prisoner density estimated effects and, 77, 78, *198–99. See also* Social Capital Benchmark Survey of 2000 (Saguaro Seminar's Social Capital Benchmark Survey of 2000)

Chicago, Illinois, and fieldwork, 134, 140–47, *142*, 149–56, 158, 219n2

civic death, 20

civic engagement, 41

civic inequality: community supervision data and, 44, 50; criminal justice and, 173, 182; mechanisms effects and, 15, 18, 105; public policies exclusion and, 18–21, *29*, 29–30; punishment effects on felons and, 18–21, *29*, 29–30; secondary marginalization and, 42; selective enforcement and, 2n86, 27–28; sentencing discrimination and, 28–29, 56, 172

Civic Voluntarism Model, 87

civil rights movement, 2, *3*, 205n4

Clear, Todd R., 129, 181

Cloward, Richard A., 136

Cohen, Cathy J., 39, 210n123

collateral consequences, 14

community experiences, with criminal justice, 12–14, 206n32

community supervision data: overview of, 6–7, 44–46, 68–74, 171–72; blacks data and, 46; block groups data and, 45–46; block groups described, 46–47, 205n14, 216n8; civic inequality and, 44, 50; criminal justice context variables and, 48–50, *49, 50*; data on, 46–50, 213n9, 213nn13–15; department of corrections data and, 47–48, 213nn13–14; descriptive analysis for adults and, 50–66, *51, 53–55, 57–62, 64–67*, 214n24; employment

opportunities and, 49; ex-felons and, 49–50; families of prisoners and, 49; financial resources in context of political participation and, 37–39, 43, 131; geocoding and, 50; Hispanic ethnicity and, 214n24; Latino ethnicity and, 46, 214n24; minority communities and, 44; Neighborhood Criminal Justice Involvement Data, 6–7, *51, 53–55, 57–62, 64–72*, 214n24; parolees and, 5, 45–46, 48, 50, 52, 63, *64–65*, 68, 72–73; political attitudes and, 49; poverty data and, 44, 46; sentencing discrimination and, 56; voting rights and, 49; youth data and, 46, 66–68, *69–72. See also* imprisonment data

crime rates, 39–40

criminal justice system: overview of, 170–71; belonging to political community and, 3–4; civic inequality and, 173, 182; civil rights movement and, 2, *3*, 205n4; collateral consequences of, 14; community experiences with, 12–14, 206n32; context variables for, 48–50, *49, 50*; context variables for imprisonment data and, 49, 50; death row data and, 10, *13*; decarceration or incarceration alternatives and, 178–79, 180–81; demobilization in relation to, 1–3, 205n4; employment data and, 10, *11*; ex-felons and voting rights, 11; families of prisoners and, 1–2, 4, 6, 13–14, 136, 171; felony convictions data and, 10, 205n10; felony disfranchisement and, 11, 22–23; financial resources and, 6; financial resources in context of political participation and, 178; immigrants and, 2, 28; imprisonment scholarship and, 10–13; individual experiences with, 12–14, 206n32; law enforcement and, 12, 170, 179–81, 206n32, 206n35, 211n137; local politics effects and, 173–75; mobilization in relation to, 1–2, 205n4; policy feedback literature and, 10–11, *11*, 12; political depopulation and, 176–78; political participation in relation to, 1–4, 12–14, 170, 179–81, 205n10; political trust and, 12, 25, 179, 206n32, 221n33; power of, 1–3, 170, 179–81; public housing restrictions for felons and, 24; racial political inequality and, 173, 175–76; sentencing discrimination and, 28–29, 172; social networks and, 6; voter turnout in relation to, 2

cultural deviance: mechanisms effects and, 9, 32–35, 210n126, 211n137; mechanisms evidence of effects and, 106–13, *111*, *112*, 129, 217n31

cultural transmission, 33–35, 107, 126

Davis, Angela Y., 26
Dawson, Michael C., 39, 210n123
death row data, 10, *13*
decarceration or incarceration alternatives, 178–79, 180–81
demobilization, 1–3, 39–40, 118, 122–24, 205n4
Democratic Party: already-registered voters and, 135; black young men mobilization efforts by, 159–60; disadvantaged communities fieldwork and, 141–42, *142*, 143, 147, *149*; disadvantaged communities mobilization and, 134, 138, 140, 145; mobilization strategies and, 141, 145–46, 152–53, 155–56, *157*, 159, 166, *167*; unregistered voter mobilization, 139–40, 145–46, 165–66; voter registration mobilization by, 145–47, 149–50, 155–56, *157*; voter turnout and, 150, 161–62. *See also* mobiliza-

tion, in disadvantaged communities; Republican Party
Denton, Nancy A., 33, 41
department of corrections data, 47–48, 50, 213nn13–14
descriptive analysis: of community supervision data, 50–66, *51*, *53–55*, *57–62*, *64–67*, 214n24; of imprisonment data, 63, 66, *66*, *67*
Diallo, Amadou, 27
direct mail, 135, 137, 140–41, 145, 151–53, *152*, 155
direct observation, 107–8, 126
Director Interviews Survey/Questionnaire, 141, *142*, 192–97
disadvantaged communities: Democrats and, 134, 138, 140, 145; political participation and, 14; Republicans and, 134–35, 141, 142, *142*, 143, 145, 147, *149*. *See also* mobilization, in disadvantaged communities
disadvantaged groups, 17–18. *See also specific groups*
disfranchisement (felony disfranchisement), 7, 11, 22–23, 160–61, 177–78
door-to-door canvassing, 39, 135, 137, 139–40, 144, *149*, 151–52, *152*, 155–56, 159, 164
drug abuse, 2n86, 18, 37–38

early voting, 150, 153, 160–61, 164, 166, *167*, 168–69
educational attainment, 17, 23, 78, 80, 178
Eller, Anja, 179, 206n35
e-mail or electronic contact, 137–38, 141, 145, 151, *152*, 154–55
employment opportunities, 10, *11*, 17, 19, 24, 37–38, 49. *See also* financial resources; poverty rates
ex-felons: community supervision data and, 49–50; data on, 49; employment opportunities and, 49; felony

ex-felons (*continued*)
disfranchisement and, 11, 22–23;
institutions serving, 49–50; political
attitudes of, 49; voting rights for, 11,
49, 103

families of prisoners: community
supervision data and, 49; criminal
justice and, 1–2, 4, 6, 13–14, 136,
171; mechanisms effects and, 32,
35–39, 40, 42–43, 87, 92; political
attitudes of individuals and, 33–35;
political participation for, 113, 116,
124–25; social disorganization effects on poverty and, 38–39
FBI (Federal Bureau of Investigation),
2, 205n4
Federal Bureau of Investigation (FBI),
2, 205n4
Federal Bureau of Prisons, 50, 180
felony convictions data, 10, 205n4
felony disfranchisement (disfranchisement), 7, 11, 22–23, 160–61, 177–78
fieldwork: analysis of mobilization,
145–47, *148*, *149*, 149–56, *152*, *154*,
157, 158; design for mobilization,
140–44, *142*
financial resources: community
supervision data and, 37–39, 43,
131; criminal justice and, 6, 178;
employment opportunities and,
10, *11*, 17, 19, 24, 37–38, 49; political participation and, 6, 178; public
policies exclusion and, 18–21, *29*,
29–30; punishment effects on felons
and, 17, 18–21, 23, *29*, 29–30, 178,
183, 208n54. *See also* employment
opportunities; poverty rates

Galvin, Daniel J., 219n2
General Social Survey, 44
geocoding, 50, 77–78
Geolytics, 45, 47, 77, 78–79

Georgia: Atlanta fieldwork and, 140–47,
142, *148*, 149–56, *157*, 158; Department of Corrections of, 48, 77,
213n13; Department of Public Health
of, 5, 44–45, 49, 77, 93, 213n15; descriptive analysis for adults and, 50,
51, 52, *54*; national data compared
with, 5–6, 205nn14–15; new prison
admissions estimated effects and,
86–87, 89, *90–91*, 216n23; political
participation in, 5–6; prisoner density estimated effects and, 76–81, *79*,
82–84, 85, 102–3, *198–99*, 214n12,
215n13, 215nn13–14, 215nn18–19;
State Board of Elections of, 80–81;
voter turnout and, 6, 86–87, 89,
90–91, 216n23
Gerber, Alan S., 144, 149
get-out-the-vote (GOTV) activities,
135, 141, 147, 149–51, 155, 157–58,
164. *See also* voter registration
Goldstein, Kenneth M., 138
GOTV (get-out-the-vote) activities,
135, 141, 147, 149–51, 155, 157–58,
164. *See also* voter registration
Green, Donald P., 144, 149
groups, and mobilization encouragement, 137–39, 142–43, 161, 164,
166, 168. *See also* mobilization, in
disadvantaged communities; *specific
groups*

Hamilton, Alexander, 178
Hanrahan, Noelle, 1
Hansen, John Mark, 123, 138
Harper, Hill, 166, *167*
health and well-being, 18
Herbert, Bob, 27–28
hierarchical linear models, 94, 214n3,
214n12, 215n13
high-imprisonment communities.
See political participation, in high-
imprisonment communities

Hispanic ethnicity: community supervision data and, 214n24; imprisonment data for, 17–18, 26, 56–57, *60*, 68; political participation and, 78; prisoner density estimated effects and, 78; punishment effects on felons and, 17–18, 26; selective enforcement and, 27–28, 179, 221n33

homeless people, 135, 139, 145, 147, 162, *163*, 164

homicide rate, 58; imprisonment data and, 46, 49, 58, *62*; political participation in high-imprisonment communities and, 78; prisoner density estimated effects and, 78

Huckfeldt, Robert, 9

immigrants, 2, 28, 135, 139, 145, 147, 160–61, 164

Immigration and Nationality Act of 1996, 28

imprisonment. *See* incarceration

imprisonment data: overview of, 6–7, 44–46, 68–74; black men and, 4; blacks and, 44, 45, 46, 56–58, *57*, *58*, *59*, 68; block groups and, 45–47, 63, 66, *66*, 216n8; criminal justice context variables and, 49, 50; criminal justice system and, 10, *12*; department of corrections data and, 48, 50; descriptive analysis for adults and, 63, 66, *66*, *67*; for disadvantaged people, 4–5; geocoding and, 50; Hispanic ethnicity adults and, 56–57, *60*; homicide rate and, 46, 49, 58, *62*; Latino ethnicity data and, 46; for men, 4; for minorities, 4–5; minority communities and, 44; North Carolina and, 45–46, 48–50, 56–58, *57*, *59–62*, 63, *66*, 66–68, *69*; poverty rates and, 44, 46, 56–58, *57*, *58*, *61*, 68; for white men, 4; youth and, 46,

66–69, *69*, *70*, *72*. *See also* community supervision data

incarceration: political depopulation and, 176–78; scholarship on, 10–13. *See also* community supervision data; criminal justice system; imprisonment data; mechanisms effects; mechanisms evidence of effects; political participation, in high-imprisonment communities; punishment effects on felons

individuals: criminal justice experiences of, 12, 206n32; educational attainment of, 17, 23, 178; individual-level analyses and, 76–77, 93–94, *96–98*, *99*, 99–101, *100*, *203–4*; political attitudes of, 24–30, 33–34

inequality, racial political, 7, 104, 173, 175–76. *See also* civic inequality

institutions: mobilization encouragement from, 137–39, 142–43, 161, 164, 166, 168; prisoner density estimated effects and, 78. *See also* Democratic Party; mobilization, in disadvantaged communities; Republican Party

IRS Master List of Exempt Organizations, 50, 93

Jencks, Christopher, 17
Johnson, Rucker C., 125
Johnson, Toylean, 44, 125

Kennedy, Randall, 176, 206n32

labor market discrimination, 17, 19, 37, 49. *See also* employment opportunities

Lamberth, John, 28
Latino ethnicity, 46, 214n24
law enforcement, 12, 170, 179–81, 206n32, 206n35, 211n137

literature distribution, 135, 151–54, *152, 154*
local politics effects, 173–75

Malcolm X, 1
Manza, Jeff, 11, 25
Marshall, Thurgood, 19–20
Massachusetts Prison Association, 40
Massey, Douglas S., 33, 41
MatchIt, 88
Mayer, Susan E., 17
McCain, John, 141, *142*, 147, *149*
mechanisms effects: overview of, 9–10, 15–17, 31–32, 41–42, 171; belonging to political community and, 15; civic engagement and, 41; civic inequality and, 15, 18; crime rates and, 39–40; cultural deviance and, 9, 32–35, 210n126, 211n137; cultural transmission and, 33–35; demobilization and, 39–40; families of prisoners and, 32, 35–39, 40, 42–43, 87, 92; incarceration as factor in increase in voter turnout and, 41; parolees and, 9, 16–17, 30, 38, 43; poverty and, 39–40, 210n10; public housing restrictions and, 35–36, 38; racial composition of communities and, 39–40; racial political inequality and, 7; rational choice theory and, 22, 136; resource deprivation and, 9–10, 17, 32, 36–37; social capital and, 26, 36, 41; social disorganization and, 9, 35–36, 182–83; social networks and, 9, 24, 35–36, 39–42, 182; sorting effect and, 41; voter registration and, 23, 30, 32, 39; voter turnout and, 30, 31, 34, 41, 42. *See also* mechanisms evidence of effects; punishment effects on felons
mechanisms evidence of effects: overview of, 8, 105–6, 131–32, 173, 181–82; belonging to political community and, 117; beta regression models and, 129, *130–31*; civic inequality and, 105; cultural deviance and, 106–13, *111, 112*, 129, 217n31; cultural transmission and, 107, 126; demobilization and, 118, 122–24; direct observation and, 107–8, 126; ordinary-least-squares regression and, 118; political efficacy and, 107–8, 110, 113, *114–15*, 126; political trust and, 108–10, *111–12*, 126, 129, 179, 218n52, 219n55; resource deprivation and, 55, *57–61*, 106, 124–26, *127–28*, 131, 217n31; Social Capital Benchmark Survey of 2000 and, 108, 113, 116, 117, 124; social disorganization and, 113, 116–18, *119–22*, 129, 217n31, 219n55; social networks and, 8, 113, 116–18, *121–22*, 123–24, 129, 131–32; social trust and, 106, 116–18, *119–20*, 123, 129, 173, 219n55; voter turnout and, 129, *130–31*, 131, 219n56
men: blacks imprisonment data for, 4, 44; black young adult mobilization efforts by, 159–60; Latino ethnicity data and, 46, 214n24; sexual abuse among prisoners data for, 18. *See also* blacks (African Americans); black youth; Hispanic ethnicity; whites; women
Mettler, Suzanne, 20, 126
Miller, Tangenea, 44
minority communities: community supervision data and, 44; educational attainment of individuals and, 178; imprisonment data and, 44; political attitudes, 26; political participation in high-imprisonment communities and, 78; prisoner density estimated effects and, 78; selective enforcement and, 27–28. *See also specific minorities*

mobilization, in disadvantaged communities: overview of, 8–9, 133–36, 162, 164–69, *167–68*, 181, 220n43; already-registered voters and, 135; belonging to political community and, 135–40; black youth and, 159–60; challenges and reengagement for, 158–62, *163*; criminal justice in relation to, 1–2, 205n4; direct mail and, 135, 137, 140–41, 145, 151–53, *152*, 155; Director Interviews Survey/Questionnaire and, 141, *142*, 192–97; door-to-door canvassing and, 39, 135, 137, 139–40, 144, *149*, 151–52, *152*, 155–56, 159, 164; early voting and, 150, 153, 160–61, 164, 166, *167*, 168–69; e-mail or electronic contact and, 137–38, 141, 145, 151, *152*, 154–55; encouragement by groups or institutions and, 137–39, 142–43, 161, 164, 166, 168; felony disfranchisement and, 160–61; fieldwork analysis and, 145–47, *148*, *149*, 149–56, *152*, *154*, *157*, 158; fieldwork design and, 140–44, *142*; homeless people and, 135, 139, 145, 147, 162, *163*, 164; immigrants and, 135, 139, 145, 147, 160–61, 164; literature distribution and, 135, 151–54, *152*, *154*; mobilization strategies and, 141, 145–46, 152–53, 155–56, *157*, 159, 166, *167*; one stop voting and, 160, 168; phone calls and, 135, 137, 139–40, 143, 145, 151, *152*, 164; social capital and, 136; social events and, 137–39, 143–45, 147, *148*, 150–51, *152*, 155–56, 159–60, 164–69, *167–68*, 220n43; unregistered voters and, 139–40, 145–46, 165–66; voter registration and, 137–41, 143, 145–51, 155–58, *157*, 160–62, *163*, 164–66, 168–69, 219n8; voter turnout and, 137–38, 140–41,

146–51, 155, 157–58, 161–62, *163*, 164; youth and, 159–60, 164, 166. *See also* Democratic Party; disadvantaged communities; Republican Party

mobilization strategies: Democrats and, 141, 145–46, 152–53, 155–56, *157*, 159, 166, *167*; Republicans and, 141, 146, 149–50, *157*, 220n43. *See also* mobilization, in disadvantaged communities

Morrell, Michael E., 110

NAACP (National Association for the Advancement of Colored People), 2, 24, 28, 147, *148*

National Action Network, 142, *142*, 147, *148*

National Association for the Advancement of Colored People (NAACP), 2, 24, 28, 147, *148*

National Commission on Civil Disorders, 1

Neighborhood Criminal Justice Involvement Data, 6–7, 50–72, *51*, *53–55*, *57–62*, *64–72*, 78–81, *79–80*, *84*, 129–31, *130–31*, *198–99*, 214n24

new prison admissions estimated effects, 76, 86–92, *90–91*, *200–202*, 215n22, 216n23

Nie, Norman H., 30, 33

North Carolina: black adults data, 56–58, *57*, *59*; black youth data and, 68; block groups data and, 45–46; community supervision data and, 45–46, 48–50, 67, *71*; criminal justice context variables and, 49; department of corrections data and, 48, 213n13; Department of Corrections of, 48, 77, 93; Department of Public Health of, 5, 44–45, 49, 77, 93; descriptive analysis for adults and, 50–52, *51–52*, *54*, 56, 63, 66,

North Carolina (*continued*)
66, 214n24; geocoding and, 50;
Hispanic ethnicity data and, 56–57,
60; homicide rate and, 49, 58, *62*; imprisonment data for, 45–46, 48–50,
56–58, *57*, *59–62*, 63, *66*, 66–68, *69*;
individual-level analyses and, 76–77,
93–94, *96–100*, 99–101, *203–4*;
national average data compared
with, 5–6, 205nn14–15; new prison
admissions estimated effects and,
86–87, 89, *90–91*, 216n23; political
participation in relation to criminal
justice in, 5–6; poverty rates and,
56–58, *61*, 68; prisoner density estimated effects and, *77*, 77–81, *79–80*,
82–84, 85, 102–3, *198–99*, 214n5,
214n12, 215nn13–14, 215nn17–19;
State Board of Elections of, 78, 80–
81, 214n5, 219n8; voter registration
and, 137, 168, 219n8; voter turnout
and, 6, *77*, 77–78, *79–80*, 86–87, 89,
90–91, *198–99*, 214n5, 216n23; youth
data and, 46, 67–68, *69*
Norton, Eleanor Holmes, 180
Nublan, Brand, 15

Obama, Barack, 134, 138, 140–41, *141*,
145–50, *149*, 155, 158–62, 165–66.
See also Democratic Party
one stop voting, 160, 168
ordinary-least-squares regression, 89,
118

parole and parolees: community
supervision data and, 45–46, 48, 50,
52, 63, *64–65*, 68, 72–73; community
supervision density and, 5; data on, 5;
mechanisms effects and, 9, 16–17, 30,
38, 43. *See also* criminal justice system
People for the American Way, 2
phone calls, 135, 137, 139–40, 143, 145,
151, *152*, 164

Piven, Frances Fox, 136
policy feedback literature, 10–11, *11*,
12, 33, 126
political attitudes, 24–30, 33–35, 49,
176
political demobilization, 1–3, 39–40,
118, 122–24, 205n4
political depopulation, 176–78
political efficacy, 34, 42, 107–8, 110,
113, *114–15*, 126
political mobilization. *See* mobilization
political participation: criminal justice
in relation to, 1–4, 12–14, 170, 179–81,
205n10; punishment effects on
felons and, 21–24, 208n44, 208n54.
See also mechanisms effects; mechanisms evidence of effects; mobilization, in disadvantaged communities;
voter registration; voter turnout
political participation, in high-
imprisonment communities:
overview of, 6–8, 75–77, 101–4,
172–73; beta regression models
and, 76, 81, *82–83*; blacks data and,
78; Civic Voluntarism Model and,
87; educational attainment data
and, 78, 80; families of prisoners
and, 113, 116, 124–25; geocoding
for voter turnout data and, 77–78;
hierarchical linear models and, 94,
214n3, 214n12, 215n13; Hispanic
ethnicity data and, 78; homicide
rate data and, 78; individual-level
analyses and, 76–77, 93–94, *96–98*,
99, 99–101, *100*, *203–4*; institutions
data and, 78; minorities data and,
78; Neighborhood Criminal Justice
Involvement Data and, 78, *79–80*,
84, *198–99*; new prison admissions
estimated effects and, 76, 86–92,
90–91, *200–202*, 215n22, 216n23;
ordinary-least-squares regression
and, 89; prisoner density estimated

effects and, 76–85, *79, 80, 82–84*, 102–3, *198–99*, 214nn3–6, 214n6, 214n12, 215nn13–14, 215nn13–19, 215nn17–19; racial political inequality and, 104; Social Capital Benchmark Survey of 2000 and, 8, 77, 92–93; voter registration and, 93–95, *96, 98*; voter turnout data and, 76–80, *77, 79–80*, 86–101, *90–91, 96–101, 198–99, 200–202*, 214n5, 215n22, 216n23, 216nn31–32; voter turnout data for new prison admissions test and, 76, 86–92, *90–91, 200–202*, 215n22, 216n23. *See also* political participation

political trust: criminal justice and, 12, 25, 179, 206n32, 221n33; mechanisms evidence of effects and, 108–10, *111–12*, 126, 129, 179, 218n52, 219n55

poverty rates: community supervision data and, 44, 46; employment opportunities and, 10, *11*, 17, 19, 24, 37–38, 49; imprisonment data and, 44, 46, 56–58, *57, 58, 61*, 68; mechanisms effects and, 39–40, 210n10; social disorganization and, 38–39. *See also* financial resources

power or authority, of criminal justice system, 1–3, 170, 179–81

prisoner density estimated effects, 76–85, *79–80, 82–84*, 102–3, *198–99*, 214nn3–6, 214n6, 214n12, 215nn13–19

public housing, 24, 35–36, 38

punishment effects on felons: overview of, 17–18, *29*, 29–30, 42–44, 171; blacks and, 17–18, 24, 26; civic inequality and, 18–21, *29*, 29–30; disadvantaged groups and, 17–18; drug and alcohol abuse data and, 18; educational attainment of individuals and, 17, 23, 178; employment opportunities and, 24; financial resources and, 17, 18–21, 23, *29*, 29–30, 178, 183, 208n54; health and well-being and, 18; Hispanic ethnicity and, 17–18, 26; political attitudes of individuals and, 24–30, 33–34; political efficacy and, 34, 42; political participation decrease and, 21–24, 208n44, 208n54; public policies and, 18–21, *29*, 29–30; racial profiling and, 26–28; selective enforcement and, 27–28; sexual abuse among prisoners data and, 18; social class and, 18–21, *29*, 29–30; social trust and, 34, 36, 41, 42; whites and, 24, 26; women imprisonment data and, 18, 26. *See also* mechanisms effects

race: community composition and, 39–40; political trust and, 129; racial political inequality and, 7, 104, 173, 175–76; racial profiling and, 26–28. *See also* civic inequality

rational choice theory, 22, 136

Raymond, Usher, 166, *167*

Republican Party: disadvantaged communities and, 134–35, 141, 142, *142*, 143, 145, 147, *149*; mobilization strategies and, 141, 146, 149–50, *157*, 220n43; unregistered voter mobilization, 140; voter registration and, 149–50. *See also* Democratic Party; mobilization, in disadvantaged communities

resource deprivation: mechanisms effects and, 9–10, 17, 32, 36–37; mechanisms evidence of effects and, 55, *57–61*, 106, 124–26, *127–28*, 131, 217n31

Richardson v. Ramirez (1974), 19–20

Ridout, Travis N., 138

Rose, Dina R., 129

Rosenberg, Morris, 117

Rosenstone, Steven J., 123, 138
Rousseau, Jean Jacques, 18

Saguaro Seminar's Social Capital
    Benchmark Survey of 2000 (Social
    Capital Benchmark Survey of 2000),
    8, 77, 92–93, 108, 113, 116, 117, 124,
    185–91. *See also* Charlotte sample
    of 2000 Social Capital Benchmark
    Survey
Scan/US, 45, 47, 77
Schlozman, Kay Lehman, 23, 87, 123,
    125, 138, 208nn54
secondary marginalization, 42
selective enforcement, 2n86, 27–28,
    179–80, 221n33
sentencing discrimination, 28–29, 56,
    172
sexual abuse among prisoners data, 18
Skogan, Wesley G., 176, 179, 206n38
social capital, 26, 36, 41, 136
Social Capital Benchmark Survey of
    2000 (Saguaro Seminar's Social
    Capital Benchmark Survey of 2000),
    8, 77, 92–93, 108, 113, 116, 117, 124,
    185–91. *See also* Charlotte sample
    of 2000 Social Capital Benchmark
    Survey
social class, 18–21, *29*, 29–30, 129, 172
social disorganization: employment
    opportunities and, 37–38; families
    of prisoners and, 38–39; mecha-
    nisms effects and, 9, 35–36, 182–83;
    mechanisms evidence of effects and,
    113, 116–18, *119–22*, 129, 217n31,
    219n55; poverty rates and, 38–39.
    See also social networks
social events, 137–39, 143–45, 147,
    148, 150–51, *152*, 155–56, 159–60,
    164–69, *167–68*, 220n43
social networks: criminal justice and,
    6; mechanisms effects and, 9, 24,
    35–36, 39–42, 182; mechanisms evi-

dence of effects and, 8, 113, 116–18,
    121–22, 123–24, 129, 131–32. *See
    also* social disorganization
social trust: mechanisms evidence of
    effects and, 106, 116–18, *119–20*,
    123, 129, 173, 219n55; punishment
    effects on felons and, 34, 36, 41, 42
sorting effect, 41
Soss, Joe, 25, 126, 129
Sourcebook of Criminal Justice Statis-
    tics Online, *11*
Sprague, John, 9
suffrage (voting rights), 2, 7, 11, 22–23,
    49, 103, 160–61, 177–78. *See also*
    mechanisms effects; mechanisms
    evidence of effects; mobilization,
    in disadvantaged communities;
    political participation, in high-
    imprisonment communities; voter
    registration; voter turnout
Survey/Questionnaire for Director
    Interviews, 192–97

TANF (Temporary Assistance for
    Needy Families), 24
Temporary Assistance for Needy Fami-
    lies (TANF), 24
Tillman, "Pitchfork" Ben, 2
Travis, Jeremy, 37
Tyler, Tom, 126

Uggen, Christopher, 11, 25
unregistered voters, 139–40, 145–46,
    165–66
U.S. Bureau of Justice statistics, *12, 13*, 17
U.S. Census Bureau (Census Bureau),
    5, 8, 47, 93, 177–78, 205n14, 213n8,
    213n9

Verba, Sidney, 15, 23, 30, 33, 87, 123,
    125, 138, 208n54
voter registration: already-registered
    voters and, 135; Democrats and,

145–46, 147, 149–50, 155–56, *157*;
GOTV activities and, 135, 141, 147,
149–51, 155, 157–58, 164; mechanisms effects and, 23, 30, 32, 39;
mobilization and, 137–41, 143,
145–51, 155–58, *157*, 160–62, *163*,
164–66, 168–69, 219n8; political
participation in high-imprisonment
communities and, 93–95, *96*, *98*; Republicans and, 149–50; unregistered
voters and, 139–40, 145–46, 165–66.
See also political participation
voter turnout: criminal justice and, 2;
Democrats and, 150, 161–62; incarceration effects on, 41; mechanisms
effects and, 30, 31, 34, 41, 42; mechanisms evidence of effects and, 129,
130–31, 131, 219n56; mobilization
and, 137–38, 140–41, 146–51, 155,
157–58, 161–62, *163*, 164; political
participation in high-imprisonment
communities and, 76–80, *77*, *79–80*,
86–101, *90–91*, *96–101*, *198–99*,
200–202, 214n5, 215n22, 216n23,
216nn31–32. *See also* political participation; voter registration
voting rights (suffrage), 2, 7, 11, 22–23,
49, 103, 160–61, 177–78. *See also*
mechanisms effects; mechanisms
evidence of effects; mobilization,
in disadvantaged communities;
political participation, in high-

imprisonment communities; voter
registration; voter turnout

Wacquant, Loïc, 20
Warren, Earl, 174–75
Weber, Max, 170
well-being and health, 18
Western, Bruce, 178
whites, 4, 24, 26, 179, 221n33; employment opportunities for, 24. *See also*
blacks (African Americans)
Wilson, William Julius, 33, 35–38
women, 18, 26, 36, 129, 172. *See also*
men

X, Malcolm, 1

youth: community supervision data
and, 46, 66–68, *69–72*; felony disfranchisement and, 7; felony
disfranchisement for, 176; imprisonment data for, 18, 46, 66–69, *69*,
70, *72*; imprisonment of, 4–6, 7, 46,
68, *72*, 74, 176, 181, 182, 205n15;
mobilization of, 159–60, 164, 166;
political attitudes of, 34–35, 176;
political trust and, 179; selective enforcement and, 27; social networks
and, 35, 182; voter registration and,
144, 145; voter turnout for, 156, 162,
176. *See also* black youth